Beyond the Kitchen Table

Black Food Justice
ASHANTÉ REESE AND HANNA GARTH, EDITORS

Black Food Justice publishes scholarship at the intersection of Black studies and critical food studies. The titles in this series explore how food studies can inform the theorization of Blackness, and how Black thought and liberation can transform meanings of food. The series aims to materially advance the protection, nourishment, and celebration of Black life by articulating new futures for Black food justice scholarship.

A complete list of books published in Black Food Justice is available at https://uncpress.org/series/black-food-justice/.

BEYOND THE KITCHEN TABLE

Black Women and Global Food Systems

EDITED BY
PRISCILLA McCUTCHEON,
LATRICA E. BEST, AND
THERESA RAJACK-TALLEY

The University of North Carolina Press
CHAPEL HILL

© 2023 Priscilla McCutcheon, Latrica E. Best, and Theresa Ann Rajack-Talley
All rights reserved

Designed by Lindsay Starr
Set in Charis
by codeMantra
Manufactured in the United States of America

Chapter 5 of this book was originally published as Ashanté M. Reese and Dara Cooper, "Making Spaces Something Like Freedom: Black Feminist Praxis in the Re/Imagining of a Just Food System," *ACME: An International Journal for Critical Geographies* 20, no. 4 (2021): 450–59.

Part of chapter 11 of this book appeared previously in somewhat different form as Shelene Gomes, "Being *Shashamane Sew*: Second Generation Caribbean Rastafari in Multicultural Ethiopia," in *Cultural Mobilities between Africa and the Caribbean*, ed. Birgit Englert, Barbara Gföllner, and Sigrid Thomsen (London: Routledge, 2021), 61–82.

Cover art: Young African woman cooking salad by Milles Studio, courtesy of Adobe Stock. Spice banner by Yaruniv-Studio, courtesy of Adobe Stock.

LIBRARY OF CONGRESS CATALOGING-IN-PUBLICATION DATA
Names: McCutcheon, Priscilla (Ph. D. in geography), editor. | Best, Latrica E., editor. | Rajack-Talley, Theresa Ann, editor.
Title: Beyond the kitchen table : Black women and global food systems / edited by Priscilla McCutcheon, Latrica E. Best, and Theresa Rajack-Talley. Other titles: Black food justice.
Description: Chapel Hill : The University of North Carolina Press, 2023. | Series: Black food justice | Includes bibliographical references and index.
Identifiers: LCCN 2023029865 | ISBN 9781469675947 (cloth ; alk. paper) | ISBN 9781469675954 (paperback) | ISBN 9781469675961 (ebook)
Subjects: LCSH: Women, Black. | Women farmers. | Women in the food industry. | Food—Social aspects. | Nutrition. | Food supply. | Businesswomen. |
BISAC: SOCIAL SCIENCE / Agriculture & Food (see also POLITICAL SCIENCE / Public Policy / Agriculture & Food Policy) | SOCIAL SCIENCE / Black Studies (Global)
Classification: LCC HD6077 .B496 2023 | DDC 338.1082—dc23/eng/20230719
LC record available at https://lccn.loc.gov/2023029865

We dedicate this book to generations of Black women across the African Diaspora—the grandmothers, the mothers, "othermothers," and daughters who for decades provided and prepared food for, and at, the kitchen table and beyond and continue to do so. We thank you, not only for nourishing us and sustaining the environment but also for your ceaseless mentorship, critical knowledge sharing, incessant commitment, and unending love—all ingredients necessary to actualize a food system that is just for all. We hope through the pages of this book your voices and values are also actualized.

Contents

viii   LIST OF ILLUSTRATIONS

ix   ACKNOWLEDGMENTS

1   INTRODUCTION. *Beyond the Kitchen Table: Exploring the Roles of Black Women in Global Food Systems* | Priscilla McCutcheon, Latrica E. Best, and Theresa Rajack-Talley

19   **PART 1. FROM THE FIELDS**
Theresa Rajack-Talley

24   CHAPTER 1. *Rural Women, Household Food Provisioning, and Dry-Season Groundwater Irrigation in Northern Ghana* | Lydia Kwoyiga and Agnes Atia Apusigah

42   CHAPTER 2. *From Farm to Kitchen: Women's Role in Three Dimensions—Production, Processing, and Consumption—in Burkina Faso* | Eveline M. F. W. Sawadogo/Compaoré and Sakiko Shiratori

59   CHAPTER 3. *The Role of Women in Sustainable Agriculture in Three Global Regions: Environmentally Friendly Practices and Passing Knowledge Along to Future Generations* | Gloria Sanders McCutcheon

74   CHAPTER 4. *Fish Farming: Women in Food Production for Improved Household Food and Nutrition Security in Ortoire Village, Mayaro, Trinidad—a Case Study* | Kenia-Rosa Campo, Wendy-Ann Isaac, Neela Badrie, and Marquitta Webb

87   **PART 2. FOOD AND SOCIAL JUSTICE**
Priscilla McCutcheon

92   CHAPTER 5. *Making Spaces Something Like Freedom: Black Feminist Praxis in the Re/Imagining of a Just Food System* | Ashanté M. Reese and Dara Cooper

106   CHAPTER 6. *Mothering in Historical Black Agrarian Pedagogies: A Historiography* | shakara tyler

124   CHAPTER 7. *Recipes for Resistance: Stories of Black Women Leading Food and Agricultural Justice Movements on Farms* | Claudia J. Ford

136   CHAPTER 8. *My Planting Is to Farm Community: Afro–Costa Rican Women's Agrarian Food Practices* | Kelsey Emard and Veronica Gordon

151   **PART 3. FOOD SECURITY, HEALTH, AND WELL-BEING**
Latrica E. Best

158   CHAPTER 9. *Black Women, Food, and Health: Exploring the Importance of Intersectionality in Population-Based Health Studies* | Latrica E. Best

173   CHAPTER 10. *I Put Food on Everyone's Table: Food Provisioning, Domestic Work, and Entrepreneurship across Three Generations of Black Women in Santiago de Cuba* | Hanna Garth

186   CHAPTER 11. *Tasting Freedom: The Rastafari Family Food Beit in Ethiopia* | Shelene Gomes

206   CONCLUSION. *Exercising Agency, Navigating Marginalization, and Maintaining Silent Control in Global Food Systems* | Theresa Rajack-Talley, Latrica E. Best, and Priscilla McCutcheon

215   CONTRIBUTORS

223   INDEX

Illustrations

FIGURES

2.1. Fried cowpea | 53

2.2. Cowpea boiled in a bag | 53

2.3. Baked cowpea | 53

4.1. World capture fisheries and aquaculture production | 77

4.2. Determinants of nutritional status | 83

8.1. Produce harvesting | 143

8.2. Learning about plants on the farm | 145

11.1. Meal prepared and served in Shashamane | 195

GRAPHS

2.1. Cowpea purchases by household | 50

2.2. Reasons for purchasing cowpea variety | 51

2.3. Recipes prepared for household members | 54

TABLES

4.1. Socioeconomic characteristics of fish farmers in Ortoire, Mayaro | 79

4.2. Women's empowerment before and after aquaculture program participation | 81

4.3. Contribution of the three empowerment dimensions to overall empowerment | 82

Acknowledgments

THE COMPLETION of this book would not have been possible without the contributions of each of our authors, high-caliber researchers, scholars, and activists. We specifically would like to acknowledge the women in the book chapters' case studies, past and present, who reside in the Caribbean, the United States, and Africa. Collectively, the chapters tell diverse stories of women who live in regions that historically made up the transatlantic slave trade. We thank you for sharing your stories that reflect strength, intellect, commitment, pain, resilience, and success.

Women's work is never separate from family and community, so we recognize the support that each of the authors received from their families and extended families. When the three editors started this project, we were at the same university and department. We have since moved to different institutions across the United States and one in Canada. The importance of the book kept us going, along with the encouragement and support of our families, friends, and mentors, whom we also graciously thank.

Special thanks to the reviewers for their pointed observations and recommendations that helped us to make the chapters in the book more connected and who helped us strengthen our introductions and conclusion. We would also like to thank our publisher and their staff, who not only believed in our editorial skills for a project that scanned the Diaspora but also recognized the importance of centering a book on Black women's food, agricultural, and health experiences, contributions, and practices.

There are many others who assisted us in different ways—you know who you are, and we are grateful for you. Thank you.

Beyond the Kitchen Table

INTRODUCTION

Beyond the Kitchen Table

Exploring the Roles of Black Women in Global Food Systems

PRISCILLA McCUTCHEON, LATRICA E. BEST, AND THERESA RAJACK-TALLEY

BLACK WOMEN have a long history and complex relationship with food systems, serving vital roles—from the production in the fields to the preparation, processing, marketing, and distribution of food—within families and among communities.[1] In the last two decades, there has been some momentum to advance gender equality and women's participation in agri-food systems. According to Jose Graziano da Silva, director general of the Food and Agriculture Organization of the United Nations, these efforts are thanks in part to the fact that women represent the majority of agricultural labor. Many UN initiatives center on the lives of women and girls, as they remain the world's most vulnerable population.[2] At the kitchen table and beyond, Black diasporic women are heavily involved in the nutrition, health, and well-being of their families, communities, and nations.[3] Both locally and globally, Black women impact the economic, political, social, and cultural segments of global food systems. Their expertise and labor often build and sustain these systems; yet Black women get little acknowledgment for their work and are rarely part of local, national, or international decision-making programs for food security.[4] Their voices are often not heard because of their positionality linked to the intersection of their race or ethnicity, gender, sexuality, culture, geography, and social class. Likewise, their roles as activists, scientists, and agents of change are not recognized or discussed. Simply, Black women are presented as victims of the agro-industrial food system without proper attention to, and acknowledgment of, the ways that Black women transform the food system. In this book, we illustrate how Black women are the backbone of this system, in large part due to their manual labor, expertise, knowledge, and dedication to creating and maintaining sustainable and secure food systems.

Research shows that it is economically and socially advantageous to educate, invest in, and empower Black women, particularly because women spend a great deal of their time in agricultural fields, kitchens, and processing and scientific spaces. Beyond the research, we know that it is the right and just thing to do to highlight women's roles in global food systems. Deciding what food is grown and cooked and how it is prepared, both inside and outside of households, has traditionally been the responsibility of women. For example, Theresa Rajack-Talley's work on poverty reveals that resources controlled by women are more likely to be used to improve family food consumption, reduce child malnutrition, and improve family welfare in general.[5] Addressing the issues women face, recognizing their contributions, providing them the support required, and working to eliminate the powerful negative effects of racism, sexism, and spatial discrimination could increase food production and improve food accessibility, availability, and consumption as well as the overall health and nutrition of Black women, Black communities, and society at large. With these efforts, Black women can continue to make major breakthroughs in food justice, food security, health, and poverty reduction on a global scale and should be central to strategic planning for food security worldwide. Recognizing Black women's roles also serves to counter other misunderstood and stereotypical beliefs about poor health and nutrition in Black families and communities.

Nutrition- and diet-related health issues are closely linked to global food systems, which can lead to significant health disparities both within and between communities.[6] While such health disparities are concerning, we acknowledge and address the complex, and often contradictory, research equating health disparities with poor health.[7] For example, there are instances in which health research pathologizes nutrition- and diet-related health issues such as obesity, where researchers overly scrutinize cultural and behavioral characteristics surrounding food, despite the significance of more pressing macrolevel social and policy concerns on health outcomes. Increasingly, research has questioned the arbitrary nature and efficacy of weight indexes, such as body mass index, in capturing one's health.[8] For example, we know that, using a food justice lens, obesity is measured through a lens of whiteness and maleness and as such does not consider physiological differences such as muscle and bone density. Julie Guthman notes that while complicated, it is possible to discuss "biological difference without resorting to genomics or vestiges of racial science—or behavioral models which fall short."[9] In other words, we can have meaningful conversations regarding Black women and health concerns such as obesity without reducing health differences to solely genetic arguments and without pathologizing Black women's health. Diet-related health issues among Black women are multifaceted and complex, and any research aimed at improving Black women's health must carefully consider individual- and structural-level sociocultural and environmental factors that shape their lived experiences and subsequent well-being. Meaningful progress in health outcomes and experiences calls for the centering of Black women's voices in research, policy, and activism.

The chapters in this book use Black women's experiences to reframe the narrative surrounding Black women's food choice and consumption. They show that the relationship to wellness starts by acknowledging and understanding the social and historical roles Black women have played in global food systems. Changes in global food systems, namely the occurrences of urbanization, modernization, and shifts in economic development, have altered not only the ways Black women cultivate and produce food but also the amounts and types of food consumed by women and their families and communities.[10] Centering Black women in conversations surrounding food and health also shifts the focus away from questionable Eurocentric measures that are often used to define the health of Black women and women of color.

Concerns related to studying Black women's health notwithstanding, the lack of adequate, nutrient-rich food has had a profound impact on health and mortality in countries where agriculture and food production have historically been vital to people's livelihoods and dietary needs. Currently, while African and Caribbean countries need to produce increasing quantities of food to satisfy their growing populations, the problem, including in the United States, is also about consuming high-quality items that have the nutritional value for healthy diets.[11] Healthy foods that are high in nutrients and low in calories, fats, sodium, and additives/processed ingredients—particularly fruits and vegetables—are important in eliminating poor health outcomes. Equally important is both the accessibility and affordability of healthy food items for everyone, including those responsible for producing them. It is, therefore, imperative that global food systems be centered on those who play key roles in a multitude of areas—production, processing and distribution, consumption, and nutrition—that is, around Black women of the Diaspora.

Intersectional Approach to Black Women and Global Food Systems

An exploration of Black women's contributions to global food systems is not complete without considering both the significance of their intersecting identities and lived experiences as well as the systems of power that create and sustain the social circumstances Black women must navigate to provide for themselves, their families, and their communities. Using intersectionality as a theoretical framework to examine Black women's relationship with food is imperative to our understanding of Black women's roles in global food systems and any subsequent efforts to assist and improve their economic and social well-being. Not only do the chapters in this book tell of the multiple roles women play in global food systems, but in each narrative, the chapters also paint a picture of women's intersecting identities as producers and nurturers; income earners; custodians of culture, knowledge, and safe environmental practices; dietitians; astute negotiators; survivors; and thrivers on the land and in food production.

For well over forty years, intersectionality has served as a foundational, theoretical perspective not only among Black feminist scholars and activists but also across various other social and academic domains. However, the core ideals of both Black feminism and, subsequently, intersectionality have been prevalent since far before Kimberlé Crenshaw named the term.[12] As Patricia Hill Collins and Sirma Bilge note, "Individual African American women had been expressing black feminist sensibilities for some time."[13] Key Black feminist texts, from Sojourner Truth's 1851 speech "Ain't I a Woman?" to Frances Beal's 1969 essay, "Double Jeopardy: To Be Black and Female," represent, historically, the issues and concerns Black women have faced navigating their gender, race, and class.[14] Though these seminal texts elucidate the intersections at which Black women's identities and experiences reside, the Combahee River Collective's 1977 "A Black Feminist Statement" provided a framework in which to understand how identity politics is linked to the systemic nature of Black women's racial, sexual, and class oppression.[15] Intersectionality's growth as a formidable form of critical inquiry can be attributed to the popularity of Crenshaw's "Mapping the Margins: Intersectionality, Identity Politics, and Violence against Women of Color."[16] Since Crenshaw, research on intersectionality and its merits has continued to increase, as scholars and activists have emphasized intersectionality's utility as a theoretical praxis, an analytical tool, and a prominent fixture in critical social theory. The presence and growth of intersectionality as a formidable theoretical framework are also evident throughout the Diaspora. In *Words of Fire: An Anthology of African American Feminist Thought*, Beverly Guy-Sheftall highlights the intersectionality of Caribbean women scholars such as Amy Jacques Garvey, Claudia Jones, and others, while in another work Clenora Hudson-Weems sets out a paradigm of Africana womanism to show how race, class, and gender must be prioritized in the fight against everyday racial dominance.[17]

According to Collins and Bilge, six key reemerging constructs define intersectionality as a framework suitable for critical inquiry: relationality, power, social inequality, social context, complexity, and social justice. From a scholarship perspective, these constructs often appear "either singularly or in combination" in intersectional research. *Relationality* offers researchers a way of thinking about the interconnectedness of categories that often goes beyond statistical differences between groups of people. The construct of *power*, according to Collins and Bilge, illustrates that "intersecting power relations produce social divisions of race, gender, class, sexuality, ability, age, country of origin, and citizenship status that are unlikely to be adequately understood in isolation from one another."[18] In taking an intersectional approach that considers power, one cannot examine adequately these categories without properly understanding and acknowledging the ways in which systems of power have created and perpetuated inequalities and differences. *Social inequality* is inherently related to power in that the uneven and discrepant nature of power relations produces a wide array of social inequalities, from race, class, and gender to age and disability. These inequalities are not separate entities, though they are often treated as such in academic research.

Another key construct of intersectionality is the importance of *social context* not only in the research process but also in the way knowledge is produced and consumed within scholarly and community/activist spaces. Changing social contexts can produce disparate outcomes of the same issue at hand, as social categories can also shift over time. As Joya Misra and colleagues note, "There is no one unified experience or 'true' experience of inequality. Rather, people face oppression in ways that reflect the variation of power and privilege and where the salience of race, class, gender, and other statuses vary according to time, space, and place."[19] Inherently, the consideration of a multitude of identities and experiences within scientific inquiry is complex. The *complexity* of research questions, however, should not deter those pursuing intersectional questions and concerns. Though it often takes a back seat in quantitatively driven research, *social justice* is another key construct of intersectionality. Social justice efforts are necessary if health equity is one of the key objectives of population health research. The concept of social justice is observed in each of the chapters, as Black women's intersectional identities across race, gender, social class, culture, and geography are both barriers and sources of agency in their fight against broader systems of inequality. Black women's agency and unique experiences of inequality and inequity throughout global food systems thread together each chapter in the book.

The geographic spread of women's narratives in the three sections illustrates that the social justice roles Black women play in global food systems are spatial and connect across the Diaspora. "Black matters are spatial matters" is a claim central to Black geographic thought.[20] In this vein, scholars of Black geographic thought center how Black people and communities occupy and make space.[21] Black geographic thought seeks to upend traditional understandings of space and place, puts emphasis on connectivity, and highlights how Black people connect their experiences to the experiences of other Black people across the Diaspora. In this book, we see that Black women's experiences with oppression impact how they seek to change the food system. This is not a new claim, as Black women have always sought to create food spaces that are freeing and liberating for themselves and others.[22] We aim to show that the "Black food geographies" that Black women create are complex, transformational, and rooted in the local and global community.[23] The connectivity evident in Black women's roles in the global food system is an important lesson for those fighting against food insecurity and for food justice. This connectivity across space accounts for the broad diversity that exists among Black women in different places and is a model for a food movement that continues to struggle to build coalitions and find commonalities.

The Book

As a group of researchers, educators, and food justice activists, we have compiled material that brings to light Black women from Africa, the Caribbean, and the United States who incorporate sustainable and environmentally safe food production practices, provide education about meal planning and healthy lifestyles, and work as or with farmers to make food accessible to low-income people and underserved women of color and their families. We also highlight the voices of Black women who establish local restaurants and urban gardens and act as food justice activists. While this book brings together the voices of authors and their research participants, we acknowledge that Black women's food networks have always existed. However, we stress the power of speaking collectively. The authors in this book, both intentionally and unintentionally, speak with one another and present the wholeness and complexity of Black women's work in global food systems. The collective voices are illustrative of how, throughout the Diaspora, Black women are consistently striving within global food systems for self-sufficiency and a fair food system that challenges racism, sexism, and classism. Black women's intersectional identities are embedded in a capitalist global food system.

The arguments, narratives, and information presented in each ensuing chapter serve to enlighten food scholars, activists, practitioners, and policymakers to reconsider the roles that Black women of the Diaspora play in local and international food and nutrition efforts. We identify the many barriers Black women face in their participation in global food systems and show that, despite the many challenges, Black women play central roles in food projects. In particular, they are critical in feeding themselves, their families, low-income communities of color, and other vulnerable populations. The approach we take also recognizes that, as vital members of their families and communities, Black women participate in global food systems, and that participation is key to understanding and addressing overall health and the potential health disparities that exist within and between communities worldwide. Black women must constantly negotiate the gendered social, economic, environmental, cultural, and political forces that impact food supply, nutrient quality, and affordability for themselves, their families, and their communities.

Beyond the Kitchen Table: Black Women and Global Food Systems is about many things. It is, in part, about Black women's role in fighting hunger and poverty as well as in achieving food security for themselves, their families, and their communities. The UN has defined food security as a situation whereby "all people, at all times, have physical, social and economic access to sufficient, safe and nutritious food that meets their dietary needs and food preferences for an active and healthy life."[24] This book is also about Black women's fight for food justice, a fight that has always been a part of Black women's history and that unfolds on the pages of this book. Likewise, this book tells the story of

Black women's current food and agricultural knowledge and how it is passed on and remembered within Black communities. Additionally, the book reveals Black women's joy, which often comes through communing with other Black women in food and agricultural spaces. While we understand the field and the kitchen to be spaces of trauma and pain, we simultaneously understand them to be spaces of joy, where women navigate their freedom. And finally, this book is about Black women's physical and emotional health, as we recognize that growing and consuming food is at the heart of sustaining this health. In the ensuing chapters, the book systematically looks at the centrality of Black women's transformative, participatory, and liberatory approach to sustainable agriculture, food justice, and family and community health and well-being.

This book brings together Black women's voices from around the globe, as we echo the growing call to listen to Black women. While this call is heard most loudly during cries for racial and social justice, this sentiment is echoed in academic circles, most noticeably in the Cite Black Women Collective.[25] In this book, we bring together a collection of articles and authors that highlight Black women's agency, assert their food voices, and combat the negative stereotypes that cast Black women's presence in global food systems in elusive and often racialized, sexist ways. Black women's food voices come through in this book to portray the women as activists, research participants, and researchers; we recognize that for many, such a strict delineation between roles does not exist. We were intentional about soliciting chapters from Black women authors and were successful. While there is increasing literature *on* Black people in global food systems, there seems to be less written *by* Black scholars, with an underlying sentiment that this scholarship does not exist. We know that this work exists and build on it in this edited volume. Most of the editors and chapter authors are Black women, and those who are not write with intention and in close community with Black women.

FROM THE FIELDS

The millions of Black women who work in agricultural fields inspired us to write this book and the first section, "From the Fields." According to the Food and Agriculture Organization, the leading international food and agriculture organization, on average, women represent 43 percent of the world's agricultural labor force and 47 percent of the workers in the global fisheries industry.[26] In "Women in Agriculture: Closing the Gender Gap for Development," part 1 of its 2010–11 *State of Food and Agriculture* report, the Food and Agriculture Organization highlighted that women produce more than half of the world's food, and in developing countries including Africa and the Caribbean, women account for 60–80 percent of food production. The Food and Agriculture Organization estimates that if the world's women farmers had the same access to resources as men, 150 million people could be lifted out of poverty. The women who come alive in the pages of our book are farmers, farmworkers, agro-processors, marketers, entrepreneurs, merchants, researchers, and innovators, who are the backbone of the world's food systems.[27] Their range of activities in the food system is intangible in their social and economic investments in community building that are unrecognized and undervalued by many. Moreover, women in the fields must navigate time, effort, and other resources while taking care of families and households. Regardless of the stage in the food chain that Black women operate, we find that they are the custodians of the land and the protectors of the environment because their families' livelihoods, health, and well-being depend on what they grow and prepare at kitchen tables. They are prone to becoming leaders of sustainable food systems and champions of food security and nutritional diets.

This section begins with Lydia Kwoyiga and Agnes Atia Apusigah, who, in their chapter, "Rural Women, Household Food Provisioning, and Dry-Season Ground Water Irrigation in Northern Ghana," show how rural women, despite being excluded from land, are still able to negotiate and produce on marginal plots because of their need to produce basic staples for their families. By devising strategies to overcome the challenges of the dry season, they are food champions in their homes and communities. The authors discuss the use of groundwater irrigation by women who break gender barriers and maintain their roles as household food providers vis-à-vis men. This transformational role of Black women is further illustrated in chapter 2 with Eveline M. F. W. Sawadogo/Compaoré and Sakiko Shiratori's case study on cowpea in Burkina Faso. The authors creatively use the cultivation, preparation, and consumption of a "women's crop" to show how some African women are taking control of household food consumption and food security on a daily basis. The next two chapters in this section highlight how Black women contribute to sustainable food systems in innovative and environmentally protective ways. Gloria Sanders McCutcheon's piece, "The Role of Women in Sustainable Agriculture in Three Global Regions: Environmentally Friendly Practices and Passing Knowledge Along to Future Generations," investigates the complexity of Black women's management of parasitic wasps in the southern United States of America, the Caribbean (Cuba), and sub-Saharan Africa (Zimbabwe). She speaks to how Black women—mothers, grandmothers, wives, and sisters—in the fields use holistic methods that are a combination of the natural and social worlds to provide environmentally friendly alternatives to chemical control in food production. Including her own experiences, Sanders McCutcheon explains how women balance their field and home responsibilities while educating children about sustainable food systems. In chapter 4, we see a comparable situation in a small rural village in the Caribbean, where a study by Kenia-Rosa Campo, Wendy-Ann Isaac, Neela Badrie, and Marquitta Webb illustrates how the integration of small-scale aquaculture in female-headed homesteads is linked to improved household food security, better nutrition for women and children, and women's empowerment. Interestingly, the researchers also make the point that women's participation in the aquaculture project is part and parcel of maintaining and building social systems resilience, particularly in rural communities.

In summation, all the chapters in this section of the book affirm that Black women in the fields engage in household food production, food security, dietary diversity, food intake, economic innovation, and women's empowerment. Moreover, the studies highlight women as managers and leaders at the very beginning of the global food systems chain. They are in many ways social justice activists and advocates taking control of both sustenance and sustainability, mitigating change and challenges in rural and urban spaces throughout the Diaspora. Similar gendered patterns of women's empowerment are also observed beyond the fields and kitchen tables, as explained in the next two sections.

FOOD AND SOCIAL JUSTICE

The chapters in this section are reflective of Black women's ability to dream and actualize a food system that is just for all. In *Freedom Dreams*, Robin D. G. Kelley speaks of his mother's ability to see with her third eye and dream of "land, a spacious house, fresh air, organic food and endless meadows without boundaries."[28] Kelley ends his seminal work with a chapter on the necessity of Black women leading liberation movements and the charge for justice. Few food studies interrogate the word "justice" and how its use might be exclusive to certain individuals or racialized groups of people. Agyeman, Bullard, and Evans are a notable exception in their conceptualization of "just sustainability," which they define as "the need to ensure a better quality of life for all, now, and into the future, in a just and equitable manner, whilst living within the limits of supporting ecosystems."[29] They implore others to consider justice broadly, without the qualifiers of food and environment. More recently, Joshua Sbicca defines food justice as "all ideas and practices that strive to eliminate oppression and challenge the structural drivers of all inequities within and beyond the food system."[30] Without addressing social, economic, and geographic inequalities, food justice can never be achieved. More recent definitions of food justice fall in line with our authors' beliefs on justice in their chapters. By centering Black women's lived experiences, they account for how all aspects of their lives influence their fight for justice. They are fighting to be fed materially but also to ensure that they have access to land to grow the food and, more important, to control over the types of food that they, their families, and their communities consume. Despite their conditions, Black women work tirelessly to ensure that they, their families, and their communities are fed, as they understand that more than equality is needed to guide our food systems.

The four chapters in this section focus on how Black women's theorization of food justice is action based and practiced through daily food and agrarian routines. In chapter 5, "Making Spaces Something Like Freedom: Black Feminist Praxis in the Re/Imagining of a Just Food System," Ashanté M. Reese and Dara Cooper explore how Black feminism can be used as a political and personal framework for food justice efforts, particularly in terms of women's leadership, relationship building, and stewardship of the earth, as well as an "ethics of care" that is not individual but based on community needs and concerns. In chapter 6, shakara tyler further pays attention to how Black women do and teach food justice in "Mothering in Historical Black Agrarian Pedagogies: A Historiography." She centers the role of mothering and "othermothering" by Black women to educate Black communities both formally and informally. Mothering is used as a teaching tool to ensure that agrarian practices are preserved and passed down to future generations. In chapter 6, tyler emphasizes that mothering and othermothering occur in civil rights and other Black-run organizations that may or may not be women focused.

Claudia J. Ford also pays close attention to the word "justice" but does so from an agrarian perspective in chapter 7, "Recipes for Resistance: Stories of Black Women Leading Food and Agricultural Justice Movements on Farms." Like Reese and Cooper, she takes a step back to focus on how the agro-industrial food system has stifled justice and the inventive ways that Black women continue to insert calls for social justice into the agrarian justice movement. For Ford, justice is reflective of Black women's desire for a system where they are free and liberated and have control over their food sources. Finally, Ford shows Black women's resistance and resilience in fighting for a just food system in both the past and the present. The idea that Black women use inventive daily methods to ensure that justice is a part of their food work is carried over into chapter 8, "My Planting Is to Farm Community: Afro–Costa Rican Women's

Agrarian Food Practices." Here, Kelsey Emard and Veronica Gordon show how Black women use acts of gathering, preparing, and serving food to fight against the broader structures, saying, "These food practices have been and are still used by Afro–Costa Ricans to resist the oppression of plantation economies, state neglect, and tourism industries that too often profit from the production of gender and racial inequalities."

Authors in this section all emphasize the importance of Black women sharing information about food practices with one another in inventive ways such as storytelling. In particular, in chapter 8, Emard and Gordon explore food practices through Afro–Costa Rican women's stories about how they feed their communities. What is fascinating about these women's stories is how innovative they are in responding to changes in the broader agro-systems. Gordon's food practices move beyond the kitchen table; they are tied to the field of production and mainly the state's inability to feed its people. The state, the individual, and the community are key to the story she is telling. In Chapter 6, tyler systematically shows that for Black women, feeding Black people is educational and actualized through Black-operated organizations, including the Black Panther Party, the Louisiana Farmers' Union, and the Freedom Quilting Bee. In these organizations, Black women's food practices are passed down from one generation to another.

Collectively, the chapters in this section underscore the need for another definition of food justice. Moreover, this definition may lie in the lived experiences of Black women who have always had to navigate a hostile food landscape. However, often in this very same hostile landscape, Black women have created food systems that are liberating and just. In "Plantation Futures," Katherine McKittrick encourages us to sit with the messiness that exists in oppressive landscapes, acknowledging the remarkable and creative ways that Black people have resisted in spite of, and often on the same site as, oppression.[31] This section also shows us that the ways Black women fight for food justice are through using care, mothering, and othermothering to ensure that their food practices are passed down. Finally, this section reminds us that the where of food work often occurs beyond the kitchen table and can happen on farms and in community spaces, among others.

FOOD SECURITY, HEALTH, AND WELL-BEING

The final section of the book, "Food Security, Health, and Well-Being," explores Black women's experiences of food security, or the lack thereof, and the health and well-being of themselves, their families, and their communities.

The presence of food security "exists when all people, at all times, have physical and economic access to sufficient, safe, and nutritious food that meets their dietary needs and food preferences for an active and healthy life."[32] The adverse relationships between food security and health, nutrition, and well-being among Black women largely can be explained by their unequal social and cultural positions within societies globally. Women serve vital roles as caretakers and household economic providers. If the health and subsequent livelihood of women diminishes, the economic, health, and food availability of households and communities may be impacted. A lack of food security can heighten the already vulnerable state of women and their households, as women in adverse circumstances must rely on a variety of coping strategies, such as selling their possessions, in order to survive.[33]

Research regarding the relationship between food security and health and well-being often neglects the heterogeneity and lived experiences of Black women both within specific countries and throughout the Diaspora. Quality social science research can greatly assist in our understanding of the issues Black women face when attempting to provide for themselves, their families, and their communities. Careful consideration of key theoretical perspectives is needed to comprehend how women contextualize food security across both their life course and familial generations. In chapter 9, Latrica E. Best takes an intersectional approach to health and food studies research on Black women in "Black Women, Food, and Health: Exploring the Importance of Intersectionality in Population-Based Health Studies." Her piece assesses both population health and food research in an effort to understand how these avenues of research can collectively address food-related health concerns among Black women. Specifically, she argues that all strands of research would benefit greatly from the inclusion of an intersectional approach to provide a more well-rounded understanding of Black women's health. Previous population health research, which often does not consider the multitude of Black women's identities and experiences, is still being used as a guide point for understanding Black women's food consumption and health outcomes. If our approach to interpreting this research lacks nuance, it is no wonder that there is little advancement in Black women's health.

The two remaining chapters in this section highlight the importance of Black women's roles in food security, the resilience these women exhibit when faced with limited resources and inadequate access to food, and the importance of intergenerational relationships in maintaining food security, identity, and health. The resiliency exhibited by the women discussed in the research throughout this section also underscores the impact of the enduring intergenerational relationships that women maintain. With each strategy women employ to make meaning of their relationships with food and food security, research shows that the women are building upon their familial understandings of food. In chapter 10, "I Put Food on Everyone's Table: Food Provisioning, Domestic Work, and Business across Three Generations of Black Women in Santiago de Cuba," Hanna Garth examines three generations of Black women in a low-income family in Santiago to capture the role of the grandmother in providing the necessary support for others to successfully engage in the labor force. Garth considers key sociopolitical and historical moments in Cuba's history to illustrate how women in each generation engaged in various forms of labor to strengthen food security and health in their families. Shelene Gomes extends on Garth's work in her chapter on intergenerational households and the importance of food to assess cultural and national identity, motherhood, and the gendered division of labor in family-run restaurants among Caribbean Rastafari migrants in urban Ethiopia, "Tasting Freedom: The Rastafari Family Food Beit in Ethiopia" (chapter 11). The importance of maintaining their cultural (Rastafari) and national (Jamaican or Trinbagonian) identities within Ethiopia has led to significant changes in how Rastafari women engage in food production, which has several implications for their overall adjustment to their new communities and vice versa.

In summation, this section goes beyond the role of Black women in the production and preparation of food to better understand how food is intertwined with women's experiences across their life course. These chapters all touch upon three key areas of research that successfully link Black women's work in establishing food security for the well-being of themselves and others. The chapters in this section provide effective examples of the importance of harnessing women's resiliency and experiences with intersectional forms of discrimination and oppression, the significance of intergenerational and life course perspectives on the meaning of food and nutrition, and the understanding of demographic and socioeconomic forces in how women make meaning of their food voices and well-being. The diversity of the subject areas displayed in these chapters illustrates the need for researchers, policymakers, and activists alike to explore broader, multifaceted conceptualizations of the terms "health" and "well-being" when discussing how Black women impact, and affect, global food systems.

This book, *Beyond the Kitchen Table: Black Women and Global Food Systems*, aims to amplify the voices of Black women, who are often silenced in larger discussions of global food systems in many academic, policy, and social justice spaces. There is often the acknowledgment that Black women's voices are important but not a willingness to actually listen to what Black women say and, more important, to pass the mantle of leadership to Black women. Historically throughout the Diaspora, Black women have served, and continue to serve, crucial roles in every aspect of food systems—from working in the fields and fighting food justice struggles beyond the kitchen table for food security and sustainability to advocating for family and community health and well-being. They exercise their human agency, challenging gender barriers and uprooting racism and other ethnic biases, while at the same time bringing awareness and establishing ethical and safe food practices. They are major players in promoting fair food economies and providing food security to low-income and underserved communities throughout the Diaspora and the world. Each chapter in the book tells a different but interrelated story of Black women's lives, struggles, successes, and sustenance. Collectively, they make visible the women who are the prime nurturers of Planet Earth and its people.

NOTES

1. McCutcheon, "Fannie Lou Hamer's"; White, *Freedom Farmers*; Williams-Forson, *Building Houses*; Smith, *African American Environmental Thought*; Carney, *Black Rice*; Collins, *Black Feminist Thought*.
2. Yakupitiyage, "More Women Owning."
3. We define the Black Diaspora as communities of African-descended people around the world whose Black identity is shaped by the geographical, colonial, and racial structures of the transatlantic slave trade. We use "African Diaspora" and "Black Diaspora" interchangeably throughout this book.
4. McCutcheon, "Fannie Lou Hamer's"; Carney, *Black Rice*.
5. Rajack-Talley, *Poverty Is a Person*.
6. Neff et al., "Food Systems."
7. Strings, "Obese Black Women."
8. Ahima and Lazar, "Health Risk of Obesity"; Anderson, "Whose Voice Counts?"; Guthman, *Weighing In*; Nuttall, "Body Mass Index."
9. Guthman, "Doing Justice to Bodies?," 1166.
10. Popkin, Adair, and Ng, "Global Nutrition Transition."
11. Rajack-Talley, "Agriculture, Trade Liberalization and Poverty."
12. Crenshaw, "Demarginalizing the Intersection of Race and Sex."
13. Collins and Bilge, *Intersectionality*, 67.
14. Collins, *Intersectionality as Critical Social Theory*.
15. Bow et al., "Combahee River Collective Statement."
16. Crenshaw, "Mapping the Margins."
17. Guy-Sheftall, *Words of Fire*; Hudson-Weems, *Africana Womanism*.
18. Collins and Bilge, *Intersectionality*, 47.

19. Misra, Curington, and Green, "Methods of Intersectional Research," 13.
20. McKittrick, *Demonic Grounds*.
21. Reese, *Black Food Geographies*; Bledsoe, Eaves, and Williams, "Introduction"; Woods and Gilmore, *Development Arrested*; Shabazz, *Spatializing Blackness*; McKittrick, "Plantation Futures"; McKittrick and Woods, *Black Geographies*; McKittrick, *Demonic Grounds*.
22. McCutcheon, "Fannie Lou Hamer's"; White, *Freedom Farmers*.
23. Reese, *Black Food Geographies*.
24. "Food Security," International Food Policy Research Institute, 2019, www.ifpri.org/topic/food-security.
25. Cite Black Women Collective, 2020, www.citeblackwomencollective.org.
26. Food and Agriculture Organization, "Role of Women."
27. Food and Agriculture Organization, "Women in Agriculture."
28. Kelley, *Freedom Dreams*, 92–93.
29. Agyeman, Bullard, and Evans, *Just Sustainabilities*, 5.
30. Sbicca, *Food Justice Now!*, 388–92.
31. McKittrick, "Plantation Futures."
32. "Rome Declaration on World Food Security," Food and Agriculture Organization, November 1996, www.fao.org/docrep/003/w3613e/w3613e00.htm.
33. Kendall, Olson, and Frongillo, "Relationship of Hunger."

WORKS CITED

Agyeman, Julian, Robert D. Bullard, and Bob Evans, eds. *Just Sustainabilities: Development in an Unequal World*. Cambridge: Massachusetts Institute of Technology Press, 2003.

Ahima, Rexford S., and Mitchell A. Lazar. "The Health Risk of Obesity—Better Metrics Imperative." *Science* 341, no. 6148 (August 2013): 856–58.

Anderson, Jenn. "Whose Voice Counts? A Critical Examination of Discourses Surrounding the Body Mass Index." *Fat Studies* 1, no. 2 (January 2012): 195–207.

Bledsoe, Adam, LaToya Eaves, and Brian Williams. "Introduction: Black Geographies in and of the United States South." *Southeastern Geographer* 57, no. 1 (January 2017): 6–11.

Bow, Leslie, Avtar Brah, Mishuana Goeman, Diane Harriford, Analouise Keating, Yi-Chun Tricia Lin, Laura Pérez, et al. "Combahee River Collective Statement: A Fortieth Anniversary Retrospective." *Frontiers* 38, no. 3 (2017): 164–89.

Carney, Judith Ann. *Black Rice: The African Origins of Rice Cultivation in the Americas*. Boston: Harvard University Press, 2001.

Collins, Patricia Hill. *Black Feminist Thought: Knowledge, Consciousness, and the Politics of Empowerment*. New York: Routledge, 1990.

———. *Intersectionality as Critical Social Theory*. Durham, NC: Duke University Press, 2019.

Collins, Patricia Hill, and Sirma Bilge. *Intersectionality*. New York: John Wiley and Sons, 2020.

Crenshaw, Kimberlé. "Demarginalizing the Intersection of Race and Sex: A Black Feminist Critique of Antidiscrimination Doctrine, Feminist Theory, and Antiracist Politics." *University of Chicago Legal Forum* 1989, no. 8 (1989): 139–67.

———. "Mapping the Margins: Intersectionality, Identity Politics, and Violence against Women of Color." *Stanford Law Review* 43, no. 6 (1991): 1241–300.
Food and Agriculture Organization. "The Role of Women in Agriculture." Prepared by the SOFA Team and Cheryl Doss. ESA Working Paper No. 11–02. Rome: FAO Agricultural Development Economics Division, 2011. www.fao.org/publications/card/en/c/8989aace-6356%E2%80%935e14-b7bf-ad8fdb7148c6/.
———. "Women in Agriculture: Closing the Gender Gap for Development." Part 1, in *The State of Food and Agriculture 2010–2011*. Rome: FAO, 2011. www.fao.org/3/i2050e/i2050e00.htm.
Guthman, Julie. "Doing Justice to Bodies? Reflections on Food Justice, Race, and Biology." *Antipode* 46, no. 5 (2014): 1153–71.
———. *Weighing In: Obesity, Food Justice, and the Limits of Capitalism*. Berkeley: University of California Press, 2011.
Guy-Sheftall, Beverly. *Words of Fire: An Anthology of African American Feminist Thought*. New York: New Press, 1995.
Hudson-Weems, Clenora. *Africana Womanism: Reclaiming Ourselves*. New York: Routledge, 2019.
Kelley, Robin D. G. *Freedom Dreams: The Black Radical Imagination*. Boston: Beacon, 2008.
Kendall, A., C. M. Olson, and E. A. Frongillo. "Relationship of Hunger and Food Insecurity to Food Availability and Consumption." *Journal of the American Dietetic Association* 96, no. 10 (October 1996): 1019–24; quiz, 1025–26.
McCutcheon, Priscilla. "Fannie Lou Hamer's Freedom Farms and Black Agrarian Geographies." *Antipode* 51, no. 1 (January 2019): 207–24.
McKittrick, Katherine. *Demonic Grounds: Black Women and the Cartographies of Struggle*. Minneapolis: University of Minnesota Press, 2006.
———. "Plantation Futures." *Small Axe* 17, no. 3 (2013): 1–15.
McKittrick, Katherine, and Clyde Adrian Woods, eds. *Black Geographies and the Politics of Place*. Toronto, ON: South End, 2007.
Misra, Joya, Celeste Vaughan Curington, and Venus Mary Green. "Methods of Intersectional Research." *Sociological Spectrum* 41, no. 1 (January 2021): 9–28.
Neff, Roni A., Anne M. Palmer, Shawn E. Mckenzie, and Robert S. Lawrence. "Food Systems and Public Health Disparities." *Journal of Hunger and Environmental Nutrition* 4, no. 3–4 (July 2009): 282–314.
Nuttall, Frank Q. "Body Mass Index: Obesity, BMI, and Health; A Critical Review." *Nutrition Today* 50, no. 3 (May 2015): 117–28.
Popkin, Barry M., Linda S. Adair, and Shu Wen Ng. "Global Nutrition Transition and the Pandemic of Obesity in Developing Countries." *Nutrition Reviews* 70, no. 1 (January 2012): 3–21.
Rajack-Talley, Theresa Ann. "Agriculture, Trade Liberalization and Poverty in the ACP Countries." In *Agricultural Development and Food Security in Developing Nations*, edited by Wayne G. Ganpat, Ronald Dyer, and Wendy-Ann P. Isaac, 1–20. Hershey, PA: IGI Global, 2016.
———. *Poverty Is a Person: Human Agency, Women and Caribbean Households*. Kingston, Jamaica: Ian Randle, 2016.
Reese, Ashanté M. *Black Food Geographies: Race, Self-Reliance, and Food Access in Washington, D.C.* Chapel Hill: University of North Carolina Press, 2019.

Sbicca, Joshua. *Food Justice Now! Deepening the Roots of Social Struggle.* Minneapolis: University of Minnesota Press, 2018.

Shabazz, Rashad. *Spatializing Blackness: Architectures of Confinement and Black Masculinity in Chicago.* Champaign: University of Illinois Press, 2017.

Smith, Kimberly K. *African American Environmental Thought: Foundations.* Lawrence: University Press of Kansas, 2007.

Strings, Sabrina. "Obese Black Women as 'Social Dead Weight': Reinventing the 'Diseased Black Woman.'" *Signs* 41, no. 1 (2015): 107–30.

White, Monica M. *Freedom Farmers: Agricultural Resistance and the Black Freedom Movement.* Chapel Hill: University of North Carolina Press, 2018.

Williams-Forson, Psyche A. *Building Houses Out of Chicken Legs: Black Women, Food, and Power.* Chapel Hill: University of North Carolina Press, 2006.

Woods, Clyde Adrian, and Ruth Wilson Gilmore. *Development Arrested: The Blues and Plantation Power in the Mississippi Delta.* 2nd ed. London: Verso Books, 2017.

Yakupitiyage, Tharanga. "More Women Owning Agricultural Land in Africa Means Increased Food Security and Nutrition." Hunger Notes, September 30, 2018. www.worldhunger.org/more-women-owning-agricultural-land-in-africa-means-increased-food-security-and-nutrition.

PART 1

From the Fields

THERESA RAJACK-TALLEY

"Women Feed the World"

Women play a decisive role in household and national food security. In rural areas—home to the majority of the world's hungry—they grow most of the crops for domestic consumption and are primarily responsible for preparing, storing, and processing food. They also handle livestock; gather food, fodder, and fuelwood; and manage the domestic water supply. In addition, they provide most of the labor for postharvest activities. Yet this women's work often goes unrecognized, and women lack the leverage necessary to gain access to resources, training, and finances.[1]

The millions of Black women who work in the fields inspired us to write this book and this section, "From the Fields."[2] Moreover, during the time we were all writing our chapters, world hunger dramatically worsened—in large part due to the repercussions of COVID-19. While the pandemic's impact has yet to be fully assessed, the World Health Organization estimates that around one-tenth of the global population—up to 811 million people—was undernourished in 2020. It will take a tremendous effort for the world to meet its goal to end hunger by 2030.[3] To envision transforming food systems to achieve food security, improve nutrition, and put healthy diets within reach of all, a focus on women in the fields is imperative.

According to the Food and Agriculture Organization of the United Nations, the leading international organization of its type, on average, women represent 43 percent of the world's agricultural labor force and 47 percent of the workers in the global fisheries industry. They produce more than half of the world's food. In developing countries, including Africa and the Caribbean, women account for 60–80 percent of food production.[4] The Food and Agriculture Organization also believes that if the world's women farmers had the same access to resources as men, 150 million people could be lifted out of poverty. In North America, there is also a resurgence in the focus on "farming while Black" for similar reasons. Leah Penniman's publication by the same name provides a blueprint for connecting Black people to the land via practical farm instruction and is also a spiritual reflection on mind, body, spirit, and land. Like other Black women in the fields in Africa and the Caribbean, she discusses the close connections to land and agriculture as well as the structural constraints of food growers.[5]

It is therefore not surprising that women's empowerment was one of the recommendations of the 2021 *State of Food Security and Nutrition in the World* report, jointly published by the Food and Agriculture Organization, International Fund for Agricultural Development, UNICEF, UN World Food Programme, and World Health Organization.[6] We recognize that such empowerment requires making women's voices heard as well as collecting and using gender-disaggregated data and gender analyses. This section of the book aims to do this by incorporating microlevel analyses of case studies on women's experiences in the fields voiced by the women themselves. The women who come alive in the pages of our book are farmers, farmworkers, agro-processors, marketers, entrepreneurs, merchants, researchers, and innovators—collectively they are the mainframe of the world's food systems. Their range of activities in the food system is intangible in their social and economic investments in their households, communities, and neighborhoods and worthy of recognition and value.

We begin the book with this section—"From the Fields"—to highlight the key roles women play before food reaches kitchen tables. As food producers, women make critical contributions to household and neighborhood food security. The experiences described in the following chapters vividly paint the conditions under which women in the fields work and the contested terrains they must navigate. Through their agency, they take control to ensure food security and consumption as well as sustainable practices. Their multitasking and highly analytical skills are essential to their survival and growth.

Food Consumption and Security

Despite the many gender barriers women face in agriculture, they continue to contribute to food security by producing food for family consumption, defying social, economic, cultural, and environmental limitations. Their tenacity to do so and the mechanisms and modi operandi they use are observed in chapters 1–4. For example, in chapter 2, "From Farm to Kitchen: Women's Role in Three Dimensions—Production, Processing, and Consumption—in Burkina Faso," Eveline M. F. W. Sawadogo/Compaoré and Sakiko Shiratori employ a case study methodology to describe how women farmers creatively dominate in the cultivation and preparation of cowpea, so much so that cowpea is commonly referred to as a "women's crop." Because cowpea is a staple for the family diet, these African women are taking control of household food security on an everyday basis. Similarly, in chapter 1, "Rural Women, Household Food Provisioning, and Dry-Season Groundwater Irrigation in Northern Ghana," Lydia Kwoyiga and Agnes Atia Apusigah examine how Ghanaian women exercise their agency to overcome the many challenges that rural farmers experience, especially in the dry season, to feed families. They discuss the use of groundwater irrigation by women who break gender barriers and maintain their roles as household food providers vis-à-vis the men. In "Fish Farming: Women in Food Production for Improved Household Food and Nutrition Security in Ortoire Village, Mayaro, Trinidad—a Case Study" (chapter 4), we see a comparable situation across the Atlantic in a small rural village in the Caribbean, where Kenia-Rosa Campo, Wendy-Ann Isaac, Neela Badrie, and Marquitta Webb examine the integration of small-scale aquaculture in female-headed homesteads. The link between aquaculture and these homesteads is associated with improved household food security, increased nutrition for women and children, and higher women's empowerment. Interestingly, the researchers also make the point that women's participation in the aquaculture project is not only helping household economies but is part and parcel of maintaining and building socioeconomic system resilience in rural communities.

Navigating Family, Community, and the Environment

Women have also always carefully balanced what they do in the fields with what they do in their homes and communities. The chapters in this section also reveal how women in the fields navigate time, labor, finances, and other resources while taking care of their families and households. They skillfully balance their domestic responsibilities and household income earnings while trying to provide fresh, healthy, and accessible foods in spaces that have been identified as rural in some spaces and as "food deserts" in more urban settings. The chapters in part 1 are predominantly case studies in rural communities and show how taking care of neighborhood families is equally important to women as taking care of their own families. This is made clear in chapter 1, where Kwoyiga and Apusigah describe why adopting a groundwater irrigation system in the dry season is important, and in chapter 2, where Sawadogo/Compaoré and Shiratori explain the production of cowpea, a "women's crop," in Burkina Faso, used by women to feed their families and others. On the other hand, in chapter 4, Campo, Isaac, Badrie, and Webb's case study of small-scale aquaculture in a rural community in Trinidad explains the economic value of what women do for themselves, their families, and the community.

Moreover, women in the fields are cognizant that their current livelihoods and the livelihoods of future generations rely on a sustainable and protected environment. They are sometimes referred to as sacred custodians of the environment and of biodiversity or as the voice of the environment. All the chapters in this section highlight the fact that regardless of the stage in the food chain that Black women operate, they assume roles as custodians of the land and protectors of the environment. The various practices they adopt demonstrate that they are leaders of sustainable food systems and champions of food security and nutritional diets. Black women's roles in environmental protection and sustainable food systems are particularly evident in Gloria Sanders McCutcheon's piece, "The Role of Women in Sustainable Agriculture in Three Global Regions: Environmentally Friendly Practices and Passing Knowledge Along to Future Generations" (chapter 3). Sanders McCutcheon provides a personal account of how women adopt biological pest control as an environmentally safe agriculture practice, while at the same time employing the practice as an educational tool for children to learn about sustainable food systems.

She argues that as the impacts of climate change become increasingly pertinent and as hunger and poverty persist or increase in some communities and countries, any strategy to effectively protect the farming environment must involve the Black women—mothers, grandmothers, wives, and sisters—who are in the fields.

Concluding Thoughts

The chapters in this section of the book affirm that Black women in the fields engage in household food production and in doing so are core elements of food security for families and communities. They continuously and bravely empower themselves to do so because their independence and their family well-being depend on their abilities to persist and be successful. The narratives in the case studies show the complexities of the lives of the women who work in the fields to bring food to their kitchen tables and those of others. They must do so while overcoming barriers, protecting the environment and their cultures, and maintaining their social responsibilities of family and community.

NOTES

1. "Women Feed the World," Food and Agriculture Organization, accessed March 28, 2023, www.fao.org/3/x0262e/x0262e16.htm.
2. "From the Fields" represents the experiences and perspectives of women who are currently actively engaged in food production practices.
3. World Health Organization, "UN Report."
4. "Women Feed the World."
5. Penniman, *Farming While Black*.
6. World Health Organization, "UN Report."

WORKS CITED

Penniman, Leah. *Farming While Black: Soul Fire Farm's Practical Guide to Liberation on the Land*. White River Junction, VT: Chelsea Green, 2018.
Tiayon, Shanna B. "Living Off the Land: The New Sisterhood of Black Female Homesteaders." *Guardian*, July 31, 2020. www.theguardian.com/us-news/2020/jul/31/living-off-the-land-the-new-sisterhood-of-black-female-homesteaders.
World Health Organization. "UN Report: Pandemic Year Marked by Spike in World Hunger." July 12, 2021. www.who.int/news/item/12-07-2021-un-report-pandemic-year-marked-by-spike-in-world-hunger.

CHAPTER 1

Rural Women, Household Food Provisioning, and Dry-Season Groundwater Irrigation in Northern Ghana

LYDIA KWOYIGA AND AGNES ATIA APUSIGAH

Introduction

The Food and Agriculture Organization of the United Nations (FAO) estimates that women are the main producers of the world's food globally. It estimates that women contribute between 60 percent and 80 percent of household food in some countries in sub-Saharan Africa. Their contributions are extended when they put their earnings from food processing and vending activities into household food needs.[1] In northern Ghana, Agnes Atiah Apusigah has noted that rural women play critical roles in both producing food and acquiring provisions that are hardly secondary or supplementary.[2] Both their on-farm and off-farm activities contribute to household food provisioning. However, challenges affecting these women's access to productive resources during the on-farm season have pushed them into off-farm alternatives, such as groundwater irrigation farming during the dry season.[3] This shift comes in addition to their normal off-farm work in the informal economy and care, which increases their work burdens, even as they face further competition in an alternative originally targeted at their male counterparts. That notwithstanding, rural women are increasingly engaging in groundwater farming in the dry season in communities endowed with such resources. As Karen G. Villholth points out, groundwater irrigation is gaining roots in sub-Saharan Africa.[4] In northern Ghana, mainly rural communities such as Sirigu, Nyangua, Doba, Mirigu, and Telania, which are endowed with groundwater resources, have become notable for women's dry-season groundwater irrigation activities.[5]

BRIDGE further notes that even though rural women make vital contributions to farming, they usually do not get credit for many of their activities.[6] In northern Ghana, rural women's dependence on groundwater for irrigation has been growing, yet existing studies in the area continue to credit only men. Where women are mentioned, their roles have been usually presented as limited and marginal, often (mis)represented as supplementary rather than complementary. In the city of Tamale in the Northern Region of Ghana, women's roles have been documented to include selling vegetables bought at the farm gate from male farmers, sourcing vegetable accompaniments to staples provided by men, assisting in fencing farm lots, harvesting crops, and even carrying water for the watering of plants. Placing women in such indirect roles suggests that women lack the agency, technical expertise, and skill to participate directly in dry-season irrigation activities in a productive role.[7] In contrast, rural women in the Upper East Region are well known for playing major/primary, rather than minor/secondary, roles. As demonstrated later in this analysis, rural women in communities endowed with groundwater-irrigation farming resources play complementary roles as primary producers rather than supplementary, reproductive roles and those in household food provisioning. For example, evidence abounds about rural women irrigators who rely on permanent wells for groundwater irrigation.[8] These women independently initiate and undertake dry-season groundwater irrigation along the entire production chain. Their agency, in this case, is brought on through the disenfranchisements they experience in their communities and households during the main on-farm season. This contrast is the focus of this study as we explore the contexts and extents to which women's agency is deployed in a food production system.

Undoubtedly, even when exercising agency during off-farm dry-season groundwater irrigation activities, the women still suffer challenges. As FAO has noted, in their quest to produce food, women often face barriers such as lack of access to land, water resources, agricultural support services, and training as well as unfavorable water resources management policies.[9] According to FAO and the Asian Development Bank, women, compared to men, on average own less land, and they are often saddled with smaller plots and challenges in transporting and marketing their produce.[10] They may also have mobility restrictions due to social norms and household care responsibilities. In Ghana, similar factors affect rural women who mostly engage in irrigation or rain-fed agriculture. They are often subjected to the stresses of marginalization and deprivations that impede access and undermine their entitlements as food producers.

Guided by women's empowerment and agency analysis, this paper interrogates the contexts in which rural women irrigators in northern Ghana journey from victimhood to agency by mitigating change and increasing women's empowerment. The analysis is premised on the argument that women's exercise of agency is driven by some compelling factors and forces that threaten their subjective positioning. Within the context of this paper, rural women's roles as household food providers will serve as the basis for interrogating the drivers, but also inhibitors, of their exercise of agency in the face of adversity.

The goal of the paper is, therefore, to examine the contexts and contributions of rural women to household food provisioning through dry-season groundwater irrigation. Specifically, it focuses on the following: (1) rural women's roles as household food providers, (2) ways through which women irrigators exercise agency, (3) opportunity structures for groundwater irrigation, (4) challenges of groundwater irrigation, and (5) ways for mitigating change. The next section of the paper outlines the methodology adopted (data collection, study area and population, and theoretical perspective). The following sections present discussions and analyses of methodology, literature, and empirical data for understanding the situatedness of rural women and groundwater irrigation and household food provisioning in northern Ghana.

Methods, Data, and Study Area

The paper is based on a qualitative study conducted between April and June 2019. According to P. A. Ochieng, a qualitative research approach allows for the understanding of phenomena deeply and in detail because it is associated with methods for the discovery of central themes and analysis of core concerns.[11] Data were obtained through in-depth interviews, informal discussions, personal conversations, participant observations, and desk reviews, resulting in the generation of both primary and secondary data. The in-depth individual interviews were with a total of 100 women irrigators, split evenly between two rural communities, Navio and Nyangua.[12] The data gathered covered themes such as the women's sociodemographic characteristics, their roles in household food provisioning, the negotiation processes for family lands, farm decisions/activities, challenges associated with farming and how they are addressed, and benefits of dry-season farming. The women were selected on a voluntary basis, depending on their willingness to participate. The interviews were conducted by a research assistant who was familiar with the study area and had interacted with the women in the past. The interviews took place on farms, in homes, and at churches at the convenience of the respondents. The interviews were conducted in local languages (i.e., Kasem and Nankam) and transcribed into English.

Nyangua is located in the Kasena/Nankana Municipality, with Navrongo as the administrative capital, while Navio is located in the Kasena/Nankana West District, with Paga as the district capital. Lying within the Guinea savanna woodland vegetative zone of northern Ghana, the two study communities have similar relief, climate, and soil conditions. The climate is characterized by dry and rainy seasons. The rainy season, of only four months, occurs from May to September; it has been getting shorter over the years. The average annual rainfall is 950 millimeters. The landscape is undulating with isolated hills. The vegetation cover is made up of savanna grassland with short trees and stumps. Savanna ochrosol and groundwater laterite are the main types of soil found in the area.

Until recently, the study communities belonged to one local government area. Hence, they have shared governance systems formally and traditionally. Apart from the formal system, they both practice the twin traditional government system of the chiefly and priestly, headed by chiefs and priests, respectively. While chiefs are political heads, priests are spiritual heads. With natural resources such as land and water critical to irrigation activities, both chiefs and priests oversee their governance. Land titles, household headships, and inheritance regimes rest with men. Marriage is also patrilocal. The patriarchal nature of their society has meant that women's interests and rights are traditionally subsumed under those of men. For instance, access to natural resources is through husbands, brothers, and sons.

The people of the rural communities are mainly agrarian and engage in food crop and animal production on a subsistence basis. They have traditionally depended on rain-fed agriculture to produce their main staples such as millet, sorghum, and maize as well as complements such as groundnuts, rice, potatoes, and vegetables. However, the impact of climate change is affecting rain-fed agriculture, pushing people toward groundwater irrigation as an adaptation strategy. Indeed, women are often left with the challenge of providing soup or sauce ingredients with or without the support of men.

Groundwater Irrigation in Ghana

Ghana is endowed with groundwater resources.[13] Rural communities often rely on groundwater as a source of potable water supply.[14] According to B. K. Kortatsi, groundwater is seen as a cheaper and more dominant means of meeting the domestic and agricultural water needs of rural, but also some urban, areas.[15] Indeed, groundwater irrigation in Africa is best understood when viewed from the perspective of the depth of groundwater utilization and funding sources.[16] In Ghana, groundwater irrigation is an activity that involves the cultivation of mostly vegetables using groundwater from wells. According to Regassa E. Namara and colleagues, the location/siting of wells is either in the riverine, usually shallow and temporal, or in the field, as mostly permanent wells.[17] Water from wells is drawn using buckets, ropes, calabashes, and sometimes pumping machines, depending on the depth of the well and its distance to the cropping area. The activity is initiated by individual farmers, both male and female. It is financed privately through personal earnings or savings. A key characteristic of groundwater irrigation here is that it is largely driven by the application of local knowledge. That is, local knowledge is applied to locate sites for the wells and to construct and maintain them. Local knowledge is further applied throughout the farming processes, from nursing seedlings and watering crops to applying chemicals, weeding, and harvesting the produce. The Upper East, Volta, and Greater Accra Regions are notable areas for groundwater irrigation farming in the country.

Northern Ghana is considered one of the poorest areas in the country due to its characteristically prolonged dry seasons now exacerbated by climate change conditions, and hunger and famine in the dry season has become a yearly norm there as food insecurity rises. Alternative livelihood activities have become crucial to provide food for the household in the off-farm season as a way of adapting to the change.[18] For communities endowed with groundwater irrigation resources, dry-season farming has become an important source for the supply of vegetables such as tomatoes, peppers, carrots, cabbages, lettuces, onions, green beans, and okras; roots and tubers such as potatoes; nuts and cereals such as rice, groundnuts, and cowpeas; and even fruits such as melons, bananas, and mangoes. These are consumed at home or sold in the market for cash.

As Namara and colleagues have noted, groundwater irrigation is contributing to offsetting food insecurity and reducing poverty.[19] It provides much-needed food and nutrition as well as employment and income for many rural households and communities during the off-farm season. In terms of gender, both men and women engage in groundwater irrigation during the dry season. Although men tend to dominate, women also actively participate either by becoming independent irrigators or by providing supporting services in the form of farm labor or the processing and marketing of produce.

Rural Women and Household Food Provisioning: Situational Analysis

Niara Sudarkasa has revealed that women in Africa play multiple roles in households. Furthermore, their roles are more complementary than supplementary.[20] In the Upper East Region of Ghana, apart from preparing food, rural women work alongside men in many of the stages of production.[21] Their traditional roles in the kitchen have entailed preparing and serving food to family members for nourishment. They often receive supplies of staple foods in the form of cereals such as millet, guinea corn/sorghum, and maize from the family produce and are left to convert that to food at the point of feeding. How the women make the conversion or provide complements to the staple foods is up to them. Basically, while women and men work together to produce staple foods as family produce, the task of converting or processing these foods into feed, and especially into soup ingredients, is left up to women. Hence, out of necessity, women are compelled to seek alternative ways to process the staples and to provide soup and sauce ingredients and cooking fuel, among others.[22] They also cultivate food crops such as nuts, beans, rice, and vegetables to complement the staples during food preparation. Apart from the complements that can be produced, women are expected to be able to buy others such as salt, spices, fish, and meat. Thus positioned, women have to engage in active production of food or income generation to complement household food provisioning.

This notwithstanding, the existing patriarchal structures and what Sudarkasa considers the deliberate implementation of colonial policies minimalize women's contributions and limit their access to important production resources.[23] Such structures and policies downplay women's primary roles as farmers and subordinate them to men. In fact, it is their so-called place in the kitchen and not outside of it—on the farm—that is valued and appreciated. Such derogatory narratives about women are even maintained during political and development discussions on both local and international platforms. For instance, in 2016 when the German press asked Nigeria's sitting president, Muhammadu Buhari, about his wife's dissident stance on his politics, he said—while standing next to German chancellor Angela Merkel, one of the world's most powerful leaders, a woman—among other things that his wife belonged in his kitchen. Though his statement received sharp criticism, his position remains a dominant notion about women and their roles in African households. Despite that misguided notion, the reality is that women perform various activities inside and outside of the kitchen to further household food provisioning and well-being.

Insofar as household food provisioning is concerned, the kitchen remains an important space for women's agency. It is a space where women experience the complexity of social positioning in all its doggedness and double-edgedness, empowerment and disempowerment. The central role that women play in food preparation and household feeding suggests women's power in feeding and nourishment. In his book *Anatomy of Female Power*, Chinweizu analyzes sites of women's power to show how women's roles in the kitchen enable them to exercise control over men.[24] Although Chinweizu's position and analysis are controversial, it is also the case that household food provisioning as a major site for women's work is also a site of power. In truth, women determine what to prepare and how to prepare it. They also determine whom to feed, how, where, and when. However, the extent to which women can exercise such power depends on what is available and what patriarchal strings exist and regulate that power. For instance, when the staple food supplier (who should be appropriately regarded as the custodian of jointly produced family foods), the household head, often male, fails to supply or undersupplies, women are thrown into a frenzy of compensating for the shortfalls or even taking on the entire burden of the household's food provisioning due to their so-called place in the kitchen. Above all, the kitchen as a symbol of domesticity has often been misappropriated to exclude women from the public sphere, where politics and decision-making around resource allocation, opportunities, and benefits reside.

Theoretical Perspectives: Women's Agency and Empowerment

It is evident that globally, women, particularly those in developing countries and rural communities, face some challenges that rob them of choice and voice.

In both the productive and reproductive arenas, rural women have to engage in the constant struggle of negotiating space for admission into decision-making in many respects. As largely agrarian farm women, they face limitations on what and how to produce or provide. In order to address these limitations, feminist scholars and others have initiated, negotiated, and sustained the push for women's empowerment, which reached a crescendo in the 1980s and '90s.[25] Over the years, however, it has become necessary to understand women's empowerment based on the extent to which they exercise agency. For this paper, where women's involvement in dry-season groundwater irrigation for household food provisioning takes place in a rather hostile environment, it is important to understand how the participating rural women exercised agency.

In designing a framework for analyzing empowerment, the term "agency" is important.[26] Emma Samman and Maria Emma Santos argue that empowerment is an expansion of agency.[27] Indeed, the only way one can recognize empowerment is through the manner in which agency is exercised. This notion resonates with Ruth Alsop and Nina Heinsohn's assertion that agency contributes to achieving a degree of empowerment.[28] It can thus be said that agency is important for women's empowerment, a demonstration of their close link. However, as Alsop and Heinsohn explain, context, or opportunity structure, is also important for their manifestation.[29] For this paper, the conceptualization of both empowerment and agency is important for understanding how marginalized rural women involved in dry-season irrigation, a predominantly male activity, in the Navio and Nyangua communities of northern Ghana, journey from victimhood to agency.

According to Amartya Sen, agency "refers to what the person is free to do and achieve in pursuit of whatever goals or values he or she regards as important."[30] He interprets agency in terms of a person's aims, objectives, allegiances, obligations, and conceptions of the good. According to Alsop and Heinsohn, agency refers to a person's ability to make a meaningful choice.[31] Naila Kabeer discusses it as a part of empowerment, which she notes to be the ability of a person to set goals and achieve them.[32]

Findings

RURAL WOMEN, GROUNDWATER IRRIGATION, AND FOOD PROVISIONING

The study showed that in the dry season, women in northern Ghana exercised agency in household food provisioning in the areas of cooking, processing, gathering firewood and fruit, and many others. In this vein, women periodically received from household heads staple food supplies from the family produce harvested during the on-farm season. The women said they contributed to preparing land, sowing seeds, weeding grass, and harvesting and storing family produce, which refers to the staple foods owned and supplied by the household head. All respondents indicated that in all stages of groundwater dry-season irrigation farming, they supported the activities of male relatives such as husbands, fathers, cousins, and brothers. In addition, they also engaged in their own food-production activities during on-farm and off-farm seasons. Asked why they had to engage in their own food-production activities, the majority of women said they preferred and opted to do so because it gave them autonomy and freedom to make decisions about the produce, especially when it came to meeting their real food-provisioning needs. A woman from Navio said this: "I have been supporting my husband in this activity, but I do not get a fair share of the benefits. Apart from being given part of the earnings from the sales of the vegetables to buy ingredients or some vegetables to prepare soup for the family, I get nothing from him. My husband keeps all the money." Thus, while assisting their husbands, about 98 percent of the women negotiated with the men for portions of irrigated land to cultivate their crops, usually vegetables for household consumption, since women in the two communities did not own land directly. Hence, they had to negotiate for such lands. Ironically, whatever is cultivated by the successful women benefits not just the woman but also her family/household. A woman from Nyangua said this: "While helping my husband weed his farm on one occasion, I requested that he give me a parcel of land to cultivate my own crops. I explained that by so doing, the burden of us depending solely on his farm for vegetables and income to buy ingredients will be reduced, which he obliged." Another woman in Nyangua said this: "When my marriage failed and I returned to my father's house with my children, I saw other women in the village engaged in dry-season farming. So I asked my brother to give me a plot of our father's land so I could also cultivate vegetables in the dry season as a way of providing food for myself and my children. My brother was glad and immediately agreed to release the land to me." Due to the exclusion of women from traditional landownership, which leaves women access to land only through their male relatives, women have tended to receive marginal lands for on-farm activities. Such lands have tended to yield marginal returns, creating food insecurity for them and their households. As a result, engaging in dry-season farming has been crucial to compensate for the shortfalls.

Of the total respondents, widows (who make up 23 percent of the total respondents) and women whose husbands had migrated (who make up 19 percent of the total respondents) indicated that they had to combine both on-farm and off-farm activities (i.e., dry- and rainy-season farming) in order to meet their household food-provisioning needs. Sometimes denied access to fertile land by male relatives, the women found irrigation farming in particular to be an important way to access productive land to produce food to complement the insecure on-farm production. A woman from Navio said this: "I sleep soundly these days because I can easily get vegetables from my dry-season farm. I no longer worry about where to get money to buy ingredients for my family soup. I get vegetables from my own farm and even sell some to buy other ingredients that I do not produce." Another woman from Nyangua said this:

> It is good to own a farm or have money. Now I cook what I want. Income earned from the sale of my vegetables enables me to prepare meals that I could not afford previously. We eat a variety of meals now, as we can now make choices about what to eat. We are not limited again by choice of food. My children are well fed now. My children even take the leftover food to school, which they eat during lunch. When they do not take food to school, I am able to give them money, which they use to buy food during lunch in school. I am glad my children no longer look on while their friends eat during the school lunch break.

Generally, all the women producers faced some challenges. As noted, groundwater irrigation in Ghana is traditionally a male-dominated activity. The existing cultural practices and socioeconomic conditions tend to marginalize women. In the process, women are traditionally pushed into providing support services for their male relatives. However, in recent times, women have been breaking barriers and engaging actively in groundwater irrigation production independently. They tend to seize the challenges and exercise agency in initiating the changes necessary to turn around their traditional situation of marginality.

FAO and the Asian Development Bank have indicated that women producers own less land, but in Nyangua and Navio, women traditionally did not own land at all.[33] However, through constant negotiations with their male counterparts, these women irrigators were able to access lands for cultivation or took over family lands and groundwater wells to cultivate vegetables on their own for the household.

Additionally, all women irrigators experienced a lack of initial capital to start groundwater irrigation. The study illustrated that money was needed to purchase seeds and seedlings, plow the land, and buy materials to fence the land being cultivated. Hired labor was also required to prepare land beds. Forty-eight percent of the total women irrigators admitted that even though some relatives offered free labor, such people expected some compensation in the form of food and drinks. The women, especially widows and women whose husbands had migrated, did not initially have the resources to meet such expectations. They were, however, able to do so later when their fortunes improved over time and, as such, they could take advantage of such benevolence.

As Pamela G. Katic corroborates, the cost of inputs such as fertilizers, chemicals, and weedicides presented a challenge for women irrigators.[34] Lacking the funds to hire labor, the women turned to friends, relatives, and children, who accepted minimal payments and noncash benefits such as food or drinks; collective labor among themselves; and exchange labor. Above all, they cultivated farm sizes that they could maintain with minimal extra farmhands. Collective labor entailed joining forces and taking turns to farm on one another's farms, desilt wells, or reconstruct broken wells. Noncash items such as farm produce, livestock, and household items were also sometimes provided in exchange for labor. This is a form of the barter system that allows women farmers to pay for labor immediately or in the future. For instance, a woman irrigator who has millet or rice could give it to a needy woman to feed her family in return for farm labor. Guinea fowl eggs can be given to needy poultry farmers to hatch and rear in exchange for farm labor. It took women irrigators with agency to negotiate such spaces to their advantage.

Drawing from Sen, agency, as the ability of a person to make a meaningful choice, was exhibited in the women irrigators' choice-making, decision-making, and goal-setting as they desilted wells, nursed and planted seedlings, mobilized materials and fenced their farms, and secured labor for their farmwork.[35] Other aspects of decision-making involved making vegetable beds, weeding, securing compost manure/fertilizer and farm tools, daily watering, harvesting, and others.

By exercising such agency, the women were able to improve their opportunities and contributions to household food provisioning. Their produce was readily available for the kitchen table and in fresh condition for preparing hearty meals. They could also sell or trade some of it to secure uncultivable or additional foods to improve their household food provisioning, nourishment, and security. In addition, all women were able to generate income, which they used to purchase complementary foods. Above all, their sheer participation and exercise of agency enabled 80 percent of the women to assert themselves, change their conditions, and even transform themselves from marginal to central players in dry-season groundwater irrigation farming.

OPPORTUNITY STRUCTURES FOR EXERCISING AGENCY

According to Alsop and Heinsohn, an opportunity structure represents the formal and informal contexts within which actors operate, and these conditions give rise to different degrees of empowerment.[36] As noted, this study's communities are endowed with groundwater resources.[37] Using local knowledge and technology, permanent wells were easily constructed in the dry season on parcels of family-owned land, which provided water in both the dry and rainy seasons. Because of these wells, as the results showed, women whose families owned the lands and wells were easily able to negotiate for and use them for cultivation.

Contrary to the portrayal of women in Tamale as lacking the technical expertise and skills required for dry-season irrigation, experience with and previous knowledge of groundwater irrigation were key motivators for 99 percent of the women in both Navio and Nyangua to engage in dry-season groundwater irrigation.[38] As noted, their male relatives who had once engaged in groundwater irrigation owned the wells. In assisting such men, the women were able to accumulate knowledge and skills over time, which they applied to their own farming activities. Of the total respondents, 28 percent of the women had accumulated such knowledge and skills even before they got married. The rest acquired such experiences in marriage.

Access to labor from family, friends, and relatives also facilitated women's engagement in dry-season farming. The results showed that 58 percent of women irrigators enjoyed free labor when it came to fencing farms; nursing seedlings; making land beds; planting seeds and seedlings; watering and weeding farmlands; applying compost manure or chemical fertilizers, weedicides, and pesticides; and harvesting, preparing and processing, storing, and marketing farm produce. Supportive husbands usually mobilized their friends to assist with desilting wells or producing farm labor. Noteworthy, however, is that the women irrigators in Nyangua benefited from the labor of their husbands' friends more than their counterparts in Navio did. This is consistent with the level of support discussed above. Also, 20 percent of the women irrigators in Navio had husbands who had migrated to southern Ghana, leaving them alone to fend for their children by themselves. Furthermore, the children of the women in both Nyangua and Navio assisted them on the farms during their free time.

The proximity of farms and the availability of security also influenced the women's engagement in dry-season irrigation. Most of these farms were in proximity to their dwelling units. Thus, less time and resources were spent visiting these farms. Though the farms were fenced, every family member also provided security both day and night in order to prevent invasion by stray animals. Eighty percent of the farms in Nyangua were near the women irrigators' homesteads, but in Navio about 38 percent of farms were located far from the women's homes.

There was also high local demand for the cultivated crops. This study found that vegetables are high on the list of foods consumed by families and households in northern Ghana, and especially so for those in rural communities. Most dishes are prepared using vegetables alone or to complement cereals. The study found that vegetables are used on a daily basis to prepare soups or sauces and other dishes for consumption. As a result, the demand for vegetables is high throughout the year. An irrigator in Nyangua said this:

> Our people in northern Ghana cannot do without vegetables. Meals prepared from vegetables are consumed daily. Unfortunately, in the dry season, because it does not rain, fresh vegetables become scarce. Therefore, vegetables we grow through groundwater irrigation are in high demand. Retailers, who are mostly women from neighboring markets, sometimes visit us on our farms to buy these vegetables, which they later repackage to sell in the markets. Matrons or cooks [most of them in Ghana are women] from some senior high schools in this part of the country also come to buy these vegetables to cook for their students in the boarding schools.

Conclusion: Enhancing Women's Agency

This study reveals that women exercised tremendous agency to turn their situation of marginality into one of centrality by converting their so-called place in the kitchen into roles as groundwater irrigators at the forefront of dry-season cultivation. By acquiring essential knowledge and skills, negotiating for resources such as land and labor, and tapping into the available opportunity structure, they were able to change their situations in spite of all the challenges they faced. With women thus established as active producers in household food provisioning, it is now crucial for policymakers to take steps to enhance women's agency for the benefit of not just the women but also households, families, and communities. It makes not just gender and welfare sense but also economic and political sense.

In the community-based engagements, farm input support was found to be crucial for women irrigators. All the respondents indicated that support in the form of tools—such as good-quality pumping machines and plows—manure, and preservatives was crucial. For instance, water-pumping machines would help them move water from wells to farmlands easily. This is because it is laborious to manually draw water from wells, transport it, and apply it to the crop. Respondents admitted that they had been given pumping machines by an NGO in the past, which they paid for on credit, but the machines broke down in a short time due to their poor quality. This explains why most of them were still drawing water out of the wells manually with buckets and ropes in spite of the task's labor-intensive and tedious nature.

Secondly, facilitating access to information and technology would help the women irrigators adopt and apply improved methods and strategies to their irrigation practices, as they were found to rely mainly on local knowledge and experience. Because of the informal nature of groundwater irrigation, formal agencies show no interest in it; hence, extension services are not available to the farmers. However, in order to adapt to the impacts of climate change on agriculture, access to information and relevant technology is important. Ninety percent of the respondents admitted that sometimes they face challenges in tackling stubborn diseases and pests because they lack the requisite knowledge or information.

Capacity building is an area that can help women irrigators overcome the challenges of dry-season irrigation. The results indicated that all women relied on local knowledge and experience they had accumulated over the years. They also took advantage of their supportive roles to learn about the trade and acquire knowledge and skills pertaining to dry-season irrigation farming before initiating action for change. Having convinced themselves of their abilities, about 97 percent of them took the necessary action to request land and undertake the cultivation themselves. By so doing, they went from being supportive to productive hands. This is a major change of status, which allowed the women to access further power in the management of their own resources and farm produce. However, the women also appreciated the fact that their knowledge and skills were limited and required further development. Hence, they requested further training regarding adopting and applying chemicals, introducing new varieties of seeds, and employing water management strategies. These women understood that to be able to sustain their gains they had to acquire more skills and knowledge. They understood that empowerment was a process that needs constant development.

Women's engagement in groundwater irrigation, which is seldom given attention in research studies, has been the highlight of this analysis. The examination of rural women's contributions to household provisioning through groundwater irrigation confirms FAO's argument that women in sub-Saharan Africa are the main producers and providers rather than supporters or idle observers or beneficiaries. In developing alternatives to contribute to household food provisioning, women in the Navio and Nyangua communities were constantly working to overcome barriers related to finances, labor, farm inputs, and technology as well as the limitations of existing patriarchal arrangements. In particular, patriarchy was said to serve as a major source of marginalization that robbed the women of access to and direct ownership of natural resources by delimiting their "place in the kitchen." Apart from falsely limiting their operational space, patriarchy also denied them their rightful entry and access to productive resources, resulting in marginalization. However, the women irrigators were able to break free of some of the traditional patriarchal binds to claim and assert their agency beyond the kitchen by engaging independently in direct food production. They were able to make and implement production decisions, which resulted in improved food provisioning. They produced food for the kitchen table and sold some for income used to purchase complementary food items. By so doing, the women were able to redefine their wrongful social positioning as reproducers to include production and were able to change their role in household food provisioning from a traditional secondary and supplementary one to an empowering primary and complementary one.

ACKNOWLEDGMENT

The study acknowledges the support of Mr. Fortunatus Kaba Agulu, which yielded the primary data in the Navio and Nyangua communities.

NOTES

1. Karl, "Inseparable."
2. Apusigah, "Gendered Politics."

3. Groundwater irrigation farming is a practice in which farmers cultivate crops, mostly vegetables, in the dry season by depending on manually constructed wells for water with the water drawn using either ropes and buckets or pumping machines.

4. Villholth, "Groundwater Irrigation."

5. Kwoyiga and Stefan, "Groundwater Development."

6. BRIDGE, *Gender and Food Security*.

7. Nchanji, "Piper Calls the Tune."

8. Apusigah, "Gendered Politics."

9. Food and Agriculture Organization, *Gender Equality*.

10. Food and Agriculture Organization, *Gender Equality*.

11. Ochieng, "Analysis."

12. The number of years these women have participated in groundwater irrigation depends on the families they were born into or the livelihood activities of their husbands. Women whose parents are irrigators or who married irrigator husbands tend to have more experience. As such, some have participated in this activity for more than thirty years.

13. Johnston and McCartney, "Inventory of Water Storage."

14. Ofosu-Addo, Jianmei, and Dong, "Groundwater Development and Evaluation."

15. Kortatsi, "Groundwater Utilization in Ghana."

16. Villholth, "Groundwater Irrigation."

17. Namara et al., "Irrigation Development in Ghana."

18. Activities are usually undertaken in the dry season, i.e., outside the normal rainy-season period.

19. Namara et al., "Irrigation Development in Ghana."

20. Sudarkasa, "'Status of Women.'"

21. Apusigah, "Gendered Politics."

22. Soup and sauce ingredients include salt, shea butter, peppers, tomatoes, smoked fish, groundnut paste or cowpea butter, and local spices such as *dawadawa* and Maggi. Women use their personal earnings or income to purchase some of them, such as salt. Others, such as shea butter, groundnut paste, and dawadawa, women process at home. Tomatoes and peppers are sometimes grown by women.

23. Sudarkasa, "'Status of Women.'"

24. Chinweizu, *Anatomy of Female Power*.

25. Cornwall, "Women's Empowerment."

26. Kabeer, "Resources, Agency, Achievements."

27. Samman and Santos, "Agency and Empowerment."

28. Alsop and Heinsohn, "Measuring Empowerment in Practice."

29. Alsop and Heinsohn.

30. Sen, "Well-Being, Agency and Freedom," 203.

31. Alsop and Heinsohn, "Measuring Empowerment in Practice."

32. Kabeer, "Resources, Agency, Achievements."

33. Food and Agriculture Organization, *Gender Equality*.

34. Katic, *Evidence for Upscaling*.

35. Sen, "Well-Being, Agency and Freedom."

36. Alsop and Heinsohn, "Measuring Empowerment in Practice."
37. Katic, *Evidence for Upscaling*.
38. Nchanji, "Piper Calls the Tune."

WORKS CITED

Alsop, Ruth, and Nina Heinsohn. "Measuring Empowerment in Practice: Structuring Analysis and Framing Indicators." Policy Research Working Papers. World Bank, 2005.

Apusigah, A. Atia. "The Gendered Politics of Farm Household Production and the Shaping of Women's Livelihoods in Northern Ghana." *Feminist Africa* 12, no. 12 (2009): 51–67.

BRIDGE. *Gender and Food Security: Towards Gender-Just Food and Nutrition Security; Overview Report*. Brighton, UK: Institute of Development Studies, 2014. https://opendocs.ids.ac.uk/opendocs/handle/20.500.12413/5245.

Chinweizu. *Anatomy of Female Power: A Masculinist Dissection of Matriarchy*. Lagos, Nigeria: Pero, 1990.

Cornwall, Andrea. "Women's Empowerment: What Works?" *Journal of International Development* 28, no. 3 (2016): 342–59.

Food and Agriculture Organization. *Gender Equality and Food Security: Women's Empowerment as a Tool against Hunger*. Mandaluyong, Philippines: Asian Development Bank, 2013.

Johnston, Robyn M., and Matthew McCartney. "Inventory of Water Storage Types in the Blue Nile and Volta River Basins." Working Paper 140. International Water Management Institute, 2010.

Kabeer, Naila. "Resources, Agency, Achievements: Reflections on the Measurement of Women's Empowerment." *Development and Change* 30, no. 3 (1999): 435–64.

Karl, Marilee. "Inseparable: The Crucial Role of Women in Food Security Revisited." *Women in Action* 1, no. 1 (2009): 8–19.

Katic, Pamela G. *Evidence for Upscaling of Dry Season Irrigation Technologies in Ghana: Market Opportunities*. Ibadan, Nigeria: International Institute of Tropical Agriculture, 2017. https://core.ac.uk/download/pdf/132692248.pdf.

Kortatsi, B. K. "Groundwater Utilization in Ghana." *Future Groundwater Resources at Risk* (Proceedings of the Helsinki Conference, June 1994), International Association of Hydrological Sciences Publication no. 222 (1994): 149–56.

Kwoyiga, Lydia, and Catalin Stefan. "Groundwater Development for Dry Season Irrigation in North East Ghana: The Place of Local Knowledge." *Water* 10, no. 12 (2018): 1724.

Namara, Regassa E., Leah Horowitz, Ben Nyamadi, and Boubacar Barry. "Irrigation Development in Ghana: Past Experiences, Emerging Opportunities, and Future Directions." GSSP Working Paper 27. International Food Policy Research Institute, 2011.

Nchanji, Eileen Bogweh. "The Piper Calls the Tune: Changing Roles of Northern Ghanaian Women in Agriculture." *Agriculture for Development* 32 (2017): 7.

Ochieng, P. A. "An Analysis of the Strengths and Limitation of Qualitative and Quantitative Research Paradigms." *Problems of Education in the 21st Century* 13 (2009): 13–18.

Ofosu-Addo, David, Cheng Jianmei, and Shaogang Dong. "Groundwater Development and Evaluation of the White Volta Basin (Ghana) Using Numerical Simulation." *Journal of American Science* 4, no. 4 (2008): 64–71.

Samman, Emma, and Maria Emma Santos. "Agency and Empowerment: A Review of Concepts, Indicators and Empirical Evidence." *Research in Progress Series*, no. 1a (2009).

Sen, Amartya. "Well-Being, Agency and Freedom: The Dewey Lectures 1984." *Journal of Philosophy* 82, no. 4 (1985): 169–221.

Sudarkasa, Niara. "'The Status of Women' in Indigenous African Societies." *Feminist Studies* 12, no. 1 (1986): 91–103.

Theis, Sophie, Nicole Lefore, Ruth Meinzen-Dick, and Elizabeth Bryan. "What Happens After Technology Adoption? Gendered Aspects of Small-Scale Irrigation Technologies in Ethiopia, Ghana, and Tanzania." *Agriculture and Human Values* 35, no. 3 (September 2018): 671–84.

Villholth, Karen G. "Groundwater Irrigation for Smallholders in Sub-Saharan Africa: A Synthesis of Current Knowledge to Guide Sustainable Outcomes." *Water International* 38, no. 4 (July 2013): 369–91.

CHAPTER 2

From Farm to Kitchen

Women's Role in Three Dimensions—Production, Processing, and Consumption—in Burkina Faso

EVELINE M. F. W. SAWADOGO/COMPAORÉ AND
SAKIKO SHIRATORI

Introduction

Agriculture is the main sector of many African countries. However, until 2019, many African countries lagged behind in ensuring food security for their population. In Burkina Faso, agriculture employs over 90 percent of the workforce, but despite efforts by the government, food insecurity remains critical in rural areas.[1] Women play a transformative role at various levels in the food system: from producing crops at the farm to preparing dishes for direct consumption via a series of processing. The roles of women in attaining food security are beginning to be taken into consideration, but more needs to be done to document this. In fact, there have been limited efforts to systematically look at the centrality of Black women in enabling participatory food security within the

African context. There is, therefore, a need to look at this centrality not only at the production level but also at the processing and consumption levels.

This paper is an evidence-based study that addresses the issue of food security and household responsibility through the role of women in Burkina Faso, a West African country. One of the crops of primary interest to us is cowpea. Among the other crops, cowpea is considered a "women's crop" and has been seen as the most promising food for nutritional improvement for Africans.[2] For instance, in the last few decades in Burkina Faso, cowpea was exclusively grown by women in their small plots. It is only quite recently, in the last two decades, that cowpea has slowly become a cash crop, and therefore more men have started to grow it for cash purposes. Also, NGO and development projects have begun to help women's associations make a cash profit from cowpea. We aim to understand the role and the power of African women regarding food consumed at the household level and to document patterns in how cowpea dishes are cooked and the reasons they are processed in such ways for family consumption.

Cowpea is a highly popular and valuable crop in Africa. It is the most planted native legume in sub-Saharan Africa and in 2016 was the second most-produced grain legume in Africa, following groundnuts.[3] Burkina Faso produced 600,000 tons of cowpea, making the country the third-largest producer following Nigeria and Niger, with its production level showing a trend of growth.[4] Cowpea plays an important role in food security because it is a "hungry-season crop"—which matures earlier than other crops and can be used before other staple foods become available—as well as a nutritional source of high-quality proteins and a wide variety of vitamins and minerals at relatively low cost, which is advantageous for households with low incomes.[5] In addition, cowpea is one of the major cash crops for farmers in West Africa.

The general objective of this study is to determine the current role women play in food security and their place in the control of resources, management of household diets, and decision-making related to food. We use cowpea as an example. We used a mixed-method approach. We conducted a household survey of more than 200 households in two regions, Po and Yako, in Burkina Faso. Additionally, we collected data to monitor and document what food is cooked, how it is cooked, and for whom (i.e., for the whole household or for children exclusively). We conducted key informant interviews and focus group discussions to pick up on concerns related to everyday opinions and practices. Finally, we collected information on demographics and dietary habits using both quantitative and qualitative methods. These data help us to understand how food is handled at the household and individual levels and to identify the specific key roles and positions of women in food systems.

This paper will first investigate the existing agricultural production systems on farms, in processing, and in market and consumption patterns in households. It will also show how determining what food is cooked at the household level is mainly the responsibility of women, giving them an important leading role in food security in Africa.

Background: The Role of Women in Food Security

In many African countries, it is a real challenge for some households to attain food security. By definition, "food security exists when all people, at all times, have physical and economic access to sufficient, safe and nutritious food that meets their dietary needs and food preferences for an active and healthy life."[6] Hunger is increasing in almost all African subregions, which makes Africa the global region with the highest prevalence of undernourishment.[7] Consistently, total food insecurity (moderate or severe), as estimated by the food insecurity experience scale, is much higher in Africa than in any other part of the world.[8]

Food security requires food availability, access, utilization, and stability. Women play key roles in food security by participating in each of those requirements. They are mostly responsible for daily food preparation in their households. They often produce food crops on farm plots that are separate from the family plots. They also sell their crops and foodstuffs at markets for cash. Women usually control the resources generated from their small plots. However, despite women's contributions to food security in many ways, the role of women in the whole agricultural value chain, including in food preparation and family consumption, has not been scientifically well documented.

While rural women may be the pillars of agricultural production and food security in Africa, they also make up a much higher percentage of the hungry people. In fact, 70 percent of these hungry people in the world are women, especially in rural areas.[9] Women reinvest up to 90 percent of their income in food, school fees, and expenses related to family health and child-rearing.[10] But there have been limited efforts to systematically examine the centrality of African women in enabling participatory food security within the African context. There is, therefore, a need to look at the centrality of women's roles not only in food production but also in food processing as well as in household food consumption.

It is also important to point out that in many rural areas in Burkina Faso, households' farms include two different kinds of farms. There is the main family farm that belongs to the whole family, led by the household head, who has power over its use. All family members work on it as their number one priority. Additionally, there are often smaller plots for individuals in the household—mainly women, but not exclusively, because even young men who are not yet married can sometimes have their own plots to grow extra crops such as groundnut, cowpea, okra, etc.

The cash income generated from these smaller plots belongs to the appropriate individuals. Nevertheless, having such a plot requires the approval of the household head, who has power and ownership over the land. When a woman is granted a plot of land, it is usually from her husband or a family member or neighbor. The income from such land is controlled exclusively in many cases by the woman herself. Previous studies have suggested that households in Burkina Faso do not efficiently allocate labor and input across plots, and as a result a household's plots are considered separately (family plots or women's plots), even though the two types of plots' incomes are both used within the household.[11] However, it is important to note that women have full control over and make decisions regarding their plots' incomes. This is important because women's control over assets (including individual farm plots) has been shown to have positive impacts on food security, child nutrition, education, and women's own well-being.[12]

Cowpea is a common legume and a source of high-quality protein. In general, the field size of a woman's plot tends to be smaller than that of a family farm. On these small plots, women generally grow groundnut, cowpea, voandzou, and okra, which are considered to be "women's crops," as opposed to the main crops grown on the family farm. However, over the last couple decades, these women's crops have gained increasing attention and are now also grown on family farms in large fields for consumption and cash income.

Despite women's long-standing role in the production of women's crops on their individual small plots and on the larger family farming plots, gender inequality persists in access to factors of production including land, credit, and agricultural input, which inhibits the empowerment of rural women. Lack of access to seeds of improved varieties is one of the major constraints to the adoption of women's crop varieties in Burkina Faso. It is believed that rural women lack all the factors that favor their participation in decision-making in their households, compared to women in cities.[13] In his study on gender and decision-making in households in Burkina Faso, B. Gnoumou Thiombiano shows that women make few decisions regarding income and health-related issues, including their social life, within the household.[14]

This study attempts to highlight some women's roles in production, processing, and consumption, because the progressive mainstreaming of gender in development and action projects has been imposed as a condition for receiving development aid. Thus, most of the positive changes in gender mainstreaming have occurred through projects and development programs funded through bilateral north-south and multilateral cooperation, though some of these changes often vanish when a project finishes and when there is no follow-up at the national level.[15] The current policy in Burkina Faso that serves as the basis for promoting women is the National Program for Economic and Social Development.[16] This plan is characterized by the consideration of gender through its broader objective of building development that takes into account regional specificities by promoting local potential.

Improving the nutrition of household members, specifically children, is an important instrument of social protection and the fight against malnutrition. Major problems identified in program reports are nondiversification, low-quality (nutritionally unbalanced) meals, insufficient quantity of food, irregularity of meals, inadequate hygiene and sanitation, inappropriate cooking methods, and unequal intrahousehold allocation, to name a few. Although local food production contributes to improving the quality, quantity, and regularity of meals, the link between local food production and school feeding remains sparsely (or not) highlighted in strategic references. Recently, the National Program for Economic and Social Development stated that we should "give to each child [of] school age at least one balanced meal per day," which is a call for local food consumption strategies for children.[17] Yet school feeding has not been sufficiently emphasized in the National Social Protection Policy as key to any development strategy so far. The national program did not specify the importance that women could play within the program either.

Methods

This paper aims to investigate existing agricultural production systems in farms and markets and consumption patterns in households; then it aims to understand women's responsibilities in making food choices and implementing usage within their households in rural Burkina Faso. We targeted 200 households in two different regions in Burkina Faso. We selected two regions (Yako and Po) and three villages in each (Gobila, Gollo, and Taonsgho in Yako and Pinyiri, Torem, and Adongo in Po), making six villages in total, taking into consideration distance and population size.

Before the interview and the survey, we conducted a census survey on all households in the six villages to establish a complete list of households. The total number of households was 625. A stratified random sampling method was then used to select target households. The households were stratified as wealthier and poorer according to the composite score constructed by the census (based on land size, housing materials, household assets such as a TV, means of transport, etc.). Target households were then randomly selected from each stratum in proportion to the number of households.

We interviewed approximately 200 households over twelve months at two-month intervals in 2018–19. Interviewers visited targeted households to conduct face-to-face interviews, carrying a tablet terminal on which the structured questionnaire was implemented. The questionnaire covered background information, household members, family plots, household characteristics (with the household head as the respondent), diet and water intake, individual diets and health, women's plots, cowpea meals, twenty-four-hour recall meals, and anthropometry (with a woman as the respondent). Each interview took up to one and a half hours and involved both the household head and his wife. In the absence of the household head, the person acting as the head was the respondent, along with the woman responsible for the household cooking and feeding. We explained our survey's content and obtained informed consent from all the household participants.

In addition to the quantitative survey, focus groups were conducted to understand the "why" and "how" questions that the quantitative survey data were not able to answer. These questions have helped us understand the reasons behind the decisions of what to cook and how to cook it. Our focus group discussions took place with mixed groups of men and women, given that we wanted to get men's thoughts on household diets and how diets are determined. The focus group discussions were recorded and transcribed. The data were analyzed around emerging themes and included content analysis.

Specifically, a total of ten mixed (male and female) focus group discussions were conducted in June and July 2019. This helped us further understand the findings from the preliminary results of the 2018 surveys. The focus group discussions were facilitated to get candid opinions concerning the changing roles of women in the agricultural value chain (with a focus on cowpea) and cooking patterns, and how these patterns were perceived. Also, the discussions made clear the responsibilities of the family members regarding what is cooked and for whom a specific meal is cooked. Further, cooked food distribution patterns were part of the discussion.

During the quantitative and qualitative data collection, in almost all cases, questions regarding the dishes cooked in the household were answered by women, who are mostly responsible for food preparation. This is very important because women play huge roles when it comes to food cooked and consumed at the household level.

Findings and Analysis

The findings revealed the importance of women's roles in agriculture and specifically in the production of the food found every day on the table for family consumption and in the collection or production of medicinal plants. Indeed, in most of the households surveyed, women prepare food for meals or medicinal purposes, and they are the ones who make decisions about what to cook and how to cook it. Also, women decide what to grow for consumption or for sale on their little plot of land.

AT THE FARM: THE ROLE OF WOMEN IN FOOD PRODUCTION

In Burkina Faso, most communities are patriarchal. As such, women generally have fewer rights than men. This includes access to and control over land (or the security of the land), financial means, means of production, and so on. In households in Burkina Faso, where arable land is increasingly scarce, women usually do not have large plots of land. The following statement from one of our focus group interviewees sheds light on this: "[*laughs*] . . . We are usually lagging behind. . . . We are strangers from our parents' and also from our husband's villages. You see, we don't belong anywhere. That's why we don't have the right to land, or even to our own children. . . . It's the reality here." The statement "We are strangers from our parents' and also from our husband's villages. You see we don't belong anywhere" implies traditional beliefs that limit women's access and control over land and forest resources. There are these kinds of beliefs behind the socioeconomic disparities between men and women.

The beliefs stated above encourage cultural and social prejudice vis-à-vis women and strongly contribute to reducing women's rights to access resources and to make decisions about land use. It appears that women can certainly cultivate the plots that are given to them, but they do not have control over these pieces of land, which are acquired through a husband, head of a lineage, or parent. As such, women invest most of their time in the family farms and spend their extra hours, such as in the early mornings or late evenings, on their own plots growing cereals, vegetables, or women's crops. They are not allowed to work on their own farms during regular working hours unless they are granted permission to do so.

Interestingly, the structured interview survey indicated that 60 percent of households have women's plots in addition to family plots. While a family plot is managed by the household head, who is responsible for the whole family's food consumption and earnings, a woman's plot is managed by women and they can decide what to grow themselves. Though women have fewer rights to land, most of them have their "own" plots. Still, women's plots tend to be smaller than family plots. For instance, in our sample households, the average sizes of women's plots were 0.4 hectare (ha) in Yako and 0.9 ha in Po; family plots on average were 1.8 ha in Yako and 5.0 ha in Po.

Our survey showed that cowpea is the second most-popular crop produced on family plots, after sorghum. On women's plots, while cereals are not a major cash crop as on the family plots, cash crops are commonly grown. In our survey, groundnut was the most popular crop produced on women's plots (in 84 percent of households with women's plots). Cowpea was also popular and was produced on women's plots in 27 percent of the surveyed households. Women also often benefit from small plots where they grow cereals and vegetables for family consumption.

FROM FARM TO KITCHEN: THE ROLE OF WOMEN IN COWPEA PROCESSING

The households surveyed cultivate crops to consume at home, sell in the market (cash crops), or both. One-third of the households that produced cowpea at the family farm in 2017 sold cowpea at the market. Compared to so-called cash crops such as soybeans (95 percent of the households that produced soybeans sold it) or cotton (77 percent of the households that produced cotton sold it), the ratio of cowpea-selling households (33 percent) is relatively low. On the other hand, compared to staple crops such as maize (17 percent) or sorghum (18 percent), 33 percent is relatively high. Cowpea is both a crop for home consumption and a cash crop.

Cowpea can be used for both purposes, that is, for home consumption and as a cash income source. It can be sold to solve cash issues a household may face. Cowpea produced in women's plots is even more likely to be sold. About two-thirds of the households that had cowpea grown in women's plots sold the cowpea that was harvested. Overall, women produce cowpea not just for their family's food consumption but to maintain a balance between food and income.

Deciding whether to consume the grown cowpea or sell it at the market differs by region. Cowpea is the main cash crop for households in Yako (a northern city), and the proportion sold is higher than that in Po (a southern city). This is because the north of Burkina Faso has better rainfall for cowpea

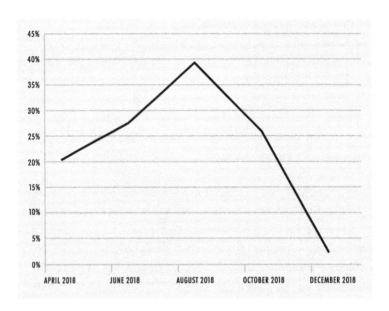

GRAPH 2.1. The percentage of households that bought cowpea in the last two months, over ten months in 2018.

production than the south, and the demand for cowpea as a cash crop is higher because there are not as many other cash crops, such as soybeans or cotton, produced as in the south.

Though some households grow their own cowpea, many households often still buy it. We asked households every other month about their cowpea production, purchase, and consumption of the last two months. We can see seasonal changes in the percentage of households that bought cowpea in the last months of 2018 in graph 2.1. Note that this question asks about the purchase over the last two months, so the survey conducted in October, for example, implies purchase in August and September. The percentage reaches its peak in August (meaning purchase in June and July), just before the cowpea harvest, which implies that the stock of cowpea has run out. It appears clear that most of the cowpea bought for consumption is during the rainy season (June to October).

The focus group interview shows that cowpea is considered the most nutritious crop, generating energy and strength. According to one of the female respondents, "Cowpea is what one needs to be able to perform well on the farm. . . . Our kids and we love it, but we cannot afford to eat it all year long. Thus, we usually set some quantity aside for the rainy season. If we don't, we definitely have to buy." Thus, women are very much aware of the nutritional content of cowpea and even associate it with strength, energy, and other positive health factors. The women are conscious about what they eat and what

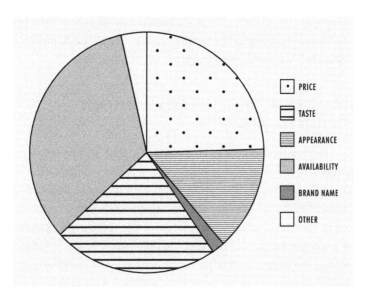

GRAPH 2.2. The most important reasons for buying a given cowpea variety.

provides calories. However, as most of them stated: "We don't have any choice sometimes; we have to eat and offer our family what is available and what is affordable for us. [*laughs*] Yes, we know good food." When it comes to selecting cowpea varieties to buy, the most important reasons for buying specific cowpea varieties are illustrated in graph 2.2. Availability, which means "there were no other varieties available," is the most popular reason. In the focus group discussion, we found that women prefer some varieties over others, depending on the recipes they use; however, we can see that farmers often do not have a choice. They usually comply with what is available either for growing or consumption purposes. However, price, taste, and appearance are sometimes considered when buying a specific variety. In most cases, women's choices are also related to how the cowpea can be cooked and to its taste, especially what appeals to their children. This was well put by one interviewee: "We like the one [cowpea] that has a sugar taste; it is my kids' favorite." On the other hand, men usually go for marketable crops that can be sold on the local market.

In sum, the availability of cowpea depends on cowpea production on family plots and women's plots; region; seasonality; and the decision to consume, sell, or buy. Most of all, it depends on a household's needs for cowpea. As households become more aware of cowpea's value in terms of nutrition and as a cash crop, their demand for cowpea increases. Because women prioritize family health more than men do, cowpea's rich nutritional value can attract them to the crop. In addition, since women are sensitive to both food needs and the cash required to meet the family's needs, they tend to produce cowpea on their own plots for family consumption or cash income.

THE HEART OF THE HOUSE: THE ROLE OF WOMEN IN HOUSEHOLD FOOD PREPARATION AND CONSUMPTION

In traditional societies, cooking is an activity that values women. Indeed, knowing how to cook is a sign of femininity in some communities in Burkina Faso. One can hear that someone "is not a woman" only because she is not capable of making *tô*, a local popular traditional dish. Modernization and the emergence of new technologies can influence the daily organization of women's tasks and have an impact on the time they spend in the kitchen. But still, in rural areas, the value in cooking is not negligible for women and still contributes to the perception of being a "real woman." A so-called real woman is a woman who knows how to cook, compared to "just a woman" or, to some extent, "not a woman," in reference to those who do not know how to cook.[18] The ability to prepare meals and to do so well is symbolic of being a better wife and a good housewife. Being a good cook has advantages for parents and brothers- and sisters-in-law and is a way of showing respect. However, food cooked for the whole family is not distributed equitably but is linked to the power and position of household members. For instance, meat is primarily intended for men, who are the head of the family and who always must have better portions. Thus, even though women take on leading roles in cooking the food, the good portions are reserved for men, especially meat. This is highlighted in the following statement: "[*laughs*] You know, one needs to take very good care of the head of the family. We always serve his part with care, even the tô. We make it properly. [*laughs*] It is like that."

Various recipes are used for cooking cowpea. A commonly cooked meal is boiled cowpea (with salt), with or without other ingredients, which 90 percent of respondents said was their most recent cowpea meal. Cowpea is often cooked with rice, millet, sorghum, or couscous. The focus group discussion helped us understand that such a "rice in the cowpea" dish is related to the changing preferences of the younger generation. Indeed, one of our interviewees attests that "my kids prefer when I cook it with rice. They will always request it, but it's not always easy to get rice. So, they have to eat it even if I cook it with couscous or millet or sometimes sorghum." When women can afford it, most of the time they prepare their kids' favorite meals. Additionally, as shown in figures 2.1, 2.2, and 2.3, there are many other cooking methods, such

FIGURE 2.1. Example of cowpea cooking method (fried). Photo by Sakiko Shiratori.

FIGURE 2.2. Example of cowpea cooking method (boiled in a bag). Photo by Sakiko Shiratori.

FIGURE 2.3. Example of cowpea cooking method (baked). Photo by Sakiko Shiratori.

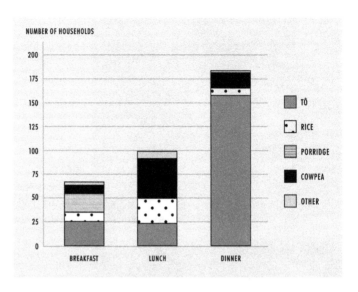

GRAPH 2.3. Recipes prepared for each meal per household, December 2018.

as frying cowpea, boiling it in a bag, or baking it like a pancake. The women explained that they can use cowpea as whole beans or flour, mix it with other ingredients, and even use its young pods and leaves in different diets. How cowpea is prepared has a considerable impact on its nutritional value.

Some decades ago, cowpea was often cooked with millet, given that rice was not common. Also, tô was mainly made from sorghum and millet flour. Nowadays, maize has become so common that it is replacing millet and sorghum. One respondent confirmed that "children don't even want to see the sorghum tô. Just last year my little son cried when he saw red sorghum tô. . . . We grow it, but we sell it to buy maize. It's the same with cowpea. They prefer it with rice than anything else." This situation sheds light on the transition in food systems and brings in the social dimensions of such systems. In this case, the responsibility falls on the women who take care of the family to determine what to cook and what not to cook and what they believe is best for the family. Their position in the shift in the food system is therefore recognized in this study.

Graph 2.3 presents the recipes women prepared for household members at home the day before the December 2018 survey was conducted. Most households eat dinner (183 households out of 212), but breakfast and lunch are less common. Meals other than breakfast, lunch, and dinner such as snacks were very rare and therefore not included in the figure. Not many households were able to eat three meals a day. As can be seen, cowpea is the second most-common food after tô, which is made from maize, millet, or sorghum. Cowpea is typically eaten at lunchtime. Most women see it as a heavy food, which is suitable for lunchtime. One woman also told us that she cooks cowpea in the morning, brings it to the field, and then eats it at lunchtime.

Discussion

Food crises have influenced consumer practices and have led women to sometimes adopt new strategies to meet the needs of their households. In addition, the quality of diets and dietary habits are changing in rural areas. The number of meals consumed in households is decreasing in rural areas, especially during the dry season (November to May). The main meal is eaten in the evening, with morning and lunchtime meals eaten less often for children and some women. Men, on the other hand, often can afford to eat outside the home during the morning and lunch periods. Thus, while there is an agreement to recognize the importance of women to food security, there are few changes being made at strategic levels to better understand women's roles and how to bring about changes in food patterns in Burkina Faso. This paper contributes to documenting and understanding the role of women in household food security through the production, transformation, and consumption of women's crops such as cowpea.

In Burkina Faso, especially in rural areas, what to cook and how to cook is mainly determined by women. They decide on recipes by considering food availability, nutritional contents, family preferences, health conditions, and so on. Then, they procure the ingredients needed and cook them for the family. In contrast, men usually consume the food put on the table without thinking about the story behind it.

Being responsible for cooking makes women responsible for their family's well-being (food, health, etc.) as well. Their role is wide-ranging and truly important. They are expected to be good mothers, good cooks, and good housekeepers. Some "domestic" qualities such as the ability to maintain the home are also required. For most women, preparing meals includes setting the table, serving the food, washing dishes and pots, cleaning the stove and sink, and sweeping the kitchen. In addition, life in rural areas evolves according to the agricultural calendar. Various tasks are linked to each season: sowing seeds in the spring, maintaining the soil in the summer, and harvesting produce in the fall. Finally, women look after children and other family members and monitor their health, diet, and care. In short, women are the cornerstones of the economy and the well-being of the family.

Conclusion

According to the qualitative data regarding decision-making processes, women have a relatively large amount of freedom in rural areas to decide what to feed their families. A woman usually does not consult her husband regarding what to cook but often has to comply with what is available. This recognized position of the woman as the decision-maker—who determines what food crops to grow on her own plot as well as what to cook for the main household meal and how to cook it—reflects her silent power within the household. However, women's roles in household food security have been largely ignored and not considered in strategic planning for food security in African countries.

This study shows that women could play transformative roles in food systems in Africa and more specifically in Burkina Faso. Having looked at the centrality of women in food systems, this article has examined the position of women in production, processing, and consumption and how they take control within such systems. It has focused on these three dimensions with regard to women and food security in Burkina Faso and found that women play central roles in all three dimensions. Cowpea was used as a case study to understand the dynamics of women cooking meals for household consumption. The results show that determining what food to cook and the way in which it is cooked in households is mainly the responsibility of women, who also decide what to eat according to the time of day and the season. Thus, women are silently in control of household food consumption patterns and food security. As such, their important role should not be neglected in strategic planning for food security in Africa and more specifically in Burkina Faso. Overall, there is a need to further and systematically examine the central role of African women in achieving food security in the African context.

NOTES

1. Food and Agriculture Organization, *Burkina Faso*.
2. Murdock, Sithole-Niang, and Higgins, "Transforming the Cowpea"; Shiratori, Sawadogo/Compaoré, and Chien, "Variation of Cowpea Production."
3. National Research Council, "Cowpea"; FAOSTAT (FAO statistics database), Food and Agriculture Organization, accessed March 28, 2023, www.fao.org/faostat/en.
4. FAOSTAT.
5. Timko and Singh, "Cowpea, a Multifunctional Legume."
6. Food and Agriculture Organization, "Food Security."

7. Food and Agriculture Organization, *State of Food Security*.
8. Food and Agriculture Organization, *State of Food Security*.
9. Badiel, "Étude sur le rôle et la place de la femme."
10. Badiel, "Étude sur le rôle et la place de la femme."
11. Udry, "Gender, Agricultural Production."
12. Quisumbing, "What Have We Learned."
13. Badiel, "Étude sur le rôle et la place de la femme"; Gnoumou Thiombiano, "Genre et prise."
14. Gnoumou Thiombiano, "Genre et prise."
15. Oouba, Tani, and Toure, *Analyse stratégique des enjeux*.
16. *Plan national de développement sanitaire*.
17. *Plan national de développement sanitaire*.
18. These are common terms used in rural communities in Burkina Faso to give credit (or not) to a woman.

WORKS CITED

Badiel, A. "Étude sur le rôle et la place de la femme dans la commune de Kaïn, province du Yatenga, région du nord (Burkina Faso)." Working paper. APROS, 2014.

Food and Agriculture Organization. *Burkina Faso: Country Fact Sheet on Food and Agriculture Policy Trends*. Rome: FAO, 2014. www.fao.org/3/i3760e/i3760e.pdf.

———. "Food Security." *FAO Policy Brief*, no. 2 (June 2006). www.fao.org/fileadmin/templates/faoitaly/documents/pdf/pdf_Food_Security_Cocept_Note.pdf.

———. *The State of Food Insecurity in the World: Economic Crises—Impacts and Lessons Learned*. Rome: FAO, 2009.

———. *The State of Food Security and Nutrition in the World: Safeguarding against Economic Slowdowns and Downturns*. Rome: FAO, 2019.

Gnoumou Thiombiano, B. "Genre et prise de décision au sein du ménage au Burkina Faso." *Cahiers québécois de démographie* 43, no. 2 (2014) 249–78.

Murdock, Larry, Idah Sithole-Niang, and T. J. V. Higgins. "Transforming the Cowpea, an African Orphan Staple Crop Grown Predominantly by Women." In *Successful Agricultural Innovation in Emerging Economies: New Genetic Technologies for Global Food Production*, edited by D. Bennett and R. Jennings, 221–32. Cambridge: Cambridge University Press, 2013.

National Research Council. "Cowpea." Chap. 5 in *Vegetables*. Vol. 2 of *Lost Crops of Africa*. Washington, DC: National Academies Press, 2006.

Oouba, Rosalie, Mariam Tani, and Zéneb Toure. *Analyse stratégique des enjeux liés au genre au Burkina Faso*. Burkina Faso: World Bank, 2010. https://documents.worldbank.org/en/publication/documents-reports/documentdetail/921061468232135539/analyse-strategique-des-enjeux-lies-au-genre-au-burkina-faso.

Plan national de développement sanitaire 2011-2020. Burkina Faso: Ministère de la Santé, 2011. www.uhc2030.org/fileadmin/uploads/ihp/Documents/Country_Pages/Burkina_Faso/Burkina_Faso_National_Health_Strategy_2011-2020_French.pdf.

Quisumbing, A. R. "What Have We Learned from Research on Intrahousehold Allocation?" In *Household Decisions, Gender, and Development: A Synthesis of Recent Research*, edited by A. R. Quisumbing, 1–16. Washington, DC: International Food Policy Research Institute, 2003.

Shiratori, Sakiko, Eveline M. F. W. Sawadogo/Compaoré, and Hsiaoping Chien. "Variation of Cowpea Production and Usage in Rural Households: A Comparison between Northern and Southern Burkina Faso." *Japan Agricultural Research Quarterly* 54, no. 3 (2020): 263–70.

Timko, M. P., and B. B. Singh "Cowpea, a Multifunctional Legume." In *Genomics of Tropical Crop Plants*, edited by P. Moore and R. Ming, 227–58. New York: Springer, 2008.

Udry, Christopher. "Gender, Agricultural Production, and the Theory of the Household." *Journal of Political Economy* 104, no. 5 (1996): 1010–46.

CHAPTER 3

The Role of Women in Sustainable Agriculture in Three Global Regions

Environmentally Friendly Practices and Passing Knowledge Along to Future Generations

GLORIA SANDERS McCUTCHEON

MY MOTHER, HATTIE MINES SANDERS, was born in 1933 in rural South Carolina. She was an avid gardener and farmer who yearned to learn more about the intricacies of the organisms that comprised the ecosystem in her fruit and vegetable gardens. She excitedly conducted field experiments on grafting and cross-pollination and was interested in making better plants and determining the impact of various insects. Were they all pests, or could some insects, such as bees, be beneficial? My mother was a high school graduate who wanted to attend college but did not have the opportunity. Nevertheless, she excelled in math and science and could teach others the basic skills of life. I, on the other hand, an African American woman in the early 1970s, earned a bachelor of science degree in zoology from Clemson University and became involved in world-class agricultural research at the Clemson University Agricultural Research Center.

There were no other scientists with a similar ethnic/racial background, and there was doubt as to whether I could fit into such an environment. After college, in the summer of 1973, I was hired as a research technologist in entomology at the Clemson University Agricultural Experiment Station to investigate alternatives to pesticides. Interestingly, my Aunt Bea was the housekeeper for the superintendent and hiring official at the research facility. While serving her delicious vegetable soup to the superintendent and his wife, she overheard the superintendent, a plant pathologist and native Canadian who was a well-respected leader in the small southern rural community, speaking excitedly of a young Black lady who had just completed her studies at Clemson during an era of desegregation in the South. As my aunt continued to listen intently, she learned that I had gotten the job and was proud to inform her boss that he was speaking of her niece's daughter.

The 1970s were an interesting time from race and gender perspectives. At that time, as I was the first and only female researcher, a women's restroom had to be installed at the facility, and local farmers assumed I was the "new cleaning woman." Although I was at the early stage of a career in this field, I presented impactful research findings to the scientific community, much to the amazement of many that a woman was involved in the science of agricultural entomology. My upbringing in rural South Carolina, the support and pride that my aunt exhibited in my career, the encouragement and interest that my mother exhibited in biological sciences, and my own research on the conservation of natural enemies all contributed to my use of a feminist lens in understanding women's roles in sustainable agriculture.

Feminist Agri-food Systems Theory

I use the Feminist Agri-food Systems Theory (FAST) to describe (1) the role of women in sustainable agriculture through the conservation of natural enemies and (2) the power of women passing knowledge to their children and other youth in sustainable agriculture in three distinct communities: the southern region of the United States, Cuba, and Zimbabwe. FAST specifically highlights the challenges that women face in agricultural communities.[1] The framework includes (1) gender equity, (2) farmer identity, (3) access to resources including land, capital, and food and farming systems, (4) roles in agricultural organizations and institutions, (5) the formation of new networking organizations for women farmers, and (6) the shaping of new food and farming systems by integrating economic, environmental, and social values.

While each element of FAST is important, in this chapter, I focus only on the sixth, that is, the three main goals of sustainable agriculture: economic efficiency, social responsibility, and quality environment.[2] Specifically, I approach FAST using agroecology, which is distinct from other approaches because it is a bottom-up process that addresses local problems. Agroecology emphasizes the co-creation of knowledge and combines science with traditional local knowledge. It places an emphasis on women's rights and empowers youth and Indigenous people.[3] FAST values the manner in which women hold significant knowledge and are major contributors to sustainable agriculture and food production through economic, social, and environmental avenues.

ECONOMIC EFFICIENCY

Economic empowerment in agriculture is critical because women comprise 43 percent of agricultural labor in developing countries.[4] Therefore, it has become more important for agricultural transformation to be inclusive by creating equal opportunities for women and men. Oxfam's conceptual framework on women's economic empowerment promotes autonomy and self-belief so that women can make changes in their lives and impact others by working at multiple levels (individual, household, community, and national/international). Women's economic empowerment is intertwined with gender equality as part of a process of empowerment along economic, political, and social lines. When women are empowered, their voices are heard and their perspectives are considered in their households, communities, economic institutions, and political spaces. Women then develop partnerships that promote ownership in local systems and smallholder agriculture.

SOCIAL RESPONSIBILITY

The social responsibility of women to sustainable agriculture and food production is equally important to economic efficiency. There are 800 million people worldwide suffering from chronic hunger.[5] At the same time, there is a disturbing rise in obesity and diet-related diseases. Obesity contributes to noncommunicable diseases such as cancer, cardiovascular disease, and diabetes, the leading causes of mortality worldwide.[6] Culturally appropriate diets provide an avenue for agroecology to contribute to food security while we move toward a healthy ecosystem.[7] Equity and justice are key to the inclusion of women in agriculture as we fight food insecurity. We should consider equity and social well-being as essential for sustainable food and agricultural systems.[8] Through agroecology, we can address gender inequity and create more opportunities for women, who make up nearly half of the agricultural workforce. Black women are already doing this work, both individually and in community service organizations. For example, women and youth are empowered to promote sustainable agriculture in Z-HOPE (Zetas Helping Other People Excel—through Mind, Body, and Spirit), the international service program of Zeta Phi Beta Sorority, Inc., a historically Black community service organization.[9] Women are empowered to become their own change agents as they address food security, health, education, and sustainable food production, all while training others in the community to promote health and protect the environment. Women's important work also includes devising inventive ways to combat the overuse of pesticides.

QUALITY ENVIRONMENT/CROP DIVERSITY

Pesticide usage has increased worldwide over the past fifty years. Approximately 2.6 million tons of pesticides are used per year, with an annual global market value of more than $25 billion.[10] In the United States alone, the use of pesticides is tremendous, reaching 324 million kilograms of pesticides (600 types) annually, with indirect environmental (impacts on wildlife, pollinators, natural enemies, fisheries, water quality, etc.) and social (human poisoning and illness) costs reaching about $8 billion each year. Over 500 species of insects and arthropods have developed resistance to more than 1,000 different types of pesticides, thus making the pesticides useless for controlling such pests chemically and harmful to the environment. Practices in agroecology can yield more efficient pollination, more efficient pest control by natural enemies such as predators and parasitoids, more reliable incomes, improved nutritional outcomes, and a cleaner environment based on agroecology and traditional agriculture.[11]

Diverse cropping systems (using multiple crops, intercropping, and rotating plant species) are known to be key to agroecology. These diverse systems promote food security and nutrition while conserving, protecting, and enhancing natural resources. Agroecologists encourage intercropping plant species and rotating crops to promote a range of production, socioeconomic, nutritional, and environmental benefits.[12] Monoculture (the use of only one plant species) is heavily dependent on pesticides. Emphasis on the interrelationships of the various components of agroecology is necessary as we produce food to feed the world without depleting the environment and disempowering communities.[13] Therefore, we can shape new food and farming systems by integrating economic, social, and environmental concerns using the FAST theoretical model (number 6), as described above. In using this model, I employ scientific inquiry and autoethnographic methods to illustrate the roles of women and girls in sustainable agriculture in three global regions.

Women's Roles in Intergenerational Learning and Promoting Sustainable Agriculture

Women of color in various cultures promote sustainable agriculture. Their practices and beliefs provide intergenerational experiences and are passed down to their children. They use agroecological strategies to combine traditional and Indigenous knowledge, producers' and traders' practical knowledge, and global scientific knowledge. Agroecological strategies include attention to the role of biological pest-control agents in sustainable farming. Formal and informal participatory processes are used to manage pests, which helps build mutual trust for promoting agricultural sustainability.[14] In the following pages, I present three cases that all exemplify (1) the role of women in sustainable agriculture through the conservation of natural enemies and (2) the power of women passing knowledge down to their children and other youth in sustainable agriculture. The case studies are based on individual, household, community, and national/international experiences related to economic, social, and environmental issues. In each case presented, I describe the biological pest issues and show the inventive ways that Black women manage them.

THE ROLE OF TWO WOMEN IN SOLVING BIOLOGICAL PEST ISSUES IN THE SOUTHEASTERN UNITED STATES

My research in the southeastern United States set the stage for my research and travel to both Zimbabwe and Cuba. There were key women in my life who made it possible for me to conduct this research and also led me to identify the many roles that women take on in conducting and enabling research on sustainable food systems. I was so excited to have the opportunity to conduct research in soybean entomology because the soybean is an important cash crop in the southern United States. As someone who had grown up in the geographic area of the Clemson University Agricultural Experiment Station, one of my first thoughts was to investigate some alternatives to chemical pesticides because I understood that the residents were being exposed to potential carcinogens. I learned quickly of the four species of major pest caterpillars that feed on and destroy leaves and pods of soybean.[15] I was anxious to contribute to insect management strategies.

The research was meticulous and labor intensive, as I demonstrated to well-established entomologists, who were all men, and also to farmers and schoolchildren that there are naturally occurring insects that can help regulate pests. I took weekly samples of insect pests of soybean using the ground cloth method for two growing seasons in three geographic areas of South Carolina and observed the samples daily for parasitism.[16] This was a very tedious task that many would not undertake because of the size (1–3 mm) of the beneficial parasitoids that emerged from pest insects, thus killing the collected sample pests. From these data, I determined the incidence and seasonal occurrence of the beneficial parasitoids.

While my mother may not have been my official research technician, it was with her assistance and persistence that we shipped hundreds of properly preserved parasitoids to the Smithsonian for confirmation and further identification, using instructions and scientific articles provided by the Smithsonian Museum of Natural History. We stayed up many late nights preparing specimens, as they each had to be identified to the taxonomic level of family and labeled with special pens on tiny labels. My mother had excellent penmanship and was careful that all labels were accurate as information was transferred from petri dishes to vials containing alcohol with the tiny labels. This research helped me realize that my mother had the determination that perhaps only a mother could exhibit as she supported me in completing the project, as she realized that it was highly significant to the future of science and the environment.[17]

Reflecting on this research has helped me realize that what made me ask questions about "who was managing crops" in both Zimbabwe and Cuba started from my own experiences as a Black woman entomologist. I knew, for example, that my mother helped me label and identify specimens to send to the Smithsonian, a task that may be performed by official lab staff in a better-resourced lab of a white male scientist. I knew that it was only after I won a major National Science Foundation grant and published in a major academic journal that my work was noticed by others. In some ways, this is just the nature of science; however, like many Black women, I have always had to prove myself differently at every stage. I, with the help of my mother, performed tasks that white male scientists probably had research support and labs to do. The people that I most remember for encouraging me to continue my studies were two female entomologists (Dr. Pat Cobb at Auburn University and Dr. Pauline Lawrence at the University of Florida), who were persistent about me continuing my studies in insect parasitism. I was supported by both women and men, including my research adviser, Dr. Sam Turnipseed, and my husband, Larry. But my support from women stayed with me and encouraged me to probe even deeper beyond the official scientific methods to determine how crops are being managed sustainably.

BIOLOGICAL PEST ISSUES IN CUBA

Since the mid-1990s, when many countries were still relying on agrochemicals for food production, policies such as the Cuban Democracy Act kept foreign subsidiaries of US companies from engaging in trade with Cuba. Some small-scale farmers have over the years learned to manage their pests with limited use of insecticides and have linked with natural resource management initiatives.[18] Having little to no access to chemicals, Cuba focused on alternative agriculture and learned to use local resources and not to rely on other countries for fertilizers and pesticides. These conditions supported agroecology, integrated pest management, and specifically, biological rather than chemical control of insect pests. In Cuba, classical biological control has received a fair amount of research attention, and it has a prominent place in developing strategies for pest management.[19] Interestingly, reports show that with the exception of some Cuban and African studies, many biological control initiatives remain isolated and miss follow-up research.[20]

In the book *Women Who Dig*, Trina Moyles provides insight into sustainable farming and women in eight countries.[21] She addresses the joys and struggles of women engaged in food production, focusing on social and environmental justice and reaching deep into the souls of women in Cuba, Guatemala, Nicaragua, the United States, Canada, Uganda, the Democratic Republic of Congo, and India. As a Food and Society Policy Fellow, I observed that popular education allowed researchers from the University of Havana (including a male entomologist and a female economist) the opportunity to go into the community at the Martin Luther King Peace Center in Havana and listen to the needs of those in the community.[22] Much like I did during my experiences in the southern United States, they found that pest management was a huge concern among farmers. However, in Cuba, the concern for food production extended far into the community and included not only young, well-educated farmers but people from all walks of life, including women and children.

In Cuba, women are the carriers of sustainability knowledge, and they transfer this knowledge to their children. Amazingly, in this agriculture project, numerous children were investigating cabbage leaves for insect eggs. They were carefully looking on the undersurface of leaves for single eggs laid by the cabbage looper moth. These activities were overseen by Cuban women, but they numbered far less than the children. The eggs of the cabbage looper are about the size of a pinhead and are often laid on the undersurface of cabbage leaves. The children, ranging in age from eight to fourteen, were searching the undersides of the exposed cabbage leaves. They would take a tiny piece of the leaf when they located an egg, place both egg and leaf into a paper container, and transport the eggs of the cabbage looper to the center of a field, where a Center for Reproduction of Entomophagous and Entomopathogenous Organisms was strategically located.[23] (Entomophagous organisms are those that feed on pest insects. Entomopathogenous organisms are those that infect insects with diseases—viruses, fungi, and bacteria.) Cuba has hundreds of such centers and is often recognized as a model in transitioning to a more sustainable, low-input style of agriculture. This knowledge is embedded in generations of people with different professional backgrounds, including teachers, lawyers, and nurses, who became farmers during the Special Period when the state struggled to produce high quantities of food to transport to the cities.

"Why was it so important to search for these eggs?" I asked about ten children and a few women working in a cabbage field outside of Havana. In response to my question about their activities, the children informed me that they were collecting the "farmer's friends" so that they can multiply and produce more farmer's friends. When asked what the "farmer's friends" were, the children informed me that they are called *Trichogramma*. These young children understood how to conserve natural resources and, in this case, the behavior and biology of these tiny one-millimeter insects (egg parasitoids). While wasps vary widely in size and color, the smallest wasps are born inside the eggs of other insects. *Trichogramma* is a small wasp that lays an egg that splits (similar to twins) inside a host (pest) egg (cabbage looper). The wasps develop inside the host egg for about a week, and then three to five adults emerge from the egg, killing that egg and eliminating any opportunity for that pest to develop. The children would collect eggs that were parasitized by the female *Trichogramma* wasp and let them develop and reproduce to use them for biological pest control.

I have vivid memories of the picturesque leafy, green, large, pesticide-free cabbage plant fields (approximately five hectares), where women and children were managing the pests using an environmentally friendly approach. At the same time, the children were learning (and teaching) science as they worked in the cabbage ecosystem. They all seemed to have ownership of the project, and this was their after-school program, in which they were making great contributions to health promotion and the environment.

ZIMBABWEAN WOMEN LEADING THE WAY IN PEST MANAGEMENT

Zimbabwe is yet another example of how women are knowledge holders in integrated pest management in other parts of the Diaspora. Leafy greens, including cabbage and *cova*, are important food staples in the Zimbabwean diet. Major pests include the cabbage looper and the diamondback moth. Insect parasitoids are important in regulating the pest insects, and they are similar to and in the same families and genera as those beneficial parasitoids documented in the United States and Cuba.

I made several visits to Zimbabwe in collaboration with peers at Africa University in Old Mutare. Global perspectives prepared me for a visit to the Children's Garden in the Eastern Highlands of Zimbabwe. This garden is associated with an orphanage at the Old Mutare Mission in Manicaland, Zimbabwe, near the campus of Africa University. On one occasion, I was escorted by children to their garden, so they could collect the "farmer's friends" from the leafy greens.

Most of the smallholder farmers were ranked into an intermediate category between integrated pest management practices and conventional insecticide use. Women are often smallholder farmers in Zimbabwe and have long focused on agricultural sustainability, mostly out of need and the lack of resources. Women on the village farms talk about various strategies to produce food, including crop rotation and the importance of determining the differences between pests and beneficial insects. They understand and communicate clearly the need to promote beneficial insects by utilizing "no-till" practices. To promote sustainability, many women have transitioned from growing one crop (potatoes) in the Nyanga District's fertile soil to growing a diversity of crops including blueberries, strawberries, peaches, avocados, and cabbages. The diamondback moth is a major insect pest of brassicas (including cabbage and cova) in Zimbabwe. The cabbage looper is also a major pest of leafy greens. Farmers use various pest control tactics, often depending upon the availability of resources.

At the orphanage, the children, accompanied by female teachers, were collecting the "farmer's friends" in the garden. Similar to the Cuban children, the Zimbabwean children provided scientific descriptions of the farmer's friends, small parasitic wasps that kill the diamondback moth. They were collecting the pupae of the farmer's friends, *Cotesia plutellae*, which develop in small (2–3 mm), white, fuzzy cocoons on the undersides of the leaves. I expanded my observations into smallholder farms in Manicaland and the Nyanga District in Zimbabwe to further investigate the role of women in sustainable farming.

The children carefully picked the cocoons containing pupae from harvested plants and simply left their tiny friends on another plant in the garden before sending the edible plants to the cafeteria. The method was to save their friends before the cova greens were washed at the cafeteria at Africa University. They understood that the more cocoons they detected, the better the chance of getting greens with fewer holes in them from pest feeding. They were very happy to be able to provide food for the cafeteria at the orphanage and at Africa University.

When we arrived at the village smallholder farm, several men pulled up logs under a large tree for us to have a seat. We engaged in a brief discussion about the production of vegetables on the farm, and the men were unable to answer any of our questions. Finally, I asked to observe some of their production practices for leafy greens. The men laughed and almost instantly said it is the role of the women. As they called three women from the kitchen, the laughter grew louder because the women realized I had asked the men about the production procedures, particularly the types and roles of the insects in the field. The women were very helpful in sharing that they manage insect pests with naturally occurring insects and pathogens. They were involved in classical biological control through the conservation of natural enemies and were able to identify several of the beneficial organisms and the pests that they attacked.

Among their list of "farmer's friends" were important natural enemies such as *Trichogramma*, ladybird beetles, hover flies, other parasitic wasps, predatory mites, ants, and some antagonistic microorganisms. I observed that some women farmers sprayed crushed marigolds on vegetables to fight pests. These traditional agricultural practices can enhance our understanding of the environment and promote sustainability. The village farmers do not have access to new chemicals, and old chemicals are harmful to the health of the community. The women apologized because they had to end our conversation early, but the knowledge that we gained beyond the kitchen table on how women sustainably manage pests was invaluable.

During another visit to Africa University and to the Nyanga District smallholder farms in 2019, we observed women farmers participating in very successful businesses, including onion production. The secretary for gender equity in Zimbabwe to the United Nations, who hosted us, was deeply invested in promoting the role of women in sustainable agriculture. She emphasized that women in Zimbabwe and other countries on the continent contribute to sustainable food production by promoting the use of beekeeping for pollination, the use of crop diversification and rotation (from potatoes only to diverse fruit and vegetable crops), and the use of naturally occurring beneficial insects such as tiny parasitic wasps on crops to regulate pest insects.

Reflections and Conclusions

My experiences as a woman were not at the forefront of my mind when I began this research. However, in reflecting on my career, I have found that being a Black woman influences my work in the field and how I work to transfer this knowledge to the community. As noted, some of my initial interests came from my mother and her desire to use as few insecticides as possible in her garden. I credit my mother for helping me prepare samples to send to the Smithsonian. While I eventually received recognition from the Experiment Station, the National Science Foundation, and the White House for my work, it was working alongside women that made many of these experiences personal and special.

My earlier experiences in the field taught me the value of sharing knowledge. I enjoyed promoting awareness at various community events. Farmers could see firsthand how beneficial, though inconspicuous, some insects are in the field. They were encouraged to consider the conservation of beneficial insects in an integrated pest management system, where beneficial insects might be the first consideration rather than the last option for the control of pests. This method decreased costs, with fewer chemical pesticide applications, and enhanced the environment, thus promoting healthier surroundings for farmers' families.

Since childhood I wanted to work in environments free of chemical insecticides in South Carolina during an era when up to twenty aerial applications of insecticide were used on large cotton farms to control boll weevils and other pests. The research that I began as a graduate student provided great insight into the potential of beneficial insects (parasitoids) in regulating soybean pest insects in South Carolina and Cuba. As a research professor, I, along with my graduate student from Zimbabwe, investigated parasitoids on pests of leafy greens (cova) in the Eastern Highlands of Zimbabwe in Mutare and Manicaland.[24] My own personal history as a woman scientist and the lessons learned from my mother provided the gendered lens to observe the role that women (and children) play in this process of sustainable agriculture and food security.

Observations from the three global areas and research data support the hypothesis that Black women promote the conservation of naturally occurring insects and diseases that fight and control pests in crop production, and they pass traditional, cultural, and scientific knowledge on to the youth at early ages. Thus, science education is enhanced in the community, as are economic opportunities and social awareness. Agroecology is the driving force because it provides the vehicle to reach out to people where they are, and it emphasizes the combination of science and traditional knowledge, with an emphasis on women's rights and the empowerment of youth and Indigenous people. The findings of this research and the FAST model show that women the world over make great contributions to sustainable agriculture through social, economic, and environmental approaches.

NOTES

1. Sachs et al., *Rise of Women Farmers*.
2. Karami, Manso, and Abadi, "Sustainable Agricultural Attitudes."
3. Gliessman, *Agroecology*.
4. Kidder, Bright, and Green, *Meaningful Action*.
5. Food and Agriculture Organization, *State of Food Security*.
6. World Health Organization, *World Health Organization Guideline*.
7. Food and Agriculture Organization, *Second Report*.
8. Food and Agriculture Organization, *Sustainability Agriculture for Biodiversity*.
9. "Z-HOPE (Zetas Helping Other People Excel)," Zeta Phi Beta Sorority, Inc., accessed November 9, 2019, http://zphib1920.org/national-programs/z-hope.
10. Food and Agriculture Organization, *Save and Grow*.
11. Altieri, Nicholls, and Montalba, "Technological Approaches"; Chen and Welter, "Crop Domestication."
12. On intercropping, see Prabhu et al., "Agroforestry." On crop rotation, see Food and Agriculture Organization, *Save and Grow*.
13. UN International Fund for Agricultural Development, *Rural Poverty Report*.
14. Holt-Giménez, *Campesino a campesino*.
15. Carner, Shepard, and Turnipseed, "Seasonal Abundance."
16. Boyer and Dumas, "Soybean Insect Survey"; Weseloh, "Host Seeking, by Parasitoids." A parasite is a small organism that lives and feeds on its host that is much larger. The parasite-host relationship is specialized, and the parasite generally weakens its host but does not kill it. If insects parasitize other insects, they are called parasitoids, and they kill their host upon emergence as they reach maturity. They are not considered true parasites because of this, and as adults they are free-living after emerging from and killing their host.
17. The results from our research revealed that we need to promote the conservation of beneficial natural resources. Each of the major pests that destroy the leaves of

the soybean plant is attacked and killed by the parasitic wasp *Cotesia marginiventris* (Cresson) and an entomopathogenic fungus. The tiny wasps hide from humans and spend part of their lives in or on the host caterpillar as they feed and develop to become free-living adults. In its short life cycle of less than one month, one female wasp can kill about 100 pest caterpillars, resulting in significant control of pests before the voracious pest caterpillars can reach larger sizes and destroy plants. The highest incidence of parasitism was in soybean looper (16 percent), and the most prevalent larval parasitoid was *Apanteles marginiventris* (Cresson), renamed *Cotesia marginiventris*. Unlike some of the other parasitoids, *C. marginiventris* is a generalist and attacks many different species of pest insects.

18. Venotola, "Integrated Pest Management."
19. Wychuys et al., "Current Status and Potential."
20. Schulthess et al., "Seasonal Fluctuation."
21. Moyles, *Women Who Dig*.
22. Deem, "Popular Education for Women."
23. Oppenheim, "Alternative Agriculture in Cuba."
24. Manyangarirwa et al., "Parasitoids of the Diamondback."

WORKS CITED

Altieri, Miguel A., Clara I. Nicholls, and Rene Montalba. "Technological Approaches to Sustainable Agriculture at a Crossroads: An Agroecological Perspective." *Sustainability* 9, no. 3 (2017): 349.

Boyer, W. B., and W. A. Dumas. "Soybean Insect Survey as Used in Arkansas." *Cooperative Economic Insect Report* 13, no. 1 (1963): 91–92.

Carner, G. R., M. Shepard, and S. G. Turnipseed. "Seasonal Abundance of Insect Pests of Soybeans." *Journal of Economic Entomology* 67, no. 4 (1974): 487–93.

Chen, Y. H., and S. C. Welter. "Crop Domestication Creates a Refuge from Parasitism for a Native Moth." *Journal of Applied Ecology* 44, no. 1 (2007): 238–45.

Deem, R. "Popular Education for Women: A Study of Four Organizations." In *Adult Learners, Education and Training*, edited by R. Edwards, S. Sieminski, and D. Zeldin, 235–49. London: Routledge, 1993.

Food and Agriculture Organization. "Human and Social Values: Protecting and Improving Rural Livelihood, Equity and Social Well-Being Is Essential for Sustainable Food and Agricultural Systems." Agroecology Knowledge Hub. Accessed November 1, 2019. www.fao.org/agroecology/knowledge/10-elements/human-social-value/en.

———. *Save and Grow: A Policymaker's Guide to the Sustainable Intensification of Smallholder Crop Production*. Rome: FAO, 2011.

———. *The Second Report on the State of the World's Plant Genetic Resources for Food and Agriculture*. Rome: FAO, 2010.

———. *The State of Food Security and Nutrition in the World 2021: Transforming Food Systems for Food Security, Improved Nutrition and Affordable Healthy Diets for All*. Rome: FAO, 2021. www.fao.org/documents/card/en/c/cb4474en.

Gilreath, M. Elizabeth, Gloria S. McCutcheon, G. R. Carner, and S. G. Turnipseed. "Pathogen Incidence in Noctuid Larvae from Selected Soybean Genotypes." *Journal of Agricultural Entomology* 3 (1986): 213–26.

Gliessman, S. R. *Agroecology: The Ecology of Sustainable Food Systems*. Boca Raton, FL: CRC, 2015.

Holt-Giménez, E. *Campesino a campesino: Voces de Latinoamérica movimiento campesino para la agricultura sustentable*. Managua, Nicaragua: SIMAS, 2008.

Karami, E., O. R. Manso, and A. Abadi. "Sustainable Agricultural Attitudes and Behaviors: A Gender Analysis of Iranian Farmers." *Journal of Environment, Development and Sustainability* 10, no. 6 (2008): 883–98.

Kidder, T., D. Bright, and C. Green. *Meaningful Action: Effective Approaches to Women's Economic Empowerment in Agriculture*. Oxfam Background Report. Oxford, UK: Oxfam, 2014.

Manyangarirwa, W., G. W. Zehnder, Gloria S. McCutcheon, J. P. Smith, P. Adler, and A. N. Mphuru. "Parasitoids of the Diamondback Moth on Brassicas in Zimbabwe." *African Crop Science Conference Proceedings* 9 (2009): 565–70.

McCutcheon, Gloria S. "Gloria Sanders McCutcheon." In *Memoirs of Black Entomologists: Reflections on Childhood, University, and Career Experiences*, edited by Eric W. Riddick, Michelle Samuel-Foo, Willye W. Bryan, and Alvin M. Simmons, 70–74. Annapolis, MD: Entomological Society of America, 2015.

McCutcheon, Gloria S., and S. G. Turnipseed. "Parasites of Lepidopterous Larvae in Insect Resistant and Susceptible Soybeans in South Carolina." *Environmental Entomology* 10, no. 1 (1981): 69–74.

McCutcheon, Gloria S., S. G. Turnipseed, and M. J. Sullivan. "Green Cloverworm (Lepidoptera: Noctuidae) as an Alternate Host for Natural Enemies of Lepidopteran Pests of Soybean in South Carolina." *Journal of Agricultural Entomology* 14 (1997): 105–19.

Moyles, Trina. *Women Who Dig: Farming, Feminism, and the Fight to Feed the World*. Regina, SK: University of Regina Press, 2018.

Oppenheim, Sara. "Alternative Agriculture in Cuba." *American Entomologist* 47, no. 4 (Winter 2001): 216–27.

Prabhu, Ravi, Edmundo Barrios, Jules Bayala, Lucien Diby, Jason Donovan, Amos Gyau, Lars Gradual, et al. "Agroforestry: Realizing the Promise of an Agroecological Approach." In *Agroecology for Food Security and Nutrition: Proceedings of the FAO International Symposium*, edited by the Food and Agriculture Organization, 201–24. Rome: FAO, 2015.

Quinn, Alicia. "Writing a Grant Proposal that Works: Leader in Action." *American Association of University Women*, Spring 1992, 9–16.

Sachs, C. E., M. E. Barbercheck, K. J. Brasier, N. E. Kiernan, and A. R. Terman. *Rise of Women Farmers and Sustainable Agriculture*. Iowa City: University of Iowa Press, 2016.

Schulthess, F., N. A. Bosque-Pérez, A. Chabi-Olaye, and G. Goergen. "Seasonal Fluctuation of *Sesamia calamistis* (Lepidoptera: Noctuidae) Egg Parasitism by *Telenomus* spp. (Hemiptera: Sceliondiae) in Maize Fields in Southern Benin." *Biocontrol Science and Technology* 11, no. 6 (2001): 745–57.

UN International Fund for Agricultural Development. *The Rural Poverty Report 2011*. Rome: IFAD, 2011. https://sustainabledevelopment.un.org.

Venotola, Vanessa. "Integrated Pest Management and Biological Control in Cuba." *Growing Culture*, 2013.

Weseloh, Ronald M. "Host Seeking, by Parasitoids." In *Encyclopedia of Insects*, edited by Vincent H. Resh and Ring T. Cardé, 526–28. San Diego, CA: Academic Press, 2003.

World Health Organization. *World Health Organization Guideline: Sugars Intake in Adults and Children*. Geneva, Switzerland: WHO, 2015.

Wychuys, K. A. G., Y. Lu, H. Morales, L. L. Vazquez, J. C. Legaspi, P. A. Eliopoulos, and L. M. Hernandez. "Current Status and Potential of Conservation Biological Control for Agriculture in the Developing World." *Biological Control* 65, no. 1 (2013): 152–67.

CHAPTER 4

Fish Farming

Women in Food Production for Improved Household Food and Nutrition Security in Ortoire Village, Mayaro, Trinidad—a Case Study

KENIA-ROSA CAMPO, WENDY-ANN ISAAC,
NEELA BADRIE, AND MARQUITTA WEBB

Introduction

The underperformance of the agriculture industry in developing countries can be linked to gender inequality regarding access to assets and resources.[1] In Trinidad and Tobago, while the vast majority of small-scale producers experience difficulty accessing resources, sociocultural norms curtail women producers' access to productive resources including education, land, technology, information, financial services, and markets. At the same time, Trinidad and Tobago's gender policy advances that differences based on sex should neither exist nor be exploited.[2] Understanding these gender inequalities leads to a need for interventions designed to be more conducive to empowering and engaging women, so that they are able to better the agricultural sector's performance.

In response to this need, this paper analyzes women's economic and social empowerment in aquaculture as a fast-growing food-production sector in the Caribbean region. It specifically investigates women's empowerment in an aquaculture project located in the fishing village of Ortoire, Mayaro.[3]

Fish production is considered one of the most effective tools to address poverty alleviation, food and nutrition security, and the economic empowerment of rural communities.[4] The socioeconomic norms of fishing groups in Mayaro, Trinidad, are not homogenous. Their enterprise comprises several categories or job classifications, such as boat owners, captains, crew members, managers, scalemen, net builders and repairers, jostlers, vendors (wholesale and retail), and engine repairers. The involvement of women is integral, as they play active roles in all aspects of southeast coast fishery, including as boat owners and managers of fishing activity on behalf of fisher husbands or sons. Additionally, women are involved in fishing groups and community organizations that promote fishermen. This is in addition to their more traditional roles as fish processors and vendors.

Aquaculture is the fastest-growing sector of food production in the world.[5] However, its income, food, and other benefits are not evenly distributed between women and men of different ages and social groups who engage in and depend on it.[6] This case study investigated women's empowerment through their participation in aquaculture activities in the rural village of Ortoire, Mayaro. This form of production was selected because, according to David J. Spielman, Javier Ekboir, and Kristin Davis, promoting agricultural innovation among smallholder farmers in developing countries is a strategic move for improving food security and enhancing productivity.[7] The study aimed to demonstrate that fishing is a major contributor to food security in the village through subsistence production and income generation. As fish farming and the incorporation of aquaculture grow, we hope that the intervention allows women to obtain their equitable share of this growth process. The well-being of other fishing communities, based on the sustainability of fish farming as a livelihood strategy, may depend on the answers we manage to find in this study.

Theory and Background

According to the National Policy of Gender and Development of Trinidad and Tobago, gender norms exist at the societal level.[8] These norms can vary significantly from one community to the next, as they are contingent upon societal identity and differ significantly depending on location. This shows that gender norms are shaped by ongoing gendered societal relations, a view supported by Bernadette P. Resurreccion and Rebecca Elmhirst, who believe gender norms are embedded in existing structural and institutional conditions that vary depending on people's daily lives.[9] Based on these statements, one can conclude that men and women behave in ways that shape and reshape the cultural norms of gender. However, a document prepared by the State of Food and Agriculture team in 2011 shows that trends in agricultural research are what frame the gender norms in the sector, as women and men often have sharply defined roles in traditional fishing communities.

As mentioned in the introduction, this chapter examines fish farming as an innovative strategy for employment regeneration and food security in Mayaro. Fish farming provides remarkable contributions to global food security and nutrition. Further, the sustainable harvesting of fish stock has ecologically determined the upper limits for increasing the contribution of fish farming toward enhancing the standards of living for many rural dwellers. This is considered a lucrative endeavor in terms of income and supply of animal protein.

The Food and Agriculture Organization of the United Nations reported that fish account for about one-fifth of the world's total supply of animal protein sources.[10] Fish is an important source of protein for many people in developing countries because fish culture is an efficient means of animal protein production that is easily assimilated, compared to other animal protein production.[11] Malnutrition affects human capital development and productivity. This is the basis for the interrelation between agriculture and nutrition. As such, in order to promote the consumption of adequate and diversified foods, the process starts by improving agricultural production and household food security. Women are crucial actors in breaking the poverty cycle and influencing the health of the entire household. There is a paucity of research aimed at assessing how maintaining or improving fish consumption benefits the diet and health of residents of Ortoire, Mayaro, as they contend with the ongoing nutrition transition characterized by an increasing demand for packaged imported foods such as canned meats, instant noodles, cereals, rice, and sugar-sweetened beverages with subsequently decreased consumption of locally produced goods.

In spite of the intervention through training, fish consumption has grown little. Moreover, despite the apparently strong markets and adequate biophysical conditions, aquaculture still has yet to be developed. According to a Food and Agriculture Organization analysis, given that many wild fisheries are fully fished (58 percent) or overfished (31 percent), it is evident that aquaculture will play a central role in filling the gap between the increasing demand

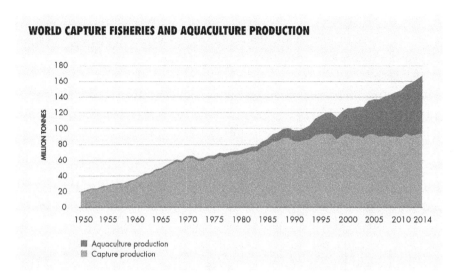

FIGURE 4.1. World capture fisheries and aquaculture production.
Food and Agriculture Organization, *State of World Fisheries*, 3.

for seafood and what capture fisheries can provide.[12] Figure 4.1 illustrates data from the 2016 Food and Agriculture Organization report on world capture fish versus fish from aquaculture production.

Aquaculture's contribution to food and nutrition security is an issue of not only where aquaculture occurs but also what is being produced and how and whether the product is as accessible as that from capture fisheries.[13] A review of studies of fish prices throughout Trinidad concluded that demand corresponds closely to price. Therefore, price is likely to be an even greater determinant of whether poor consumers buy fish or not. Where aquaculture production dominates the market, farmed fish should be cheaper, as a result increasing economic access. Farmed fish are also different in terms of their nutrient content, a result of the species being grown and of different rearing methods.

Methods

This case study was conducted in one of the six villages in Mayaro, Trinidad and Tobago. Data were collected over a ten-month period between February and November 2015, using focus group discussions, key informant interviews, and qualitative methodology adopted from the Consultative Group on International Agricultural Research's GENNOVATE initiative.[14] This method focused on how gender norms shape men's and women's innovation and adaptation to technology in agriculture programs. Data were collected from a total of sixty participants; only eight participants were women.

Semistructured interviews with individuals, along with focus group discussions in small groups, were conducted to explore the profile of the community. For the purposes of this case study, we looked at gender and participation from a theoretical perspective to explain how gender manifested itself in participation and why women have limited benefits from the fishing industry. Then, we highlighted the barriers that seemed to preclude women from participating, which included institutional embedded norms and financial, sociocultural, and reproduction roles. As such, women's empowerment was assessed across two dimensions, specifically agriculture production and income use. By using the gender lens to analyze issues of sustainability, we sought to establish the differential contributions of women and men to production and value addition within this sector and to bring into the spotlight the varying degrees of economic and social returns they obtain. Three measures of empowerment were selected for this study: women's decision-making ability in their households, spending ability, and access to assets and resources. These parameters for empowerment were explained to the women taking part in the study, and they were asked for their perceived extent of empowerment, taking into account their situations before and after their participation in the aquaculture program.

Findings and Discussion

Understanding the individuals involved in fish farming is important; therefore, the study sought to explore the demographics of the participants. Evidence from the descriptive analysis of socioeconomic characteristics of participants in table 4.1 shows that men constituted about 87 percent of the fish farmers, compared to approximately 13 percent female farmers. A gendered analysis of the overall project and a discourse on whether the "feminization" of fishing in the village impacts the fishers' livelihoods are only just beginning to emerge. It is unclear whether the adoption of aquaculture would aid in increasing or decreasing overall income in fish farming villages, as vegetables can also be sold to increase revenue.

The mean age of the fish farmers was twenty-eight years, and most of the participants were between twenty-one and thirty years old. The results show that relatively younger individuals are engaged in fish farming. This indicates that most of the fish farmers engaged in aquaculture fall into the "active age"

	RANGE/ CLASSIFICATION	FREQUENCY (N)	PERCENT (%)	CUMULATIVE (%)
AGE (YEARS)	21–30	24	40	40
	31–40	19	31.7	71.7
	41–50	17	28.3	100
SEX	Male	52	86.7	86.7
	Female	8	13.3	100
EDUCATION	Nonformal	8	13.3	13.3
	Primary	28	46.7	60
	Secondary	16	26.7	86.7
	Tertiary	8	13.3	100
MARITAL STATUS	Single	6	10	10
	Married	14	23.3	33.3
	Common law	40	66.7	100
EXPERIENCE FISHING	Less than 5 years	30	50	50
	5–10 years	22	36.7	86.7
	More than 10 years	8	13.3	100
HOUSEHOLD INCOME, WEALTH INDEX	Men	36	60	60
	Women	24	40	100

TABLE 4.1. The socioeconomic characteristics of fish farmers in Ortoire, Mayaro.

category. Therefore, training, extension services, and the spread of knowledge should be effective for fish farmers of this age.

The farmers were said to be literate, as only a small proportion of them had no formal education. The average level of schooling was primary, which is quite common in rural areas of Trinidad and Tobago, according to the 2018 National Policy of Gender and Development of Trinidad and Tobago. It is important to note that many fish farmers are illiterate yet have become entrepreneurs in aquaculture. Further, fish farmers who graduated from high school and above have also adopted the profession. No matter what their educational background, these rural individuals have come forward to participate in aquaculture.

In this case study, most of the fish farmers (72.5 percent) operated on state-owned land. About 75 percent of the farmers were able to raise their capital from bank loans. Some capital was also obtained from grants from the Mayaro Initiative for Private Enterprise Development, according to that initiative's own data. The disparity in age of male and female processors may be due to the amount of household responsibility placed on female processors compared to their male counterparts at an early stage of life, especially as it concerns children's upbringing and other household responsibilities that may be expected of the female gender, many of whom may also be tasked with taking care of the household with little or no assistance.

Fishing associations' influence on fish consumption was reviewed in the study based on fish's contribution to household food and nutrition security. In their 2007 study on fishery management and community fishery associations, Rosemarie Kishore and Himawatee Ramsundar found a reliance on availability, access, and cultural and personal preferences, with access to community meetings largely determined by location and with enthusiasm influenced by seasonality and price. However, at the individual level, fish consumption also depends on a person's physiological and health status; how fish is prepared, cooked, and shared among household members; and their willingness to consume the product.[15] The sustained and rapid expansion of aquaculture over the years has resulted in more than 40 percent of all fish now consumed being derived from farming, as aquaculture produce is increasingly featured in the diets of many locals in suburban areas on the island and is much less apparent among those living in rural settings such as Ortoire, Mayaro.

There was a significant positive relationship between empowerment and training in the program. The findings showed that women appeared to be gaining more decision-making influence. Although women comprise on average 43 percent of the agricultural labor force in developing countries and produce the bulk of the world's food crops, their presence in decision-making bodies, especially in leadership positions, remains weak, and their needs as farmers are seldom accounted for in policy and resource allocation.[16] As a result, women farmers do not produce to their full capacity.

After ten months, only 20 percent of the women in the control group reported that they had any money of their own and that they could decide how to use it without their husband's permission. The randomized control trial, which studied sixty villagers from Ortoire, Mayaro, showed that homestead food production in fishponds improved food security, dietary diversity, food

EMPOWERMENT DIMENSION	MEAN		T-VALUE FOR DIFFERENCES OF MEANS
	BEFORE	AFTER	
DECISION-MAKING ABILITY	3.90	4.03	-11.52*
SPENDING ABILITY	3.42	4.21	-10.47*
ACCESS TO ASSETS AND RESOURCES	3.45	3.92	-9.82*

*$p < 0.01$

TABLE 4.2. Scores obtained from women in the three dimensions of empowerment before and after their participation in the aquaculture program (N=15).

intake, and women's empowerment. Ortoire was chosen out of three districts (Manzanilla and Mafeking being the other two) because it was categorized in a 2012 Mayaro Initiative for Private Enterprise Development survey as the most resource-deprived district. The longitudinal research design employed in the end-line survey had the households interviewed at baseline revisited to assess changes over time.

The study showed that women play a significant role in agriculture and food production but earn 20 percent less than men for the same work. In 30 percent of the households interviewed, women played an active role in fishing, selling fish, and mending nets for income-generation purposes. The extent of their empowerment was positively correlated to exposure to aquaculture training as well as participation in aquaculture activities. The integration of this small-scale aquaculture project sought to build women's confidence and influence in decision-making through greater income-generation opportunities.

At the end of the project, we observed that the percentage of women who were the primary decision-makers regarding food-crop farming choices increased by 20 percent. At the end of the ten-month study, we discovered that only 9 percent of the women were the primary decision-makers regarding major household expenditures. The data presented in tables 4.2 and 4.3 indicate that there was an improvement in the empowerment of women in the village after they participated in the aquaculture program. The mean empowerment scores before and after participation for decision-making, spending ability, and access to assets clearly indicate this improvement, further supported by the t-values in the t-test.

Employment and income remained an insufficient measure of the gendered nature of poverty in the village. The "capabilities approach" emphasized access

EMPOWERMENT DIMENSION	MULTIPLE R	COEFFICIENT OF DETERMINATION R^2	PERCENT OF VARIATION EXPRESSED (%)
DECISION-MAKING ABILITY	0.652	0.374	37.2
SPENDING ABILITY	0.983	0.961	3.4
ACCESS TO ASSETS AND RESOURCES	0.722	0.496	25.0

TABLE 4.3. Stepwise multiple regression analysis showing the contribution of the three empowerment dimensions to the overall empowerment score obtained.

to food security, nutrition, health, and education as capabilities that lead to "functioning," indicating human well-being.[17] These dimensions of well-being determined the parameters of the study as it was correlated to both access to employment and labor productivity. However, we lacked adequate data on the disparities in access and outcomes among men and women in relation to health and nutrition.

Conclusion

This case study, conducted in 2015, confirmed that fisheries are important for the livelihoods of Ortoire Village's rural poor, as the harvesting, handling, processing, and distributing done in fisheries provides their livelihood. Based on the results generated, women played the main role in agriculture and food production but earned less than men for the same work. The integration of this small-scale aquaculture project sought to build women's confidence and influence in decision-making through greater income-generation opportunities. It can be concluded that the empowerment status of women in Ortoire, Mayaro, can be significantly improved by increasing their involvement in income-generation activities such as aquaculture. The findings led to the conclusion that if technical organizations, such as the University of the West Indies, promote agricultural innovations, they need to go beyond cataloging gender gaps if they are to engage more closely with the underlying gender norms of the communities they wish to impact, meaning that gender norms are likely to affect the capacities of women and men to adopt and innovate new practices in agriculture.

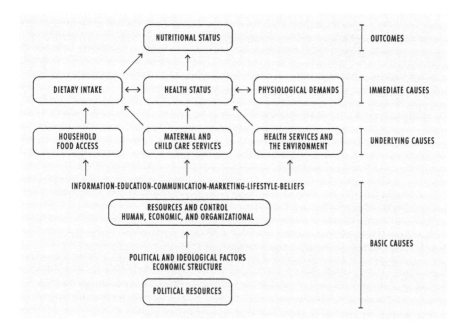

FIGURE 4.2. Determinants of nutritional status. Modified from Kawarazuka and Béné, "Linking Small-Scale Fisheries"; and UNICEF, *Strategy for Improved Nutrition*.

Understanding these relations between men and women in fish farming unveiled gender-based opportunities and constraints along the value chains of the industry. A gender discourse perspective on the participation of the subjects in the study further facilitated an understanding of the complex and subtle ways in which gender is represented, constructed, and contested in the wider society.

Generally, it was observed that women had little influence over types of fishing sites, markets, and access to financing of their businesses.[18] A gender-transformative agenda is therefore required to proactively facilitate changes in some entrenched institutional norms, as is having greater access to financial services and new technologies in order to enhance women's full participation in and equal benefits from fish farming.

The conceptual model of how nutritional status is determined by these various causal factors is shown in figure 4.2. From this model we can deduce that individual nutritional status is directly correlated to nutrient intake, care, and health, and nutrient intake is governed by the food that is purchased and shared within households, which is often an underlying cause of malnutrition. The same model can be used by the fish and aquaculture industries to improve household food security.

Finally, results showed that when women engaged in aquaculture and fishery-related activities such as processing and trading, a greater proportion of household income was spent on food. With more income, households are able to increase the number of daily meals and buy more and better-quality food. This shows that an increased income makes a significant contribution to stabilizing food security at the household level.

NOTES

1. Food and Agriculture Organization, "Role of Women."
2. Republic of Trinidad and Tobago, "National Policy on Gender and Development of the Republic of Trinidad and Tobago," (unpublished manuscript, 2009), https://oig.cepal.org/sites/default/files/trinidad_y_tobago_2009_genero_y_desarrollo.pdf.
3. Mayaro is the name of a county on southeastern Trinidad island, in Trinidad and Tobago. Ortoire Village runs alongside the Ortoire River in Trinidad and Tobago. The river forms the boundary between Nariva County and Mayaro County in east Trinidad.
4. Halwart, Funge-Smith, and Moehl, "Role of Aquaculture."
5. Subasinghe, Soto, and Jia, "Global Aquaculture."
6. Ndanga, Quagrainie, and Dennis, "Economically Feasible Options."
7. Spielman, Ekboir, and Davis, "Art and Science."
8. Republic of Trinidad and Tobago, "National Policy."
9. Resurreccion and Elmhirst, *Gender and Natural Resource*.
10. Food and Agriculture Organization, *State of World Fisheries*.
11. Song et al., "Arabidopsis EPSIN1."
12. Food and Agriculture Organization, *State of World Fisheries*.
13. "Capture fishery" refers to all kinds of harvesting of naturally occurring living resources in both marine and freshwater environments.
14. GENNOVATE is a qualitative, comparative research initiative across the Consultative Group on International Agricultural Research that addresses the question of how gender norms and agency influence men, women, and youth to innovate in agriculture and natural resource management. See Petesch, Badstue, and Prain, *Gender Norms*.
15. See Kishore and Ramsundar, "Community-Based Fisheries Management," for a detailed timeline of the evolution of southeast coastal fishing associations.
16. Food and Agriculture Organization, "Role of Women."
17. Sen, *Quality of Life*.
18. Kolawole, Williams, and Awujola. "Indigenous Fish Processing."

WORKS CITED

Asong, R. H., Ma L. Mabunay, D. Aure, E. Seraspe, R. Braganza, and D. E. Corda. "Alternative Livelihoods in Coastal Villages." Paper presented at Global Symposium on Women in Fisheries, Kaohsiung, Taiwan, November 2001. http://pubs.iclarm.net/Pubs/Wif/wifglobal/wifg_asia_alternative.pdf.

Berkes, Fikret, ed. *Managing Small-Scale Fisheries: Alternative Directions and Methods*. Ottawa, ON: International Development Research Centre, 2001.

Fisheries Division. *1998/1999 Annual Report*. Chaguanas, Trinidad and Tobago: Ministry of Agriculture, Land and Marine Resources, 2000.

Food and Agriculture Organization. "The Role of Women in Agriculture." Prepared by the SOFA Team and Cheryl Doss. ESA Working Paper No. 11–02. Rome: FAO Agriculture and Economic Development Analysis Division, 2011. www.fao.org/publications/card/en/c/8989aace-6356%E2%80%935e14-b7bf-ad8fdb7148c6.

———. *The State of World Fisheries and Aquaculture 2016: Contributing to Food Security and Nutrition for All*. Rome: FAO, 2016. www.fao.org/3/i5555e/i5555e.pdf.

———. *The State of World Fisheries and Aquaculture 2020*. Rome: FAO, 2020. www.fao.org/state-of-fisheries-aquaculture/2020/en.

Halwart, Matthias, Simon Funge-Smith, and John Moehl. "The Role of Aquaculture in Rural Development." Working paper. Rome: Food and Agriculture Organization, 2003. www.fao.org/3/y4490e/y4490e04.pdf.

Jentoft, Svein. "Fisheries Co-management as Empowerment." *Marine Policy* 29, no. 1 (January 2005): 1–7.

Kawarazuka, Nozomi, and Christophe Béné. "Linking Small-Scale Fisheries and Aquaculture to Household Nutritional Security: An Overview." *Food Security* 2, no. 4 (December 2010): 343–57.

Kishore, Rosemarie, and Himawatee Ramsundar. "Community-Based Fisheries Management: A Case Study of Fishing Communities from Ortoire to Guayaguayare, Trinidad." *Proceedings of the Gulf and Caribbean Fisheries Institute* 59 (2007): 99–109.

Kolawole, Oluwatoyin, Stella Williams, and A. F. Awujola. "Indigenous Fish Processing and Preservation Practices amongst Women in South-Western Nigeria." *Indian Journal of Traditional Knowledge* 9, no. 4 (October 2010): 668–72.

Ndanga, Leah Z. B., Kwamena K. Quagrainie, and Jennifer H. Dennis. "Economically Feasible Options for Increased Women Participation in Kenyan Aquaculture Value Chain." *Aquaculture*, no. 414–15 (November 2013): 183–90.

Petesch, Patti, Lone Badstue, and Gordon Prain. *Gender Norms, Agency, and Innovation in Agriculture and Natural Resource Management: The GENNOVATE Methodology*. Mexico City: International Maize and Wheat Improvement Center, 2018. https://gender.cgiar.org/wp-content/uploads/2018/02/GENNOVATE-Methodology_Feb2018_FINAL.pdf.

Resurreccion, Bernadette P., and Rebecca Elmhirst, eds. *Gender and Natural Resource Management: Livelihoods, Mobility and Interventions*. London: Earthscan, 2008.

Sen, Amartya. *The Quality of Life*. Oxford, UK: Clarendon, 1993.

Song, Jinhee, Myoung Hui Lee, Gil-Je Lee, Cheol Min Yoo, and Inhwan Hwang. "Arabidopsis EPSIN1 Plays an Important Role in Vacuolar Trafficking of Soluble Cargo Proteins in Plant Cells via Interactions with Clathrin, AP-1, VTI11, and VSR1." *Plant Cell* 18, no. 9 (September 2006): 2258–74.

Spielman, David J., Javier Ekboir, and Kristin Davis. "The Art and Science of Innovation Systems Inquiry: Applications to Sub-Saharan African Agriculture." *Technology in Society* 31, no. 4 (November 2009): 399–405.

Subasinghe, Rohana, D. Soto, and Jiansan Jia. "Global Aquaculture and Its Role in Sustainable Development." *Reviews in Aquaculture* 1, no. 1 (February 2009): 2-9.

UNICEF. *Strategy for Improved Nutrition of Children and Women in Developing Countries*. Policy review paper. New York: UNICEF, 1990.

WorldFish Center. "Blue Frontiers: Managing the Environmental Costs of Aquaculture." Policy brief no. 2011-24. Penang, Malaysia: WorldFish Center, 2011. https://hdl.handle.net/20.500.12348/1147.

PART 2

Food and Social Justice

PRISCILLA McCUTCHEON

WE ALWAYS BEGIN by thanking our ancestors.[1] "Specifically, food justice includes all ideas and practices that strive to eliminate oppression and challenge the structural drivers of all inequities within and beyond the food system. Food justice also advocates for the right to healthy food that is produced justly, recognizes diverse cultural foodways and historical traumas, and promotes equitable distribution of resources, democratic participation, and control over food systems."[2]

"Food justice" is not a term gifted to Black women by others but is one we have defined for ourselves and our communities. The chapters in this section show us that for Black women, food justice has always been informed by the past, actualized in the present, and forward-looking. In a talk at Harvard University, farmer and food and agrarian justice activist Leah Penniman poignantly stated, "We always begin by thanking our ancestors," as she recalled what her family taught her about food, growing practices, community, freedom, and Black liberation. In paying attention to history, the authors, and those they work with in the community, are essentially paying homage to their ancestors and centering them in their food justice work. Importantly, the authors writing in this section understand the fluidity of time. In *Beyond Settler Time*, Mark Rifkin argues for a different engagement with time, saying, "Rather than approaching time as an abstract, homogeneous measure of universal movement along a singular axis, we can think of it as plural, less as a temporality than temporalities."[3] For Black women and Black communities, the "past" is not linear in how we contextualize their engagement with food justice, agrarian justice, and liberation. While the ancestors that Penniman speaks about are not in their bodily form on earth, they are ever-present, as Black women continue to rely on their knowledge to define ongoing practices around food justice, agrarian justice, and liberation. In our understanding of food justice, briefly explored below, we consider Black women's engagement with the past, the past/present, and the past/future.

The Past

The chapters in this section explore the many avenues through which Black women have practiced and taught justice. In chapter 7, "Recipes for Resistance: Stories of Black Women Leading Food and Agricultural Justice Movements on Farms," Claudia J. Ford is intentional about naming the Black foremothers of food and agrarian justice and liberation. For example, Ford connects the prominence of present-day New Orleans chefs to Black women such as Leah Chase, whose deep contributions to New Orleans cuisine are unparalleled. Ford also names great Black historical figures such as Zora Neale Hurston, Ella Baker, and Fannie Lou Hamer, writing, "While I briefly mention the work of some of these important foremothers, I am primarily concerned with how their legacies are presently expressed." In chapter 6, shakara tyler's work, "Mothering in Historical Black Agrarian Pedagogies: A Historiography," encompasses the history of Black women and Black placemaking practices of the movement. Through the concept of "mothering," she examines how agrarian knowledge is passed down by Black women generationally. Through this passing down, Black women are responding to the needs of the community, thus providing a road map for food justice work in the present and the future. For authors writing in this section, the historical example of justice and liberation work is a Black woman or a movement led by a Black woman. For example, the two chapters mentioned above, along with Ashanté M. Reese and Dara Cooper's "Making Spaces Something Like Freedom: Black Feminist Praxis in the Re/Imagining of a Just Food System," lift up Fannie Lou Hamer as a seminal figure in Black women's food justice and food liberation movements. Hamer created a vision of cooperative development, actualized it, and mapped it for future generations.[4] Important to this section, the naming of Hamer as an ancestor shifts the focus of who and what is central to Black women working in and writing about food justice and food liberation.

The Past/Present

Black women food justice activists' ongoing practices are transforming their communities and their world. "Past/present" signifies that these practices are informed by a continuous engagement with the ancestors, who continue to speak to the food system's ongoing and changing conditions. Reese and Cooper combine Black feminism with food justice, making a vital intervention. They "explore how Black women build Black feminist practices through critiques of patriarchy and capitalism, development of relational leadership, responsible stewardship of the earth, and reciprocal caregiving. In doing so, these leaders use food justice as one avenue to reimagine a more just world." Reese and Cooper explore these practices, specifically "care," in the National Black Food and Justice Alliance. Importantly, they do not limit themselves to one way of conceptualizing "food justice"; in doing so, they would leave important people and movements out who do not align themselves with the term. The National Black Food and Justice Alliance actively defines where food justice and Black feminism meet through its principles and daily practices. In chapter 8, "My Planting Is to Farm Community: Afro–Costa Rican Women's Agrarian Food Practices," Kelsey Emard and Veronica Gordon write beautifully about Afro–Costa Rican women's community-building practices through food and agriculture. Gordon, the coauthor of the chapter, is also one of the main focuses of the chapter, wherein she and Emard discuss how Gordon uses food and agriculture to feed community, build community, improve the physical health of the community, and preserve Afro–Costa Rican culture. They provide an expansive view of what justice is that includes economic security for their families and communities, which is similar to Psyche Williams-Forson's understanding of the economic impact of food cooked by Black women as presented in *Building Houses Out of Chicken Legs*.[5]

The Past/Future

It is clear throughout the chapters in this section that creating a better food and agricultural system for the future is vital to Black women across the globe. Reese and Cooper note that "it is through this commitment to interconnectedness that a care-based system rooted in Black feminist values counters the extractive, patriarchal labor expectations that seek to predetermine the care work that we can and should do." In this section, we understand the future through a care-based system and also a future not dictated by Western notions of time. Simply, this future is not so far away that we are unable to see it. For the Afro–Costa Rican women that Emard and Gordon speak of, the future is currently being made on the land. Gordon's vision of permaculture is rooted in her faith, which guides her to utilize sustainable growing practices in the present. She and her husband left their farm to open a restaurant and are, like the other women in the chapter, deeply engaged in the agrotourism industry. Afro–Costa Rican women's care work is complicated as they seemingly move in and out of what they must do to survive a neoliberal food system that they are unable to escape. They are growing better futures while simultaneously fighting an oppressive present reality.

Concluding Thoughts

In this section of the book, we return to the importance of naming in food justice work for Black women. All the authors focus on the ancestors, their foremothers, their grandmothers, and Black women in general who came before them to show them what food justice is and how food justice work should be done. While only chapters 4 and 5 are coauthored, Dara Cooper, Kelsey Emard, Claudia Ford, Veronica Gordon, Ashanté Reese, and shakara tyler are all seemingly working in the community with one another. Moreover, they are working with a community of Black women food and agrarian justice scholars, activists, and scholar-activists who work within, and write from, a place of community. Within the realm of food justice, many of these messengers are Black women who are in conversation with one another and are vitally concerned with working through the nuances of a movement that we know from this section has a long and storied history.[6] None of the authors spent much, if any, time defining food justice, as there is an increasing number of discussions on this topic in the literature, though rarely do they include Black women's voices and contributions. On the contrary, the discussions in this section and in the book overall are grounded in Black women. The important practice of naming and citing Black women does not just pay homage to Black women in individual communities or organizations. Rather, naming is a practice and arguably care work, where section authors are clear about the history and influence of Black women on their work. It is almost as if Black women have created an alternative world view where justice work is being done that is futuristic yet real. This work is merely hidden from the landscape.

NOTES

1. Leah Penniman in Hooks, "Leading the Fight."
2. Sbicca, *Food Justice Now!*, 385–90.
3. Rifkin, *Beyond Settler Time*, 2.
4. McCutcheon, "Fannie Lou Hamer's"; White, *Freedom Farmers*.
5. Williams-Forson, *Building Houses*.
6. Garth and Reese, *Black Food Matters*; Reese, *Black Food Geographies*; Jones, "Dying to Eat?"; White, *Freedom Farmers*.

WORKS CITED

Garth, Hanna, and Ashanté Reese. *Black Food Matters*. Minneapolis: University of Minnesota Press, 2020.

Hooks, Cody. "Leading the Fight for Food Justice." Harvard Divinity School News, September 18, 2009. https://hds.harvard.edu/news/2019/09/18/leah-penniman-fight-food-justice.

Jones, Naya. "Dying to Eat? Black Food Geographies of Slow Violence and Resilience." *CME: An International Journal for Critical Geographies* 18 no. 5 (2019): 1076–99.

McCutcheon, Priscilla. "Fannie Lou Hamer's Freedom Farms and Black Agrarian Geographies." *Antipode* 51, no. 1 (January 2019): 207–24.

McKittrick, Katherine. *Dear Science and Other Stories*. Durham, NC: Duke University Press, 2021.

Reese, Ashanté M. *Black Food Geographies: Race, Self-Reliance, and Food Access in Washington, D.C.* Chapel Hill: University of North Carolina Press, 2019.

Rifkin, Mark. *Beyond Settler Time*. Durham, NC: Duke University Press, 2017. Kindle.

Sbicca, Joshua. *Food Justice Now! Deepening the Roots of Social Struggle*. Minneapolis: University of Minnesota Press, 2018. Kindle.

White, Monica M. *Freedom Farmers: Agricultural Resistance and the Black Freedom Movement*. Chapel Hill: University of North Carolina Press, 2018.

Williams-Forson, Psyche. *Building Houses Out of Chicken Legs: Black Women, Food, and Power*. Chapel Hill: University of North Carolina Press, 2006.

CHAPTER 5

Making Spaces Something Like Freedom

Black Feminist Praxis in the Re/Imagining of a Just Food System

ASHANTÉ M. REESE AND DARA COOPER

Introduction

There is a pervasive idea in the sustainable food movement that simply returning to a food system of the past would right all that is wrong in the food world. However, history does not show that there has ever been a time when our food system was fair or just. Reflecting through my eyes, the eyes of an African-American woman, I see a system that from the earliest days of the founding of America was built on the annihilation of Native Americans and enslavement of Africans.
—LADONNA REDMOND

In 2009, LaDonna Redmond wrote an essay for *The Nation* from which the above quotation comes. In it, she outlined what many at the time failed to see or acknowledge: That food production, distribution, and consumption are not simply a matter of where to grow food and how to get people to consume healthier foods. Instead, food is a barometer through which we can measure the failures of the United States as a nation-state that has long profited from the land and free labor of Indigenous and Black people. For some, especially many in the sustainable food movement, this was an eye-opener. What LaDonna Redmond was suggesting was that "knowing your farmer" and "voting with your fork"—strategies that had become slogans for alternative food movements—would not adequately address or resolve widespread food inequities. Addressing these issues requires reckoning with the roots that lie in a racial calculus that made possible the theft of land from Indigenous people to create a nation-state that enslaved Black people, exploited Black people's labor through sharecropping, and continued the work of dispossession through US Department of Agriculture policies and procedures engineered to disenfranchise.[1] These historical conditions in part contribute to the present situation. What so often gets framed as an issue of "access" is much more complicated. Food is a site of power and struggle.[2] Under the guise of a market economy that is neither race-neutral nor interested in meeting people's basic needs, Black neighborhoods (regardless of income) are more likely than their white counterparts to lack access to grocery stores and good-quality food.[3]

In response to food inequities in the United States, a robust though sometimes fragmented food justice movement has emerged. This movement—or what could be argued is a set of related movements that range from reformist approaches to radical redistribution of resources[4]—grew out of a larger movement for environmental justice and seeks to address the disparities and harm within food systems through urban and peri-urban agriculture, alternative production and distribution systems, policy reforms, and local and national organizing on behalf of Black farmers, land stewards, and communities.[5] Academic literature on these movements has varied, focusing on the processes and outcomes as well as the barriers that food justice organizations face.[6] Black women leaders and Black feminist praxis have guided much of this work, though there has been little exploration of how Black feminist leadership manifests within food justice movements.

Black feminism springs from a genealogy that is too long and complex to account for in this essay. We take up Jennifer Nash's capacious definition of Black feminism to account for the nuances within Black feminist leadership:

> I treat black feminism as a varied project with theoretical, political, activist, intellectual, erotic, ethical, and creative dimensions; black feminism is multiple, myriad, shifting, and unfolding. To speak of it in the singular is always to reduce its complexity, to neglect its internal debates and its rich and varied approaches to questions of black women's personhood. I treat the word "black" in front of "feminism" not as a marker of identity but as a political category, and I understand a "black feminist" approach to be one that centers analyses of racialized sexism and homophobia, and that foregrounds black women as intellectual producers, as creative agents, as political subjects, and as "freedom dreamers" even as the content and contours of those dreams vary.[7]

In this essay, we examine Black feminist leadership in food justice movements. In the first section, we lay out what we see as central tenets of a Black feminist praxis and intervention in food justice. Drawing from Christina Sharpe's notion of an ethic of care that emerges when attempting to make spaces of freedom, in which "care" is a form of "shared risk," we explore how Black women build Black feminist practices through critiques of patriarchy and capitalism, development of relational leadership, responsible stewardship of the earth, and reciprocal caregiving.[8] In doing so, these leaders use food justice as one avenue to reimagine a more just world. Lastly, we turn to the organizing origins and reflections from the National Black Food and Justice Alliance to engage Black feminist freedom dreams and food justice possibilities.

Care as a Black Feminist Framework

In 1967, Fannie Lou Hamer, a longtime activist, founded Freedom Farm Cooperative (FFC) in Sunflower County, Mississippi. Starting as an antipoverty strategy, FFC combined self-reliance and collective work to meet the material needs of some of the poorest Black residents in the country. It was also a mechanism through which Black women organized around the immediate and long-term needs of their families and communities. As Monica White describes, when the National Council for Negro Women donated fifty female pigs toward the start of a pig bank, it was the women who built a barn for them.[9] It is unlikely that these women called themselves feminists or formally organized themselves around gender politics that placed Black women's leadership at the center. However, following the dynamic leadership of Hamer, these unnamed women became concerned with a fundamental question that united them in a holistic vision: Who is going to feed our communities?

It is not unusual that these women were concerned with food and nourishment, as they prepared and often produced the food they ate. Historically, women have been associated with domesticity and home spaces, though the distinctions between "the home" and "public" spaces are complicated for Black women because of threats of violence, being seen and treated as ungendered laborers, and the need for multiple income streams to support a single household, which often required Black women to be in white women's homes more than their own.[10] When Fannie Lou Hamer founded FFC and these women offered their labor, excitement, and care to the work of building a local, self-determining economy at which food was the center, they furthered the ancestral work that we continue: the work of making spaces something like freedom, spaces in which Black people can and do exist outside of and beyond subjection and abjection.[11]

Black women's presence alone does not define a Black feminist praxis. Not all Black women identify as feminists, even when they are the subject of feminist inquiry or critique. Rather, we see Black feminisms in the vein articulated by Hortense Spillers as "a repertoire of concepts, practices, and alignments, [that] is progressive in outlook and dedicated to the view that sustainable life systems must be available to everyone; it also stands up for the survival of this planet, which pits it against the kleptocratic darkness that now engulfs us. If we're going to reach a different place—and it is difficult these days to be hopeful, I would acknowledge—then black feminist ideas and ideals might be one of the lights leading us there."[12]

If Black feminisms are lights that help us imagine new ways of being and relating, then how we think about and enact care is the energy that animates those lights. In their introductory essay to a special issue on care, Hiʻilei Hobart and Tamara Kneese define radical care as "a set of vital but underappreciated strategies for enduring precarious worlds."[13] Carefully laying out a genealogy of care in both academic and activist lineages, Hobart and Kneese stress that while care is most often associated with a feeling, it has meaning and application well beyond that of a feeling for others. They write, "Theorized as an affective connective tissue between an inner self and an outer world, care constitutes a feeling with, rather than a feeling for, others. When mobilized, it offers visceral, material, and emotional heft to acts of preservation that span a breadth of localities: selves, communities, and social worlds."[14]

This understanding of care does not preclude the possibility of interpersonal feelings of attachment to another being. Rather, it broadens the scope to think of care as organized and often collective responses to structural inequities.

Within her framework of the wake and wake work, Sharpe insists that "thinking needs care ('all thought is Black thought') and that thinking and care need to stay in the wake."[15] In this context, "the wake" is both a metaphorical and material formulation of the outer world that Hobart and Kneese suggest, and the work of care is the work of survival and communal re/imagination. Sharpe continues:

> Living as I have argued we do in the wake of slavery, in spaces where we were never meant to survive, or have been punished for surviving and for daring to claim or make spaces of something like freedom, we yet reimagine and transform spaces for and practices of an ethics of care (as in repair, maintenance, and attention), an ethics of seeing, and of being in the wake as consciousness; as a way of remembering and observance that started with the door of no return, continued in the hold of the ship, and on the shore.[16]

In food justice, Black feminist practices are at the heart of many of these reimaginings and transformations. This notion of "care" problematizes mainstream thinking about Black being and interrupts the violence enacted by the state and its attending actors. In other words, here we consider care as practices that do not seek to extend suffering.[17] In food justice, as in other spaces where liberation is centered, we respond to Derrais Carter's call to "create spaces, platforms, environments, partnerships, theories, methods, and art that witness our freedom in their very creation."[18] The practices at the center of Black feminist food justice leadership are "living experiments in freedom."[19]

According to patriarchal norms, care work is expected from women and is rooted in domination. In the context of Black feminist food work, however, care takes on different meanings. Rooted in multiple forms of nourishment, Black feminist food work presumes that if our care starts with and among Black women, then it will extend to others. Given that Black women's physical and emotional pain is not always taken seriously by physicians, that we are not fairly compensated for our work despite our qualifications, and that our life expectancy is less than that of white women, care as a central component of Black feminist food politics offers a direct affront to white supremacist patriarchy.[20]

Taking Black women's leadership in food justice seriously extends beyond issues of representation. In a Western orientation in which one's being is presumed to be fragmented and individualized, a Black feminist approach to food justice seeks to rejoin or heal these fractures through care-based practices that recognize multiple layers of interconnectedness: between past, present, and future; between the spiritual and physical realms of the human experience; and between us and the land.[21] It is through this commitment to interconnectedness that a care-based system rooted in Black feminist values counters the extractive, patriarchal labor expectations that seek to predetermine the care work that we can and should do. A Black feminist praxis is an expressed and intentional divestment from sexist patriarchy, which also entails divestment from destructive patterns of domination that extend to the land and all that inhabit it. Black feminism is Black liberation *and also* eco-justice — an understanding that our liberation is inextricably linked to the earth. We see this expression in the many ways our foremothers and ancestral practices teach us to pay homage to our ancestors in addition to honoring our connection to the earth.

Black Feminists at Work on the Ground: The National Black Food and Justice Alliance

> As food justice activists and organizers, we have to make the connection between food justice and a whole host of issues that food, land, and the exploitation of Black bodies intersect with in highly sophisticated and systematic ways each and every day. We must be unapologetic in charging the current food system in its engagement in modern-day lynchings that mirror Jim Crow policies, and posturing that marginalizes Black communities from any semblance of food sovereignty, self-determination, and land.
> —BEATRIZ BECKFORD, cofounder, National Black Food and Justice Alliance

"Care as shared risk" is not a theoretical construct absent of application. Instead, we understand it to be an overarching, aspirational, and relational framework that has and can be employed in a variety of organizational structures. In this section, we turn to the National Black Food and Justice Alliance (NBFJA, or the Alliance) to reflect on some of the ways care gets framed and deployed beyond narrow gender stereotypes associated with care work. The 2016 launch of the Alliance—a coalition of Black leaders, farms, and organizations invested in fighting state violence and building alternate systems of power that center on Black dignity, nourishment, agency, and self-determination via food and land justice—began with two radical Black feminists, Dara Cooper and Beatriz Beckford. With foundations in the Malcolm X Grassroots Movement, racial justice organizing in New York City, as well as various food movements, Cooper and Beckford saw an opportunity to explicitly build a food justice movement in which Black feminist principles would be central to furthering Black liberation.[22] An intentional and expressed commitment to gender-based equity and justice from the organizers of a formation is noteworthy. Patriarchy instructs us to position cis men as supreme, more intelligent, charismatic leaders, as architects, strategists, and thought leaders, while women are relegated to second-class positions or made to be invisible. Therefore, having two radical Black feminists as the founding architects, theorists, strategists, and primary founding spokespersons for NBFJA as we set out to build radical food, economic, and social structures rooted in care is significant. Seeing the possibilities of this Black feminist-led food justice work, Malik Yakini, executive director of the Detroit Black Community Food Security Network and a prominent food movement leader, joined as a third cofounder.

The founders understood they needed to deliberately resist, dismantle, and unlearn white supremacy and patriarchy to build a food system that was rooted in care rather than exploitation. Thus, the ideological backgrounds and affiliations of the organizers are important to note. Taking a revolutionary orientation toward food justice meant establishing a critique of anti-Blackness, racial capitalism, patriarchy, and white supremacy. It also meant theorizing and positioning Black people as being able to self-determine the means to sustain and nourish our communities. When the Alliance was founded, the goal was to bring Black people together to define a collective path toward liberation. As revolutionary Black feminists, the cofounders were not interested in integrating into or reinforcing the US empire, which has never seen or respected Black humanity or autonomy. Instead, we aim to fortify our communities, boldly fight against the current system, and create new systems that are essential to our means to be truly self-determining.

NBFJA's objectives are to bring together Black leaders and to unearth the possibilities of Black leadership rooted in radical Black organizing in the food movement for the greater purpose of Black liberation. Organizers have focused on building an intentional foundation and agreements rooted in systems outside of white supremacy, patriarchy, and racial capitalism. These include an ongoing practice of collective democratic governance, political education, and what we call "creating togetherness" and kinship care. Here, Black feminist praxis looks like caring for the political development of every member; curating safe and creative spaces for members to bring their whole selves; creating tighter networks to protect and invest in the well-being of members; and enabling ongoing experimentation with the many forms that collective decision-making, governance, and agency can take. For example, this in part means experimenting with collective stewardship and redistribution of millions of dollars to Black land institutions and projects throughout the country. Such action requires an ongoing practice around democratic decision-making and resource sharing. Our Black feminist praxis also looks like actively deconstructing false divisions while building intergenerational wisdom (the founding leadership team members range from eighteen to seventy years of age) rooted in experience, analysis, expertise, and valuable work in urban and rural areas and municipalities.

NBFJA members participate in ongoing economic examinations and experimentations rooted in collective care via what we call "self-determining food economies." These are economies rooted in community care and resilience with the aim of increasing agency among Black people in local food systems. Through self-determining food economies, we do the aspirational work of divesting from the destructive, corporate-controlled industrial agricultural system and invest in designing economies that are rooted in nourishment and care for the earth, our communities, and each other. This work is inspired by the local food systems work of the Black Oaks Center for Sustainable Renewable Living (an off-grid forty-acre eco-campus in Pembroke, Illinois, led by Dr. Jifunza Wright, who studied with the late holistic healer Dr. Alvenia Fulton) and Fred Carter, who teaches Black communities to be self-sufficient and resilient through sustainable energy, food, building/housing, and our relationships. The Detroit Black Community Food Security Network runs a seven-acre urban farm that grows over thirty different varieties of fruits, vegetables, and herbs; offers a "Food Warriors" youth food justice program; and recently launched the Detroit "People's Co-op" and community food commons. These systems include shared Black leadership among various parts of the food system (and beyond), the creation of cooperative economies, and a deepened sense of interconnectedness that confronts individualism and competition in direct ways.

Along the same lines, our land justice work provides another example of experimentation with divestment in patriarchy. Initiated by member organizations Southeastern African American Farmers Organic Network and Land Loss Prevention Project, this work initially began in response to the urgent lack of land and spaces stewarded by Black people in which organizers can train and meet. While our work focuses on the protection of Black farmers and their land from rapid and often violent land loss, we have invested in a politic of nonextraction, a commitment to removing land from the speculative market, and an explicit rejection of the commodification and private ownership of land. Instead, our focus is to preserve land and move our communities toward collective, community-controlled processes that reshape our relationship with each other and with the earth.

Our final Black feminist reflection on NBFJA is that many of its members and organizers have been influenced by the many radical Black feminists who shape the movement to abolish prisons as we know them. Members frequently engage in discussions examining what an abolitionist framework looks like with the US industrial food system. The contemporary food system serves as the "last plantation," and many NBFJA organizers argue that the work to end slavery will only be achieved through the abolition of the prison industrial complex *and* the abolition of the US industrial food system.[23] Abolition requires the complete destruction of carceral institutions alongside the promotion of expansive imaginations to create more just institutions. NBFJA members are working to do just that, looking beyond carceral and destructive food systems to new imaginaries of freedom, nourishment, sustainability, and affirmations of Black dignity and humanity.

The difficult work of developing systems to nourish Black communities in the most dignified, considerate, healthy, and sustainable ways possible is the practice of Black feminist food futures work. While land justice work and cooperative economics have long been an essential part of Black community work, here we examine the practical influence of Black feminism via NBFJA.[24] Through an ethic of care grounded in experiments in how to govern and create structures that are not rooted in extraction and exploitation, the Alliance offers insight into how Black-led food movements provide strategic paths forward within a larger movement for Black liberation.

Conclusion

In this essay, we outlined key tenets of a Black feminist practice as it is currently articulated in food justice movements as Black women's leadership, cooperative economics, and care rooted in a pursuit of Black liberation. We cite Fannie Lou Hamer's work as an early, documented example of how, in the context of racism, patriarchy, and the continued failures of the state, Black women co-created the cooperative mechanisms needed to provide nourishment for malnourished southerners.[25] FFC faced many of the same problems that current movements face, including funding crises, racist backlash, and the ever-present threat of corporatization. However, FFC is part of a longer tradition of Black radical imagination that fuels past and present freedom movements.[26] We acknowledge, however, that Black feminism is capacious and shows up in food justice organizing and praxis in ways that are not outlined here. We also acknowledge that this article focuses on US food justice work, though Black feminist leadership in food movements is global in scope.[27] Our goal is not to preclude the possibility of other examples or forms of Black feminist leadership but to highlight a gap in the literature on food justice leadership and open up possibilities for additional research and writing in this area.

The work of Black feminists in the food justice world is broad and deep—from the Black women leading the Black Farmers Urban Growers Conference, one of the largest conferences for Black urban growers and farmers; the award-winning leadership of Leah Penniman and Soul Fire Farm; and Shirley Sherrod's stewardship of the Southwest Georgia Project; to decades of urgent legal strategizing under the leadership of Savi Horne at Land Loss Prevention Project; investment in sustainable alternatives via Southeastern African American Farmers Organic Network; and the significant body of trainings and the field of Afroecology developed primarily by Black feminist farmers via Black Dirt Farm Collective. What is clear from these initiatives is that Black women's leadership and resistance around food systems are robust.

Like the work of Black feminists in the food system and beyond, this essay is aspirational. While we believe that care is a necessary and capacious framework for doing food justice work, "care" is also laden with racialized, gendered expectations that render Black women leaders as caretakers while at the same time reproducing them as the targets of violence and harm. In the crosshairs of white supremacy and patriarchy, Black feminists are often doing the work of institution building while also huddling together outside the spotlight to offer advice, affirmation, and tangible support to recover from violence and aggression aimed at them. Sometimes, this violence and aggression arise simultaneously from outside *and* within Black food movement spaces. The challenges to Black feminist leadership are many, and yet we believe it to be potentially transformative for the way we see, think, and imagine new (food) worlds.

In writing this essay, we call on the names of our foremothers in food work: Fannie Lou Hamer, Vertamae Smart-Grosvenor, Edna Lewis, Dr. Alvenia Fulton, Wangari Maathai, Cynthia Hayes, Dorothy Wise, our own grandmothers, and the many unnamed women who planted, harvested, and fed communities.

We looked to the work of our peers and mentors for inspiration in the current moment: Monica White, Leah Penniman, Savi Horne, Melbah Smith, Alice Parrish, LaDonna Redmond, Aleya Frasier, Kirtrina Baxter, Dean Jackson, Brenda Thompson-Duchene, Chef Nadine Nelson, Psyche Williams-Forson, Kimberly Nettles-Barcelón, Rafia Zafar, Francia Marquez, Charo Minas Rojas, Priscilla McCutcheon, Erika Allen, Karen Washington, Alsie Parks, Shirley Sherrod, Sthandiwe Yeni, Darnella Burkett, Estelle Apperwhite, Lindsay Lunsford, Desiree Lewis, Donna Andrews, Tiffany Washington, and many others whom we cannot name. The work we draw from and do provides a vision for relating and being that we try to operationalize on a daily basis. While still a work in progress, this vision is, as Hortense Spillers suggests, a light—perhaps the most hopeful guide we have.

NOTES

1. Daniel, *Dispossession*; Grim, "Politics of Inclusion"; Davy et al., "Resistance."
2. Patel, *Stuffed and Starved*.
3. Reese, *Black Food Geographies*; White, *Freedom Farmers*; White, "Sisters of the Soil."
4. Holt-Giménez, "Food Security, Food Justice."
5. Alkon and Agyeman, *Cultivating Food Justice*; Alkon and Guthman, *New Food Activism*.
6. White, "Sisters of the Soil"; Reynolds and Cohen, *Beyond the Kale*; Alkon and Guthman, *New Food Activism*.
7. Nash, *Black Feminism Reimagined*, 5.
8. Sharpe, *Monstrous Intimacies*, 131.
9. White, *Freedom Farmers*; McCutcheon, "Fannie Lou Hamer's." *ACME: An International Journal for Critical Geographies*, in which this chapter was originally published, is committed to interrogating multiple forms of oppression—including those forms that result from human use and exploitation of animals. During the review process we were asked questions about how the pigs were treated, and those are questions that we do not have answers to. Though it is beyond the scope of this chapter both in terms of content and historical context, we want to acknowledge here that FFC's visions for liberation were intimately connected to and in part reliant on the labor and sacrifice of the female pigs collected. This is a connection that is worthy of exploration—in the context of interrogating both speciesism and anti-Blackness that often renders Black women as ungendered and unworthy of protection. For a recent exploration of the connections between (anti-)Blackness and animality, see Jackson, *Becoming Human*. For examinations of connections between veganism, speciesism, anti-Blackness, gender, and the creation of ethical foodscapes, see A. Breeze Harper's body of work, which includes her longtime blog, *Sistah Vegan* (see www.sistahvegan.com).

10. Allen and Sachs, "Women and Food Chains"; Hartman, *Lose Your Mother*; Sharpe, *Monstrous Intimacies*; Williams-Forson, *Building Houses*.

11. Sharpe, *In the Wake*.

12. Spillers, "Scholarly Journey."

13. Hobart and Kneese, "Radical Care," 2.

14. Hobart and Kneese, "Radical Care," 2.

15. Sharpe, *In the Wake*, 5.

16. Sharpe, *In the Wake*, 130–31.

17. Sharpe, *In the Wake*, 5, 130–32.

18. Carter, "Black Study," 41.

19. Carter, "Black Study," 39.

20. On pain, see Hoffman et al., "Racial Bias." On compensation, see Mandel and Semyonov, "Going Back in Time?"

21. On spiritual and physical realms of the human experience, see Geronimus, "Weathering Hypothesis"; and Geronimus et al., "'Weathering' and Age Patterns."

22. To learn more about the Malcolm X Grassroots Movement, see https://freethelandmxgm.org.

23. "The last plantation" is what many activists labeled the US Department of Agriculture, particularly during the era of Black farmer activism that resulted in the *Pigford v. Glickman* settlement against the Department of Agriculture for racial discrimination against Black farmers. Here we apply this term to the entire contemporary industrial food system.

24. Nembhard, *Collective Courage*.

25. White, *Freedom Farmers*; Dickinson, *Feeding the Crisis*.

26. Kelley, *Freedom Dreams*.

27. One such example is the Critical Food Studies: Transdisciplinary Humanities Approaches project led by Desiree Lewis at the University of the Western Cape. Infused with Black feminist practices, the project bridges fields in the humanities while partnering with communities outside the university.

WORKS CITED

Alkon, Alison Hope, and Julian Agyeman, eds. *Cultivating Food Justice: Race, Class, and Sustainability*. Cambridge: Massachusetts Institute of Technology Press, 2011.

Alkon, Alison Hope, and Julie Guthman, eds. *The New Food Activism: Opposition, Cooperation, and Collective Action*. Berkeley: University of California Press, 2017.

Allen, Patricia, and Carolyn Sachs. "Women and Food Chains: The Gendered Politics of Food." In *Taking Food Public: Redefining Foodways in a Changing World*, edited by Psyche Williams-Forson and Carole Counihan, 23–40. New York: Routledge, 2012.

Carter, Derrais. "Black Study." In *The Fire Now: Anti-racist Scholarship in Times of Explicit Racial Violence*, edited by Azeezat Johnson, Remi Joseph-Salisbury, and Beth Kamunge, 38–43. London: Zed Books, 2018.

Daniel, Pete. *Dispossession: Discrimination against African American Farmers in the Age of Civil Rights*. Chapel Hill: University of North Carolina Press, 2013.

Davy, Dãnia C., Savonala Horne, Tracy L. McCurty, and Edward "Jerry" Pennick. "Resistance." In *Land Justice: Re-imagining Land, Food, and the Commons in the United States*, edited by Justine M. Williams and Eric Holt-Giménez, 40–60. Oakland, CA: Food First Books, 2017.

Dickinson, Maggie. *Feeding the Crisis: Care and Abandonment in America's Food Safety Net*. Berkeley: University of California Press, 2019.

Geronimus, Arline T. "The Weathering Hypothesis and the Health of African-American Women and Infants: Evidence and Speculations." *Ethnicity and Disease* 2, no. 3 (Summer 1992): 207–21.

Geronimus, Arline T., Margaret Hicken, Danya Keene, and John Bound. "'Weathering' and Age Patterns of Allostatic Load Scores among Blacks and Whites in the United States." *American Journal of Public Health* 96, no. 5 (May 2006): 826–33.

Grim, Valerie. "The Politics of Inclusion: Black Farmers and the Quest for Agribusiness Participation, 1945–1990s." *Agricultural History* 69, no. 2 (Spring 1995): 257–71.

Hartman, Saidiya. *Lose Your Mother: A Journey along the Atlantic Slave Route*. New York: Macmillan, 2008.

Hobart, Hiʻilei Julia Kawehipuaakahaopulani, and Tamara Kneese. "Radical Care: Survival Strategies for Uncertain Times." *Social Text* 38, no. 1 (March 2020): 1–16.

Hoffman, Kelly M., Sophie Trawalter, Jordan R. Axt, and M. Norman Oliver. "Racial Bias in Pain Assessment and Treatment Recommendations, and False Beliefs about Biological Differences between Blacks and Whites." *Proceedings of the National Academy of Sciences* 113, no. 16 (April 2016): 4296–301.

Holt-Giménez, Eric. "Food Security, Food Justice, or Food Sovereignty." In Alkon and Agyeman, *Cultivating Food Justice*, 309–30.

Kelley, Robin D. G. *Freedom Dreams: The Black Radical Imagination*. Boston: Beacon, 2002.

Kwate, Naa Oyo A. "Fried Chicken and Fresh Apples: Racial Segregation as a Fundamental Cause of Fast Food Density in Black Neighborhoods." *Health and Place* 14, no. 1 (2008): 32–44.

Mandel, Hadas, and Moshe Semyonov. "Going Back in Time? Gender Differences in Trends and Sources of the Racial Pay Gap, 1970 to 2010." *American Sociological Review* 81, no. 5 (September 2016): 1039–68.

McCutcheon, Priscilla. "Fannie Lou Hamer's Freedom Farms and Black Agrarian Geographies." *Antipode* 51, no. 1 (January 2019): 207–24.

Nash, Jennifer C. *Black Feminism Reimagined: After Intersectionality*. Durham, NC: Duke University Press, 2018.

Nembhard, Jessica Gordon. *Collective Courage: A History of African American Cooperative Economic Thought and Practice*. University Park: Pennsylvania State University Press, 2014.

Patel, Raj. *Stuffed and Starved: The Hidden Battle for the World Food System*. New York: Melville House, 2012.

Reese, Ashanté M. *Black Food Geographies: Race, Self-Reliance, and Food Access in Washington, D.C.* Chapel Hill: University of North Carolina Press, 2019.

Reynolds, Kristin, and Nevin Cohen. *Beyond the Kale: Urban Agriculture and Social Justice Activism in New York City*. Athens: University of Georgia Press, 2016.

Rifkin, Mark. *Beyond Settler Time*. Durham, NC: Duke University Press, 2017. Kindle.

Sbicca, Joshua. *Food Justice Now! Deepening the Roots of Social Struggle*. Minneapolis: University of Minnesota Press, 2018. Kindle.

Sharpe, Christina. *In the Wake: On Blackness and Being*. Durham, NC: Duke University Press, 2016.

———. *Monstrous Intimacies: Making Post-slavery Subjects*. Durham, NC: Duke University Press, 2009.

Spillers, Hortense J. "The Scholarly Journey of Hortense Spillers." Interview by Faith Lois Smith. BrandeisNOW, February 1, 2019. www.brandeis.edu/now/2019/february/hortense-spillers-qa.html.

White, Monica M. *Freedom Farmers: Agricultural Resistance and the Black Freedom Movement*. Chapel Hill: University of North Carolina Press, 2018.

———. "Sisters of the Soil: Urban Gardening as Resistance in Detroit." *Race/Ethnicity: Multidisciplinary Global Contexts* 5, no. 1 (2011): 13–28.

Williams-Forson, Psyche A. *Building Houses Out of Chicken Legs: Black Women, Food, and Power*. Chapel Hill: University of North Carolina Press, 2006.

CHAPTER 6

Mothering in Historical Black Agrarian Pedagogies

A Historiography

SHAKARA TYLER

Introduction

Black agrarianism is a pedagogical thought, praxis, and social movement. Black agrarian pedagogies are the processes by which we teach and learn with one another through the exchange of knowledge that ranges from basic survival necessities on how to feed, shelter, and clothe ourselves to cultural stories that affirm our identities and value as dignified human beings. These pedagogical processes were characterized through groups of people forming institutions and organizations by teaching and learning with the ultimate goal of pursuing "Negro uplift" and self-reliance through land and food matrices.[1] Mothering, as a nurturance process, guides the interdependent wellness of the mind, body, and spirit to ensure the survival of the people—the cultural continuance.[2] The mothering of Black agrarian pedagogies illuminates the cultural labor of women, specifically "community othermothers" who creatively crafted Black agrarian educational environments based on responding to felt community needs to convivially promote political and academic education under Black women's leadership.

This chapter illuminates Black women's work in agrarian educational environments throughout the magnetic movement-building of the twentieth century that centered on "the resilience of the search for a place where Black people could be made whole."[3] The chapter makes the argument that this wholeness has intrepidly been led by and through the mothering of Black women as cultural laborers, educators, and organizers. Thus, mothering becomes an essential component in the pedagogical construction and maintenance of Black agrarian movement building. This chapter examines the concept of mothering through "community othermothers" as the birthing art of how Black agrarian communities shared, understood, retained, and catalyzed knowledge into action.[4] Black women—via intersectional and historical women's roles—mothered food as a historical tool of consciousness-raising and mobilization "so that vulnerable members of the community will be able to attain the self-reliance and independence essential for resistance."[5]

Mothering

Drawing from contemporary Black feminist philosophy, specific pedagogical processes reveal the prominent role of "mothering" in the theory and practice of Black agrarian pedagogies. Historically, the diversity of Black motherhood as a concept has been of central importance in the philosophies of people of African descent, particularly in African liberation movements.[6] The concept of mothering enables education as a channel for empowerment and "racial uplift" rather than for focusing solely on technical skill development for employability. It symbolizes "important connections among self, change, and empowerment in African-American communities."[7] Community othermothers contributed to building different types of communities in often hostile political and economic surroundings, through the "mothering of the mind [body] and soul" as a process of cultural continuance.[8] In "African Diaspora Women: The Making of Cultural Workers," Bernice Johnson Reagon posited a mothering generation as a community organizing tool to nurture the present and future communities for cultural continuance.[9] She maintained:

> Among all living things in the universe, there is a nurturing process. It is holding of life before birth, the care, and feeding of the young until

the young can care for itself. This process is called mothering. When applied to the examination and analysis of cultural data, it can reveal much within the historical picture of how culture evolves and how and why changes occur in order to maintain the existence of a people. It is important, as you review the data, to look for the nurturing space or ground. Look for where and how feeding takes place. Look for what is passed from the mothering generation to the younger generation.

Following this formulaic analysis of the cultural data, I understood creatively crafted pedagogical spaces such as family homes, one-room schoolhouses, churches, and other family and community gathering places as the nurturing sites. As I looked for how feeding took place, I recognized four thematic traces of mothering in the transfer of information: response to felt community needs, conviviality, political and academic education, and women's leadership. Through this particular feeding process incubated in these nurturing spaces, what was passed on was the mind, body, and soul skill sets needed to resiliently survive the violence perpetrated by the "imperialist white supremacist capitalist patriarchy."[10]

Methodology

All histories are selective. This historiography uses historical and contemporary literature of the past to (re)interpret the pedagogical history of Black agrarianism in ways that question assumptions about the present. This history, like all histories, is a (re)interpretation of Black agrarian pedagogical history that addresses the erasure of Black women from the historical record. Four Black agrarian institutions—"Negro" farm home demonstrations in Florida, the Freedom Quilting Bee (FQB), the Black Panther Party (BPP), and Freedom Farm Cooperative (FFC)—are highlighted in this historical articulation due to their explicit pedagogical processes of mothering the community through agrarian pathways.

In the effort to write Black women back into the historical record, the historiographical analysis unfolds in four main parts. First, I provide an overview of historical mothering in Black agrarian pedagogies. Second, I chronologically explain the four institutions that developed throughout the twentieth century, using secondary and tertiary sources such as academic journal articles and books. Third, I highlight the four thematic traces of "mothering" within Black agrarian pedagogies as they relate to each institution's development. Finally, I summarize and conclude with how these institutions employed mothering in

Black agrarian pedagogies in their quests for economic self-sufficiency, social cohesion, and communal empowerment.

Historical Mothering in Black Agrarian Pedagogies

Historically, Black women were assigned the mission of promoting the consciousness and practice of resistance.[11] In "Black women's role in the community of slaves," Angela Davis theorizes the consciousness of women's oppression and needs of unrelenting resistance as sustained through their sense of community, which had to be removed from the most immediate areas of domination: the plantation fields, the master's house, and other public spaces. It could only be located in and around the living quarters, the area where the basic needs of physical life were met.[12] While the women were out in the fields plowing and planting just like the men, it was also the women's responsibility to nurture the home front through child-rearing, cooking, and cleaning, based on the male supremacist ideology of white America and patriarchal traditions in certain parts of Africa.[13] Because the women dominated the home space, the exact space where resistance was incubated, women have always been endowed as the pedagogical experts in Black communities.

Reagon confirmed this theory in her observation of women throughout the African Diaspora arguing that women were central to the continuance of many traditional practices, as heads of our communities and the keepers of our traditions.[14] As a central part of the community structure and process, there is an element of transformation in all of our work to resolve conflict and "maintain, sometimes create, an identity that was independent of a society organized for the exploitation of natural resources, people and land."[15] Through their unconditional care and nurturance and creative protection and resistance, women became the keepers and teachers of agrarian cultures. This, essentially, is the mothering of Black agrarian pedagogies.

From 1915 to 1992, select historical Black agrarian institutions and their pedagogical practices utilized the praxis of "mothering" by responding to felt community needs to convivially promote an educational ethic of political and academic education under Black women's leadership. In times of post-emancipation sharecropping, peonage, tenancy, and landownership, Black women were often the backbone of Black education, which continued throughout Jim Crow segregation, civil rights desegregation, and Black Power socialism. While not all institutions were women centered, the philosophy of mothering is present through visible and invisible women's work. Debra A. Reid and Evan P. Bennett argue that there were a variety of "personal agendas, grassroots politics, educational initiatives and economic strategies that helped Black landowning farm families challenge white agrarianism and white supremacy."[16] I intend to show how many of these were pedagogical processes of mothering the community through agrarian pathways. What follows are brief profiles of Black agrarian institutions of the twentieth century that exemplify the mothering pedagogies that facilitated community upliftment and empowerment.

Profiles of Black Agrarian Institutions of the Twentieth Century

NEGRO HOME DEMONSTRATION IN FLORIDA

By 1915, Negro home demonstration served as a means of assisting the development of Black rural communities through educational programs intended to increase the quality of life. Various phases of the Negro extension work funded by the government evolved into home demonstrations carried out with women and girls to capture the importance of socially constructed traditional women's work, exclusively in the home and community. Black women's home demonstration in Florida acted as a vehicle for "integrating worlds wedged apart by both official and self-segregation" and as a vehicle to preserve rural populations.[17] These rural university-trained and government-appointed women learned that having success as an agent meant diplomatically negotiating and collaborating with the women who were deemed recipients of the extension services.

FREEDOM QUILTING BEE

The FQB of Alberta, Alabama, began in 1966 when women in sharecropping families began making quilts and selling them to augment family incomes. The cooperative bought twenty-three acres in 1968 to build a sewing plant and also to sell land to sharecropping families who had been evicted from their homes for registering to vote or participating in civil rights activities. By 1992, the 150-member cooperative, the largest employer in town, owned a day care center and operated an after-school tutoring program and a summer reading program.[18]

BLACK PANTHER PARTY

In 1966, the BPP headquartered in Oakland, California, dedicated to socialist radical politics, unapologetic armed self-defense, and creative racial self-determination, emerged as the offspring of the rural BPP in Lowndes County, Alabama. The roots of the BPP lie in the Lowndes County Freedom Organization, also known as the Black Panther Party, which was started in 1965 under the direction of the Student Nonviolent Coordinating Committee. Though the Oakland chapter is known as an urban violent revolutionary organization, its rural agrarian roots solidify its validation as a Black agrarian organization. The Marxist politics and socialism in action came in the form of the Free Breakfast for Children Program, free health clinics, liberation schools, and legal aid seminars.

FREEDOM FARM COOPERATIVE

In 1969, Fannie Lou Hamer led the development of FFC on 33 percent of the Black-owned land in Sunflower County, Mississippi, as a strategy to end starvation and build power. FFC was an "institutionalized structure and process for low-income and destitute rural people to feed themselves, own their homes, farm cooperatively, and create small businesses together in order to support a sustainable food system, land ownership, and economic independence" for a one-dollar monthly membership fee.[19] As a "long-term scheme for Black rural survival," FFC was driven by five projects: (1) a "pig bank" that allowed any FFC family to receive a pregnant pig, (2) the building of a sustainable food system via landownership and food preservation, (3) an affordable housing co-op initiative, (4) educational grants and scholarships for FFC students, and (5) a business development plan supporting Black-owned businesses.[20]

Findings: Mothering in Black Agrarian Pedagogies

Based on the historical accounts detailing the philosophy and activities of these profiled institutions, education is the inter- and intra-sharing of information to improve the social, economic, and political conditions of the oppressed communities under the strangles of racism, classism, capitalism, and urbanism. Black agrarian pedagogies constructed an educational environment based on responding to felt community needs to convivially promote political and academic education under Black women's leadership. Strategically, by centering agrarian lifeways, the pedagogical strategies orchestrally worked to mother the mind, body, and soul. This mothering encompasses the ways the pedagogical occupancy of Black women influenced the philosophy and practices carried forth by the community institutions committed to expressing ethics of care and personal accountability rather than domination and control to ultimately "bring people along."[21] The mothering of Black agrarian pedagogies, via a historical lens, strategically emphasizes how women's leadership in the food arena has been used as a historical tool of consciousness-raising and mobilization by way of Black women's cultural work as political work in building alternatives to oppressive systems. A thematic discussion is contextualized below on how the historical institutions illustrate mothering as an important aspect in the pedagogical construction and maintenance of Black agrarian movement building.

RESPONDING TO FELT COMMUNITY NEEDS

The institutional cases demonstrate how mothering meant building educational climates around the needs of the communities, because working on behalf of the community means addressing the multifaceted issues within it.[22] Black women's intersectional and historically designated societal positions indubitably ushered in women's leadership in the food arena, which meant serving the needs of the community. Doing so often meant employing personal experiences as political educative opportunities.

FLORIDA NEGRO DISTRICT HOME DEMONSTRATION

The home demonstration program endogenously created responsive educational environments, which employed Black women as extension agents because they were part of the community they served. This insider perspective caused the women to bypass state or national prescriptions for rural reform in favor of the more relevant and necessary work for "practical, customized improvements chosen by farm women and implemented in their backyards and kitchens."[23] The programs were more closely tailored to women's needs and interests, and the agents' teaching strategy simply offered knowledge without demanding the women do something meaningless and impossible. The women cared less about the work being done in other states or what the US Department of Agriculture's annual goals were and put their "farm economy and their family needs" first.[24]

FREEDOM QUILTING BEE

In parallel terms of responsiveness, the FQB cooperative's day care center provided needed cooperative childcare for the women working in the quilting facility. As Patricia Hill Collins articulated, the "Black cultural value placed on cooperative childcare traditionally found institutional support in the adverse conditions under which so many Black women mothered and arose from how

African-influenced understandings of the family have been continually reworked to help [Black] communities collectively cope with and resist oppression."[25] The necessity of cooperative childcare contributed to the successful educational environment of the institution, which appeared to be centered on experiential learning.

FREEDOM FARM COOPERATIVE

As a similar women-centered institution, FFC was established out of community necessity, providing housing, health care, employment, education, and access to healthy food that the white power structure of rural Mississippi denied Black women then.[26] FFC targeted women, especially women heads of household and women farm laborers, which reflected the needs of Fannie Lou Hamer's community, being that Sunflower County had more women-headed households than ever before at the time.[27] Hamer, as a community organizer, voting rights activist, mother, and fired sharecropper, understood that the most pressing community needs determined one's political agenda.[28] She used food as a mobilizing tool, given how central it was to the daily lives of the people deeply entrenched in starvation, homelessness, increasing mortality, and absent voting rights.

BLACK PANTHER PARTY

The BPP's free socialist-type programs in the areas of human sustenance, health care, education, and criminal justice were central to the party's identity and ideological composition, and the ideology directly connected to the needs of the people through informal community classes sponsored weekly by local branches focused on the ten-point program.[29] The survival programs, such as the Free Breakfast Program, operated under the guises of food injustices being addressed interdependently with other human needs.[30] Responding to felt community needs was at the core of the BPP's educational development and delivery.[31] A huge component of building awareness and recruiting communities into the social movement processes was political and academic education, sometimes intertwined and other times separately facilitated in a variety of spaces.

POLITICAL AND ACADEMIC EDUCATION

Academic education, combined with political education or the political delivery of academic education, has been important to Black agrarian pedagogical continuums across rural and urban spaces. Many of these self-help and upliftment spaces prioritized academic or literacy education out of the sentiment of "racial upliftment," which meant gaining access to literacy in order to navigate the societal structures based on literacy measures. In discussing "the impact of black women in education" in the *Journal of Negro Education*, Collier-Thomas states, "The history of black education in America begins with the struggle of antebellum slaves, who were willing to risk their lives to learn how to read and write."[32] Learning how to read and write possibly led to increased autonomy in feeding, sheltering, and clothing communities.

FLORIDA NEGRO DISTRICT HOME DEMONSTRATION

As Collins states, Black women have long integrated economic self-reliance and mothering.[33] Attaining the skills necessary to control their well-being was a political education process. The ways in which the women were inspired and encouraged to pull from traditional agrarian knowledge (e.g., composting and natural fertilizers) passed down through generations was a political act that stressed the value of ancestry and inherited practices extending back to enslaved cabin gardens.[34] Reclaiming these agroecological land management practices strengthened their communities culturally, economically, and aesthetically. The whole premise of home demonstration was to empower rural women by involving them in the decision-making process and teaching them the skills necessary to improve their garden lots and their families' well-being.[35]

FREEDOM QUILTING BEE

In the FQB, elder women, with minimal academic education caused by the forcible tending of cotton fields the majority of the time, used quilting as a political tool to position the community to attain the academic skills the quilters themselves did not have the privilege of attaining. To mother the mind, the FQB implemented a summer reading program and after-school tutoring program for community children.[36] It also became the largest employer in town, providing an experiential educational environment for women to hone their quilting skills as an economic and social mobility tactic.[37]

FREEDOM FARM COOPERATIVE

Hamer organized landworkers while actively participating in political education campaigns to educate residents of Sunflower County, using flyers and pamphlets that informed residents about their right to participate in the political process by voting.[38] Facilitating more food security through the farm cooperative positioned the institution to educate the community on the politics of voting rights and what it meant for their freedom as a nonvoting populace. Cases such as these "illustrate the importance of political education in building the capacity of grassroots communities to pursue strategies that lean toward freedom."[39]

BLACK PANTHER PARTY

Mothering the community into literacy within agrarian ideals became the survival tactic of the Black Power era. The BPP also taught the critical skills of reading and writing in addition to providing lectures about party ideology.[40] The intertwined academic and political education design uniquely demonstrates how the academic supported the political. The Free Breakfast for Children Program was founded at academic and political intersections. The connection between undernourished bodies and underdeveloped minds was understood in that children must be fed each morning if they were to feed their minds at school during the day and establish fundamental skills in math and reading necessary for socioeconomic mobility and political mobilization.[41] This was a prime example of "mothering the mind" not only through literacy measures but also through the political education of becoming more aware of the realities and the reasons behind the existence of the realities.[42]

CONVIVIALITY

Conviviality was the affable aspect in historical Black agrarian community building that often manifested through churches as inconspicuous sites of social, political, and cultural communion. W. E. B. DuBois often claimed churches as cornerstone social institutions in Black community building.[43] The church functioned as a safe space, as a place where people could talk about and exercise spiritual, religious, and economic cooperation. It was the site of insurrections and interracial efforts and encouraged literacy through Sunday school. The ways that the home demonstration program, FFC, and the BPP used churches as tools of knowledge sharing and networking also point to another significant aspect of mothering in that Black women's lives revolved around churches as sociocultural sites of knowledge production and transmission. Churches were "homeplaces," or sites of resistance created by women of color in intimate spaces such as kitchen tables and church basements for the purposes of conducting anti-oppression work.[44] An example of this lies in the way Black women's creativity could be expressed through music, much of it within Black churches.[45] Black women's activities in families, churches, community institutions, and creative expressions mitigate pressures stemming from oppression by facilitating knowledge exchanges under the guises of sociocultural survival, preservation, and empowerment.[46]

FLORIDA NEGRO DISTRICT HOME DEMONSTRATION

Churches played a significant role as the community focal points that the Florida home demonstration women prioritized rebuilding, rather than their individual homes. Additionally, local financial support for the home demonstration program often came from churches in the racialized absence of national and state funding.[47] Women's leadership in positioning churches as incubators for social movement resistance toward education for economic empowerment, self-sufficiency, self-improvement, and racial uplift birthed a kind of mothering rooted in the gregariousness and well-being of the community, where the mind, body, and soul were centered in the pedagogical practices of agrarian struggles and triumphs.

BLACK PANTHER PARTY

The close practical alliance the BPP had with community churches allowed it to house the Free Breakfast Program and receive community donations.[48] Joan Kelley, the national coordinator of the Free Breakfast Program, said, "We try to teach children not so much through indoctrination but through our practice and example about sharing and socialism."[49] It was less about schooling them on historical facts and more about offering lighthearted yet invigorating content in an artistic manner to care for the total child. This meant mothering the mind through academic education, mothering the soul through cultural history, and mothering the body through nutritious food, which culminated in congenial sustenance that could sometimes be rare beyond the school walls.

FREEDOM FARM COOPERATIVE

FFC also became a church-like site, as Hamer was often celebrated for singing and preaching about joining the movement for Black liberation in and outside of literal church spaces. Most of the movement songs impelled people to action through their visionary, empowering lyrics that foretold the drawing of a new society. Freedom songs such as "Ain't Gonna Let Nobody Turn Me 'Round," "We Shall Overcome," "Keep Your Eyes on the Prize," and "This Little Light of Mine" emphasized individual perseverance while encouraging steadiness of purpose and the elimination of fear.[50] These freedom songs contributed to a convivial environment that bonded people together and facilitated learning through heart-to-heart connections on cooperatively owned land built to preserve the agrarian knowledge base of the Black agrarian communities of the Mississippi delta.

BLACK WOMEN'S LEADERSHIP

Women's leadership visibly and invisibly influenced the educational and overall organizational development of Black agrarian movement building throughout the twentieth century. Women's leadership in the food arena, in particular, suggests how food has been used as a historical tool of consciousness-raising and mobilization, specifically through the utility of the themes noted above. According to Deborah King, "Black women often held central and powerful leadership roles within the black community and within its liberation politics. We founded schools, operated social welfare services, sustained churches, organized collective workgroups and unions, and even established banks and community enterprises. . . . We were the backbone of racial uplift, and we also played critical roles in the struggle for racial justice."[51]

This is what Collins termed "spheres of influence," in that crafting independent and oppositional identities for Black women embraces a form of identity politics that catalyzes a worldview valuing lived Black experience as important to creating a critical Black consciousness and crafting political strategies.[52] This was a pedagogical act that understood the relationship between land, labor, love, and the liberation, or "upliftment," of the Black communities surviving post-emancipation white terrorism, the Great Depression's extreme destitution, and the civil rights movement's white reprisal.

FLORIDA NEGRO DISTRICT HOME DEMONSTRATION AND THE FREEDOM QUILTING BEE

Flavia Gleason, the Florida state home demonstration director, was one of the most instrumental figures in creating, securing, and funding the Black home demonstration agent position and insisted that the work be free from "male control."[53] Under her leadership, the Freedom Quilting Bee prioritized health clinics for local families, and schools became vehicles for extensive health initiatives such as National Negro Health Week, a movement started by Booker T. Washington in 1915 to galvanize health care by and for Black people.[54] Though it was steered by men nationally, women powered it on the ground through home demonstration work topics on health and sanitation, and in 1931, 1,000 families reported receiving immunizations through home demonstration club activities.[55]

FREEDOM FARM COOPERATIVE

As a leader of the civil rights movement, Hamer used songs to teach and inspire, which positioned her as a charismatic leader and dynamic mobilizing force for the movement.[56] As a committed Student Nonviolent Coordinating Committee organizer, Hamer believed in "local autonomy [as] the basis of sustained militancy" as well as in the committee's belief that the movement was best served by building "pockets of community leadership."[57] The women-led and primarily women-served FFC aimed to do this by engaging the community in survival projects. Out of all the FFC initiatives, "the pig bank seems to have done the best, perhaps because it was the best capitalized . . . was not capital- or labor-intensive and was run by women."[58]

BLACK PANTHER PARTY

Women made up almost 50 percent of the BPP's total membership base by 1973, and their influence within the organization was amplified due to their highly educated status as a group.[59] BPP member Erica Huggins argued that "behind the scenes, women ran almost every program, were involved in every level of the party, even the most behind the scenes."[60] The way the BPP used the party newspaper, community centers, and churches to enlist the assistance of "Mothers, Welfare Recipients, Grandmothers, Guardians and others who are trying to raise children in the Black Community" points to the significance of women's roles and the "mothering" associated with the Free Breakfast for Children Program as an agrarian response to a pervasive impoverishment.[61]

Conclusions

The mothering of historical Black agrarian pedagogies exemplified how the institution of Black motherhood consists of a series of constantly renegotiated relationships that Black women experience with one another, with Black children, with the larger Black community, and with themselves.[62] This pedagogical praxis mothered the Black agrarian movement by responding to felt community needs to convivially promote an educational ethic of political and academic education under Black women's leadership. The "personal agendas, grassroots politics, educational initiatives and economic strategies that helped Black landowning farm families challenge white agrarianism and white supremacy" were the pedagogical processes of mothering the community through agrarian pathways.[63]

The Negro home demonstration work literally lifted the community by alchemizing the natural environment around them and remembering their ancestral roots of agroecological land management. The FQB ensured the survival of their community as sharecroppers turned cooperative landowners through the utility of ancestral artistries and collective care and responsibility for the needs of the entire community. The BPP revolutionized urban resistance to poverty through free food coupled with political education, understanding that hunger couldn't be tackled in a vacuum without addressing racial and broader socioeconomic inequality. The FFC also centered the poverty of the grieving communities under the stranglehold of white supremacist ideologies through survival projects and spiritual nourishment.

These were anti-oppression pedagogies led by mothering spirits to manifest socioeconomic, sociopolitical, and sociocultural transformation based on connectedness with others and ethics of caring and personal accountability that are intended to move communities forward.[64] In the same way that the "personal becomes political," Black women continually used cultural work as political work to build alternatives to the oppressive system.[65] As community othermothers, they honed their intersectionality and historically designated roles navigating multiple terrains with multiple responsibilities within the targeted quest of mothering the mind, body, and soul into community wellness.

Final Conclusion

As articulated here, education is the inter- and intra-sharing of information to improve the social, economic, and political conditions of the oppressed communities under the strangleholds of racism, classism, capitalism, and urbanism. The mothering of Black agrarian pedagogies constructed a system of education as a way of (re)building grounded self-identities and uplifted thriving communities led by the cultural labor of women, the community othermothers, who fearlessly mothered for the survival and liberation of their communities. Black agrarian institutions formed the social movements epitomizing community development, racial upliftment, and economic autonomy and utilized Black agrarian pedagogies birthed from matriarchal lineages. Women used food as a historical tool of consciousness-raising and mobilization via the synergy of the cultural work, reflecting personal experiences, as political work. The mothering of Black agrarian pedagogies nurtured the historical movement building that continues to cradle the liberation praxis through the feeding of knowledge as not merely power alone but an overall responsibility to cultivate dignified wellness for communities.

NOTES

1. Rickford, "'We Can't Grow Food,'" 960.
2. Collins, *Black Feminist Thought*; Reagon, "African Diaspora Women."
3. Rickford, "'We Can't Grow Food,'" 960.
4. Collins, *Black Feminist Thought*.
5. Collins, *Black Feminist Thought*, 208.
6. Collins, *Black Feminist Thought*; Icheli, "Mother-Spirit-Nation."
7. Collins, *Black Feminist Thought*, 210.
8. Reagon, "African Diaspora Women"; Collins, *Black Feminist Thought*, 215.
9. Reagon, "African Diaspora Women."
10. hooks, *Writing beyond Race*, 12.
11. Davis, "Reflections."
12. Davis., "Reflections."
13. Davis., "Reflections."
14. Reagon, "African Diaspora Women."
15. Reagon, "African Diaspora Women," 79.
16. Reid and Bennett, *Beyond Forty Acres*.
17. Minor, "Justifiable Pride," 207.
18. Nembhard, *Collective Courage*.
19. Nembhard, *Collective Courage*, 221; Lee, *For Freedom's Sake*.
20. Nembhard and Edmondson, "Making It Safe"; Lee, *For Freedom's Sake*.
21. Collins, *Black Feminist Thought*, 208.
22. Collins, *Black Feminist Thought*, 208.
23. Minor, "Justifiable Pride," 207.
24. Minor, "Justifiable Pride," 215.
25. Collins, *Black Feminist Thought*, 197.
26. White, *Freedom Farmers*.
27. Lee, *For Freedom's Sake*.
28. Lee, *For Freedom's Sake*.
29. Kirkby, "'Revolution.'"
30. Potorti, "Feeding Revolution."
31. According to Kirkby ("'Revolution,'" 50), "When stripped of the niceties that went along with serving hot breakfasts to children, teaching adults how to read, and providing free medical care, the survival programs . . . were ultimately consciousness-raising devices to reveal the structural inequities of American capitalism."
32. Collier-Thomas, "Impact of Black Women," 174.
33. Collins, *Black Feminist Thought*.
34. Minor, "Justifiable Pride"; Glave, "'Garden So Brilliant.'"
35. Minor, "Justifiable Pride." Allowing "the women to choose what the service would become in their communities" (Minor, 205) was a political pedagogical process

in an era when Black women were often dictated tasks and they held very little control over their lives, struggling to gain autonomy in a white patriarchally dominant societal system.

36. On "mothering the mind," see Collins, *Black Feminist Thought*. On the FQB programs, see Nembhard, *Collective Courage*.
37. Nembhard, *Collective Courage*.
38. White, *Freedom Farmers*.
39. White, *Freedom Farmers*.
40. Kirkby, "'Revolution,'" 45.
41. Potorti, "Feeding Revolution."
42. On "mothering the mind," see Collins, *Black Feminist Thought*, 215.
43. White, *Freedom Farmers*.
44. hooks, "Homeplace." Despite the brutal reality of racial apartheid, of domination, one's homeplace was the one site where one could freely confront the issue of humanization, where one could resist. Black women resisted by making homes where all Black people could strive to be subjects, not objects, where we could be affirmed in our minds and hearts despite poverty, hardship, and deprivation, where we could restore to ourselves the dignity denied us on the outside in the public world. hooks, "Homeplace," 42.
45. Collins, *Black Feminist Thought*.
46. Collins, "Learning from the Outsider."
47. Minor, "Justifiable Pride."
48. The BPP liberation schools organized in June 1969 replaced the Free Breakfast Program during the summer months and worked to create genuine relationships with the people they were serving and to establish stronger connections in the community, which meant interacting with the children through games, songs, and general chit-chat. Kirkby, "'Revolution.'"
49. Potorti, "Feeding Revolution," 46.
50. Lee, *For Freedom's Sake*.
51. King, "Multiple Jeopardy, Multiple Consciousness," 54.
52. Collins, *Black Feminist Thought*, 204.
53. Minor, "Justifiable Pride," 214.
54. Minor, "Justifiable Pride."
55. Minor, "Justifiable Pride."
56. Lee, *For Freedom's Sake*.
57. Lee, *For Freedom's Sake*, 23.
58. Nembhard, *Collective Courage*, 186. Women's leadership is also reflected in the National Council of Negro Women's role as a key funder of the cooperative during FFC's inaugural year. White, "Pig and a Garden."
59. Spencer, "Engendering the Black Freedom Struggle."
60. Spencer, "Engendering the Black Freedom Struggle." The police particularly targeted male Panthers because they assumed that they were the leaders, and this targeting by COINTELPRO created an organizational crisis that, ironically, provided fertile ground for women's leadership. Under Black women's leadership, the BPP food programs, which began with a single breakfast program in Oakland, exploded to over thirty-six sites nationwide by 1971. Potorti, "Feeding Revolution." Mothering one of

the most vulnerable segments of the community—children—with basic nourishment is undoubtedly a praxis of mothering as a demonstration of the women-led nurturance that occurred through the Free Breakfast Program.

61. Quote in Kirkby, "'Revolution,'" 40.
62. Collins, *Black Feminist Thought*.
63. Reid and Bennett, *Beyond Forty Acres*, 15.
64. Mogadime, "Black Girls."
65. Quote in Lorde, *Sister Outsider*.

WORKS CITED

Collier-Thomas, Bettye. "The Impact of Black Women in Education: An Historical Overview." *Journal of Negro Education* 51, no. 3 (Summer 1982): 173–80.

Collins, Patricia Hill. *Black Feminist Thought: Knowledge, Consciousness, and the Politics of Empowerment*. New York: Routledge, 2002.

———. "Learning from the Outsider Within: The Sociological Significance of Black Feminist Thought." *Social Problems* 33, no. 6 (December 1986): 14–32.

Davis, Angela. "Reflections on the Black Woman's Role in the Community of Slaves." *Massachusetts Review* 13, no. 1–2 (Spring 1972): 81–100.

Glave, Dianne. "'A Garden So Brilliant with Colors, So Original in Its Design': Rural African American Women, Gardening, Progressive Reform, and the Foundation of an African American Environmental Perspective." *Environmental History* 8, no. 3 (July 2003): 395–411.

hooks, bell. "Homeplace: A Site of Resistance." In *Yearning: Race, Gender, and Cultural Politics*, 382–90. Boston: South End, 1999.

———. *Writing beyond Race: Living Theory and Practice*. New York: Routledge, 2013.

Icheli, I. "Mother-Spirit-Nation: The Centrality of Mothering in African Liberation Movements." Unpublished manuscript, 2018. Microsoft Word file.

King, Deborah K. "Multiple Jeopardy, Multiple Consciousness: The Context of a Black Feminist Ideology." *Signs* 14, no. 1 (Autumn 1988): 42–72.

Kirkby, Ryan J. "'The Revolution Will Not Be Televised': Community Activism and the Black Panther Party, 1966–1971." *Canadian Review of American Studies* 41, no. 1 (2011): 25–62.

Lee, Chana Kai. *For Freedom's Sake: The Life of Fannie Lou Hamer*. Chicago: University of Illinois Press, 2000.

Lorde, Audre. *Sister Outsider: Essays and Speeches*. Berkeley, CA: Crossing, 2012.

Minor, Kelly. "Justifiable Pride: Negotiation and Collaboration in Florida African American Extension." In Reid and Bennett, *Beyond Forty Acres*, 205–28.

Mogadime, Dolana. "Black Girls/Black Women–Centered Texts and Black Teachers as Othermothers." *Journal of the Association for Research on Mothering* 2, no. 2 (November 2000): 222–33.

Nembhard, Jessica Gordon. *Collective Courage: A History of African American Cooperative Economic Thought and Practice*. University Park: Pennsylvania State University Press, 2014.

---. "Principles and Strategies for Reconstruction: Models of African American Community-Based Cooperative Economic Development." *Harvard Journal of African American Public Policy* 12 (June 2006): 39–56.

Nembhard, Ingrid M., and Amy C. Edmondson. "Making It Safe: The Effects of Leader Inclusiveness and Professional Status on Psychological Safety and Improvement Efforts in Health Care Teams." *Journal of Organizational Behavior* 27, no. 7 (September 2006): 941–66.

Potorti, Mary. "Feeding Revolution: The Black Panther Party and the Politics of Food." *Radical Teacher* 98 (2014): 43–51.

Reagon, Bernice Johnson. "African Diaspora Women: The Making of Cultural Workers." *Feminist Studies* 12, no. 1 (Spring 1986): 77–90.

Reid, Debra A., and Evan P. Bennett. *Beyond Forty Acres and a Mule: African American Landowning Families since Reconstruction*. Gainesville: University Press of Florida, 2012.

Rickford, Russell. "'We Can't Grow Food on All This Concrete': The Land Question, Agrarianism, and Black Nationalist Thought in the Late 1960s and 1970s." *Journal of American History* 103, no. 4 (March 2017): 956–80.

Spencer, Robyn C. "Engendering the Black Freedom Struggle: Revolutionary Black Womanhood and the Black Panther Party in the Bay Area, California." *Journal of Women's History* 20, no. 1 (Spring 2008): 90–113.

White, Monica M. *Freedom Farmers: Agricultural Resistance and the Black Freedom Movement*. Chapel Hill: University of North Carolina Press, 2018.

---. "A Pig and a Garden: Fannie Lou Hamer and the Freedom Farms Cooperative." *Food and Foodways* 25, no. 1 (February 2017): 20–39.

CHAPTER 7

Recipes for Resistance

Stories of Black Women Leading Food and Agricultural Justice Movements on Farms

CLAUDIA J. FORD

Introduction

When I began writing this essay, Leah Lange Chase had just died. She grew up during the Great Depression, working on her family's farm from early childhood in segregated, economically impoverished Madisonville, Louisiana. Leah Chase was the chef and co-owner of Dooky Chase's Restaurant, established in 1941 in New Orleans.[1] She fed leaders of the freedom movement such as Rev. Martin Luther King Jr. and James Baldwin, entertainers such as Lena Horne and Cecily Tyson, and a few US presidents, including Barack Obama and George W. Bush. Leah Chase hosted and cooked for frontline civil rights organizations such as the People's Defense League and the NAACP at a time when there was no other place for activists to eat or congregate during the tense, violent days of Jim Crow segregation and months-long civil rights demonstrations. She perfected the recipe for community resistance: inspiration at the crossroads of food sovereignty and racial justice, a unique Black American story of solidarity and resilience, the hope of freedom, and a legacy of feeding the bodies and dreams of our community.

As I finished writing this essay, we were in the midst of the COVID-19 pandemic and a surge of state-sanctioned violence against Black people and communities. Black Americans in the spring of 2020 were profoundly impacted by the concurrent brutal murders of George Floyd, Breonna Taylor, and Ahmaud Arbery, while battling a serious illness that viciously robbed us of our education, our employment, our eldest family members, and our lives. Amid these overlapping crises, it is precisely the stories of our leaders that encourage us to continue meeting, planning, and strategizing. In our liberation and civil rights struggles, we are bound to our leaders' stories of hope and resilience. We are encouraged by women, such as Leah Chase, who lead us to liberation through food and agricultural justice.

There are few sources that provide detailed or accurate pictures of the critical historical role that Black women have played in American food justice movements. In this essay, the circumstances under which Black women are leading these movements are articulated through these women's brief stories of their work. Stories are a methodology of investigation and inquiry. It is crucial to privilege our individual stories, create new community narratives, and change the discussion around Black women's leadership in justice movements. In choosing stories as a form of inquiry, I am mindful that the dominant historical discourses have silenced and failed us, as the achievements and aspirations of Black women have been largely absent from them. This essay does not use storytelling at the level of formal narrative analysis; however, stories perform the function of tying individual identities to community narratives in a way that places stories as often more persuasive to analysis than arguments. In this exploration of Black women leading food and agricultural justice movements their stories create narratives, and these narratives control the discourse of resistance to injustice.[2]

I come from a familiar, rather ordinary background of Black American relationships to food and land. I am a woman who, as a post–World War II child, was raised by southern Black aunties. These were my grandmother's sisters, internal migrants, participants in the Great Migration to New York City yet still firmly planted in the rich southern soil of our extended family's Virginia farmland. These formidable women were dedicated to seeing that no one, family, hangers-on, or strangers, left their kitchen tables without being completely satiated in stomach and spirit. In my upbringing, food was everything. In family-owned restaurants, I sat in the bustling kitchens on a tall metal stool and was fed homemade succotash from heaping, steaming bowls. At the heavily laden Thanksgiving tables, we gathered with my brother and cousins, listening to mostly good-natured feuds and squabbles over which auntie made the best chocolate cake or potato salad. I picked tomatoes and grapes in my grandmother's garden in the Bronx and helped uncles pick ripe sweet peaches under the sticky southern heat in Newport News, afterward joining the family get-together over important conversations about the news of the day and home-churned vanilla ice cream, as peach mash was stomped for brandy the old-fashioned way—in a huge wooden vat under my great grandfather's meticulously scrubbed feet. Food, family, and the stamina and resistance necessary to get us through the violent insults of Jim Crow and segregation, these things framed the stories of my civil-rights-era childhood.

I am interested in the relationship between foodways and culture and in the motivations for agricultural and food activism. This essay emphasizes the resiliency of the Black American community, fighting against systems that have sought to warp our understandings and practices around food and farming. The purpose of the essay is to address a key question about food and agricultural justice: How is the cultivation of food being used to heal, connect, transform, and preserve Black community? I do not attempt, however, to fully record the achievements of the vast numbers of Indigenous, brown, Latina, Asian, and other women of color leading effective change efforts in the North American food system. I acknowledge our debt to all Indigenous North American food systems pioneers, but I do not include their work in this essay. Similarly, I do not include the important food justice work undertaken in the African Diaspora. Fortunately, others have uplifted the names and work of specific activists.[3]

In truth, it is difficult to disengage civil rights activism from food activism. Black people created American agricultural wealth, and we come from farming traditions. As such, our movements for freedom and justice have an enduring relationship to food and land. I focus here on the way in which growing food and tending the land itself are focal points of Black women's activism in the United States. Tending the soil is as critical to justice as tending a cooking pot or joining a protest. I am interested in uplifting those activists who have their hands in the dirt, those who toil through the seasons under the sun, rain, wind, and cold to bring the love of the land and healthy fresh food to their people. I am interested in the stories of women farmers who are working to shift the currently oppressive and dysfunctional food system on behalf of themselves, their families, and their communities.

Motivations for Resistance

When we examine the hopes and legacies of Black American women in agricultural, land, and food justice we must acknowledge our established queens—Harriet Tubman and Sojourner Truth—and give honor to Zora Neale Hurston, Vertamae Smart-Grosvenor, Callie House, Leah Chase, Sylvia Wood, Georgia Gilmore, Ella Josephine Baker, Edna Lewis, Princess Pamela, Fannie Lou Hamer, and Shirley Sherrod. While I briefly mention the work of some of these important foremothers, I am primarily concerned with how their legacies are presently expressed.

While much has been written about both Black foodways and Black landownership, very few sources provide details about the specific contributions of Black women to changing these systems. We know from the work of Owusu Bandele, and others, that "women played a significant role in early extension initiatives as part of the Negro Cooperative Extension Service. More than 100 such women served in the South by 1923. In 1920, these women reported that their clients completed 17,311 demonstrations involving home beautification with lawn and flower gardens. They also documented that African American woman cultivated 20,494 vegetable gardens that year."[4]

The oppressive histories of slavery, sharecropping, and discriminatory lending practices contribute to a modern American agricultural landscape where Black farmers are currently severely underrepresented. While Black Americans once made up 14 percent of the United States' farmer population, today they make up only 1.4 percent. Land dispossession is just one facet of what farmer and activist Leah Penniman describes as "racism in the DNA of the US agricultural and food system."[5] The general exclusion of Black Americans from land and farm ownership exacerbates our lack of access to fresh, healthy, and affordable food, a challenge that activist farmers are eager to overcome.

Environmental injustice connected to agriculture is another key motivator for food system activism. At this point in our societies, the environmental costs of industrialized agriculture are intolerable. Our contemporary agricultural system is among the primary forces behind biodiversity loss, declining animal and public health, pollution, and degradation of ecosystems. Black Americans have always been strongly impacted by environmental injustice and consequently have emerged as leaders in redressing these issues. As bell hooks reminds us, "Recalling the legacy of our ancestors who knew that the way we regard land and nature will determine the level of our self-regard, black people must reclaim a spiritual legacy where we connect our well-being to the well-being of the earth."[6]

Reclaiming the History of Resistance

To uncover the connections between histories of resilience and contemporary responses to injustice, we should be mindful of Black agricultural history in the United States; however, I do not recount the entirety of this history here. We are aware this is a history of white supremacy and racism, beginning with the legacy of Manifest Destiny, which attempted to justify settler-colonists' stealing of land from the Indigenous peoples living on the North American continent. Black agricultural history is also a reminder that despite an oppressive postslavery legal system and the never-fulfilled promise of reparations granting the formerly enslaved "40 acres and a mule," Black Americans purchased 121,000 farms by 1890. By 1910 Black farmers had accumulated 219,000 farms and nearly 15 million acres. By the 1920s, Black farmers owned 926,000 farms on 16 million acres, a representational 14 percent of the total farm acreage in the country. As a result of these land purchases, Black landowners established independent towns, even as more than 4,000 Black Americans were lynched between 1877 and 1950. Black landowners were specifically targeted for murder for not "staying in their place," that is, for not settling for life as sharecroppers.[7] For Black American women to persist with farm ownership today is an act of defiance and resistance that is rooted in the courage of our enslaved and newly freed foremothers.

Remembering the history of Black women farmer activists, we uplift the story of Fannie Lou Hamer's Freedom Farm Cooperative, which, in 1969, provided land, food, scholarships, and a "pig bank" to distribute thousands of livestock animals to Black farmers in Mississippi. Monica White states that "Hamer's background as a sharecropper and domestic worker with a sixth-grade education fed—rather than impeded—the sophistication of her intellectual achievements. . . . She galvanized resources to respond to the immediate concerns of poverty, including hunger, shelter, health care, and housing. Hamer envisioned a model in which the community could achieve self-sufficiency, even within the context of the racially contentious Jim Crow state of Mississippi. Freedom Farm represented a piece of her long-term strategy of self-sufficiency."[8] Black agricultural history includes the establishment of one of the country's first land trusts through New Communities, a farming collective founded in 1969 in rural Georgia by Shirley Sherrod and her husband, Charles. At its height, New Communities was 5,700 acres—the largest tract of Black-owned land in the country—and had about a dozen families living on and working the land full-time before it went out of business in 1985.[9]

Black women were the leaders of many crucial efforts for community resilience and upliftment, maintaining an understanding of the connection between landownership and food and social justice. Edward Pennick, Heather Gray, and Miessha N. Thomas tell us that "women revealed . . . that they were well aware that land ownership played an important role in providing a place for people to live when they were forced off the land for voting in the 1960s."[10] We do well to learn, remember, and reclaim these and other aspects of the history of Black women in agriculture and food justice in this country if we are to make substantive changes in the food system. The story of our agricultural roots and the legacy of the farm as a site of resistance and self-sufficiency is continued through contemporary farm-based Black women activists.

Stories of Food Justice

Achieving justice in the food system is a battle between historical and contemporary systems of oppression and injustice, not just a fight about individual food choices and lifestyles. University researcher and community activist E. Jemila Sequeira tells us, "I hope to . . . explore the possibilities that can exist when the sustainability of our food systems places a high value on everyone experiencing 'dignity' in their relationship to food—whether as a consumer, entrepreneur, farmer, composter, or activist."[11] However, presently the food system is characterized by the undignified circumstance that about 4 million Americans live in extreme poverty and food insecurity, and 50 million Americans of all races are food insecure, meaning they are often unsure as to where they will get their next meal.[12] Half of those individuals live in neighborhoods where it is difficult or impossible to access affordable, healthy food.

These circumstances are not race neutral. White neighborhoods have an average of four times as many supermarkets as predominantly Black neighborhoods. This lack of access to healthy food has dire consequences for Black communities. The incidence of diabetes, obesity, and heart disease are on the rise in all populations, but the greatest increases have occurred among African Americans and Native Americans. These illnesses are fueled by diets high in unhealthy fats, cholesterol, and refined sugars and low in fresh fruits, vegetables, and legumes. In vulnerable communities, children are being raised on processed foods, and over one-third of children are overweight or obese, a fourfold increase over the past 30 years. This puts the next generation at risk for lifelong chronic health conditions.[13] Thus, contemporary activists have built their food justice work from the foundational inspiration of historical figures; their motivation to address the multiple injustices of food, health, and environment; the exact needs of their specific communities; and the immense possibility for addressing all these issues through rural and urban farming and gardening.

The critical question is, how is the cultivation of food being used to heal, connect, transform, and preserve Black community? When we think of food justice, we can look to the story of Kanchan Dawn Hunter, the codirector of the nonprofit Spiral Gardens Community Food Security Project.[14] Hunter works at the intersection of urban organic gardening, food security, environmental justice, youth advocacy, and plant medicine. From the organization's website: "Spiral Gardens strives to model and enable a healthy alternative to our current food economy. For almost two decades we have been part of the ever-growing movement to recreate a resilient and local food system that ties people directly to their sources of sustenance and is proof against economic fluctuations and the corporatization of food systems." Emphasizing community education, Hunter and Spiral Gardens provide a farm, plant nursery, and produce stand. The farm is dedicated to food production, and the harvest is not sold but "shared between the volunteer growers, low-income senior residents in the adjacent apartments, and other neighborhood folks who need it."[15]

Food justice is at the heart of the stories of Karen Washington and Lorrie Clevenger of Rise and Root Farm, who both work with urban farms and community gardens in New York City.[16] As an organization, Rise and Root "care[s] about justice and equity and in building a strong local food economy." Rise and Root maintains productive organic farmland outside the city, in rural Chester, New York. The farm is committed to being "a place where food and agriculture can make a big difference in areas like social justice, community development, health, and equity."[17] Washington and Clevenger are two of the six cofounders of the farming cooperative. Washington is a nationally recognized public speaker and food justice activist who also cofounded the Garden of Happiness in the Bronx and the national organization Black Urban Growers.[18] Clevenger is a community organizer and activist who is now a full-time farmer at Rise and Root. For both, farming is about reclaiming food sovereignty while creating and sustaining community.[19]

The story of Barbara Norman is another example of Black food justice activism.[20] Norman is the owner and operator of a blueberry farm in Covert, Michigan, not far from Chicago and Detroit. Norman is a third-generation farmer, tending the land that was settled by her great-grandfather during the early part of the Great Migration and passing on her farming skills to her grandchildren. Because of this deep generational connection, Norman is aware of the need for Black Americans to have a connection to land. She reminds us, "Some people think money is power. I think power gets you money, and I think *land* is power."[21] The farm is open to nearby communities so that people may experience the meaning of this relationship to land, specifically connecting to the dozens of schoolchildren who visit from the three states that surround it: Michigan, Illinois, and Indiana.

The work of food justice is also found in the story of Edith Floyd, who established Growing Joy Community Garden.[22] Floyd is motivated by reclaiming community in a neighborhood that has suffered the absolute worst of urban decline and abandonment, East Side, Detroit. This is where she tends an urban farm on land that would normally be considered vacant lots. As the properties around her home were abandoned, Floyd reclaimed them for cultivation, making it possible for her neighbors to make healthier food choices.

Activism for food justice is at the foundation of the work of Leah Penniman, a nationally recognized author and speaker.[23] Penniman is the cofounder of Soul Fire Farm, an organization that seeks to dismantle racist and unjust practices in food systems. Penniman started Soul Fire Farm along with her husband, Jonah Vitale-Wolff. A major inspiration for Soul Fire Farm was the opportunity to provide fresh and healthy food to a struggling community in Troy, New York. "With deep reverence for the land and wisdom of the ancestors, the farm works to reclaim our collective right to belong to the earth and to have agency in the food system."[24] For Penniman, dismantling racism in the food system is about dispelling the myth that the relationship of Black Americans to land is solely the traumatic history tied to slavery and sharecropping.

Monica White writes about contemporary urban and rural relationships to farming and reminds us that "we tend to be more familiar with the history of slavery, sharecropping, and tenant farming and the exploitation and oppression agriculture involved. That history is full of pain, trauma, exploitation, and even death. But the blossoming and expansion of the current African American agricultural movement encourage us to dig deeper, ask another set of questions, and, therefore, expand what we thought we know about black people's relationship to the land."[25] What is demonstrated in these few stories of hope and resilience is that Black American women are addressing food injustices by growing food on their own land, distributing it to the neediest in their communities, and teaching their neighbors how to farm.

La Via Campesina says, "Food is not a commodity and eating is not merely a matter of individual choice. Food systems are about dignity, sovereignty, and justice."[26] Many communities are committing themselves to food justice by reclaiming the cultivation, harvest, and cooking of traditional, nonprocessed foods as an essential strategy for decolonizing and sustaining their cultures, bodies, lands, and waters.[27] Small-scale agriculture also has the potential to enhance sustainable solutions to environmental degradation. What we grow, how we grow it, who grows it, how it is harvested and distributed, and how it is prepared and served are all issues of food justice. The stories of farmer activists remind us that all conversations around food justice span from soil to table.

Conclusion: Recipes for Resistance

What we observe in the historical and contemporary stories of Black American women who are fighting for the liberation of their communities is the following: since reaching the shores of this continent, Black women's resistance against oppression and activism for justice has consistently been marked by a commitment to family, while simultaneously being the social conscience of their communities. Black American women, specifically those who have led the fight for food and agricultural justice on behalf of or from Black-owned farms, are dedicated to food, family, and resilience—the nurturance of their loved ones and sustenance of their neighbors. This is our legacy of activism, a Black American struggle that continues from the times of enslavement through the first decades of the twenty-first century.

The stories of the women highlighted here, and those of many other gardeners and farmers, are about the cultivation and management of a variety of properties and programs, both rural and urban. There is great diversity in the manifestation of their aspirations; however, there is simultaneously great unity in the meaning of this vision of Black agricultural and food justice. At the heart of these women's work is a movement to reclaim dignity and sovereignty from a food system that has been unfair and discriminatory for generations, depriving Black American communities of the right and opportunity to grow and choose healthy food. These Black women have joined their love and labor in the soil of their gardens and farms to their people's need for better food security, improved community health, and protected environmental and social justice. As farmers and leaders, they have committed to a combination of cultivating fresh vegetables and cultivating community empowerment. They are actively tending the soil while tending the spirit of the land and the self-sufficiency of their communities. This is the recipe for resistance.

NOTES

1. Dooky Chase's Restaurant (website), accessed March 28, 2023, www.dookychaserestaurants.com.
2. I did not conduct interviews with the contemporary Black women activists and farmers discussed in this essay. I accept that this choice presents some limitations in the depth of knowledge of these women's lives and work. I relied on written accounts of their work on their websites, in their books, in secondary sources, and in publicly available articles and interviews.
3. Bowens, *Color of Food*; Opie, *Southern Food*; Penniman, *Farming While Black*; White, *Freedom Farmers*.
4. Bandele, "Deep Roots," 84.
5. Penniman, *Farming While Black*, 8; Penniman, "By Reconnecting with Soil."
6. hooks, *Sisters of the Yam*, 179.
7. Penniman, *Farming While Black*, 263–70.
8. White, *Freedom Farmers*, 70.
9. Penniman, *Farming While Black*.
10. Pennick, Gray, and Thomas, "Preserving," 162.
11. Sequeira, "Entering into a Community," 9.
12. See Elsheikh and Barhoum, *Structural Racialization*; and Sbicca, "Growing Food Justice."
13. Mernit, "For the Homeless."
14. Spiral Gardens Community Food Security Project, accessed March 28, 2023, www.spiralgardens.org.
15. "Kanchan Dawn Hunter," Women's Earth Alliance, accessed September 1, 2020, https://womensearthalliance.org/2019-us-accelerator/kanchan-dawn-hunter.
16. "Karen Washington," Rise and Root Farm, accessed September 1, 2020, www.riseandrootfarm.com/karen-washington; "Lorrie Clevenger," Rise and Root Farm, accessed September 1, 2020, www.riseandrootfarm.com/index#/lorrie-clevenger.
17. "Home," Rise and Root Farm, accessed September 1, 2020, www.riseandrootfarm.com.
18. Black Urban Growers, accessed March 28, 2023, https://blackurbangrowers.org.
19. Penniman, *Farming While Black*.
20. Adewunmi, "Black Farmers Grapple."
21. Adewunmi, "Black Farmers Grapple."
22. Crouch, "New Agtivist."
23. "Leah Penniman," Chelsea Green Publishing (website), accessed March 28, 2023, www.chelseagreen.com/writer/leah-penniman.

24. "Mission," Soul Fire Farm, accessed September 1, 2020, www.soulfirefarm.org.
25. White, *Freedom Farmers*, 141.
26. "Food Sovereignty," La Via Campesina, accessed September 1, 2020, https://viacampesina.org/en/food-sovereignty.
27. Lambert-Pennington and Hicks, "Class Conscious, Color-Blind."

WORKS CITED

Adewunmi, Bim. "Black Farmers Grapple with an Uncertain Economy." *BuzzFeed News*, September 29, 2017. www.buzzfeednews.com/article/bimadewunmi/black-farmers-grapple-with-an-uncertain-economy.

Bandele, Owusu. "The Deep Roots of Our Land-Based Heritage: Cultural, Social, Political, and Environmental Implications." In *Land and Power: Sustainable Agriculture and African Americans*, edited by Jeffrey L. Jordan, Edward Pennick, Walter A. Hill, and Robert Zabawa, 79–92. Waldorf, MD: Sustainable Agriculture Research and Education, 2007.

Bowens, Natasha. *The Color of Food: Stories of Race, Resilience and Farming*. Gabriola Island, BC: New Society, 2015.

Crouch, Patrick, "New Agtivist: Edith Floyd Is Making a Detroit Urban Farm, Empty Lot by Empty Lot." *Grist*, December 8, 2011. https://grist.org/urban-agriculture/2011-12-08-new-agtivist-edith-floyd-is-making-an-urban-farm-lot-by-lot.

Elsheikh, Elsadig, and Nadia Barhoum. *Structural Racialization and Food Insecurity in the United States: A Report to the U.N. Human Rights Committee on the International Covenant on Civil and Political Rights*. Berkeley: Haas Institute for a Fair and Inclusive Society, University of California, Berkeley, 2013.

hooks, bell. *Sisters of the Yam: Black Women and Self-Recovery*. New York: Routledge, 2015.

Lambert-Pennington, Katherine, and Kathryn Hicks. "Class Conscious, Color-Blind: Examining the Dynamics of Food Access and the Justice Potential of Farmers Markets." *Culture, Agriculture, Food and Environment* 38, no. 1 (2016): 57–66.

Mernit, Judith Lewis. "For the Homeless, There's More to Eating Than Food." *Civil Eats*, May 28, 2018. https://civileats.com/2018/05/28/for-the-homeless-theres-more-to-eating-than-food.

Opie, Frederick Douglass. *Southern Food and Civil Rights: Feeding the Revolution*. Charleston, SC: History Press, 2017.

Pennick, Edward, Heather Gray, and Miessha N. Thomas. "Preserving African American Rural Property: An Assessment of Intergenerational Values toward Land." In *Land and Power: Sustainable Agriculture and African Americans*, edited by Jeffrey L. Jordan, Edward Pennick, Walter A. Hill, and Robert Zabawa, 153–73. Waldorf, MD: Sustainable Agriculture Research and Education, 2007.

Penniman, Leah. "By Reconnecting with Soil, We Heal the Planet and Ourselves." *Yes!*, Spring 2019, 18–22. www.yesmagazine.org/issue/dirt/2019/02/14/by-reconnecting-with-soil-we-heal-the-planet-and-ourselves.

———. *Farming While Black: Soul Fire Farm's Practical Guide to Liberation on the Land*. White River Junction, VT: Chelsea Green, 2018.

———. "Why Farming Is an Act of Defiance for People of Color." *Bon Appétit*, October 31, 2018. www.bonappetit.com/story/leah-penniman-farming.

Sbicca, Joshua. "Growing Food Justice by Planting an Anti-oppression Foundation: Opportunities and Obstacles for Building a Social Movement." *Agriculture and Human Values* 29, no. 4 (December 2012): 455–66.

Sequeira, E. Jemila. "Entering into a Community-University Collaboration: Reflections from the Whole Community Project." In "Food Dignity," special issue. *Journal of Agriculture, Food Systems, and Community Development* 8, no. A (July 2018): 9–11.

White, Monica M. *Freedom Farmers: Agricultural Resistance and the Black Freedom Movement*. Chapel Hill: University of North Carolina Press, 2018.

CHAPTER 8

My Planting Is to Farm Community

Afro-Costa Rican Women's Agrarian Food Practices

KELSEY EMARD AND VERONICA GORDON

BLACK WOMEN'S SIGNIFICANT contributions to global food systems have received little attention.[1] This is especially true of Black women in Latin America, where the very presence of Black populations has been obscured by national narratives of a mythical ethnic homogeneity.[2] In actuality, Afro-descendants comprise approximately a quarter of Latin America's population.[3] In Central America, specifically, Afro-descendants arrived both during the period of brutal colonial enslavement and during multiple free migrations since that time, most notably from Caribbean islands in the 1800s to work on US economic projects in the area including the Panama Canal, railroad infrastructure, and banana plantations.[4] Afro-Caribbean migrants settled on Costa Rica's Caribbean Talamanca coastline in the late 1800s, where they have farmed for over a century.[5]

In this chapter, we view Afro-Costa Rican women's practices of growing, harvesting, and preparing food on the Talamanca coast as a Black agrarian geography that offers important insights for building sustainable and equitable food systems. To do so, we draw on and contribute to the growing scholarship on Black Geographies, a body of work that highlights the spatial practices and experiences of Black people to reimagine an equitable and just world.[6] We use this approach to understand Afro-Costa Rican women's practices on the farm as both a response to legacies of racist systems in Central America and the active reimagining of their futures on farms in ways that resist racist dynamics.[7] In other words, Afro-Costa Rican women's food practices reveal the oppressive systems of racism, capitalism, and patriarchy they struggle against, while also offering visions for more just food systems.

This chapter developed from conversations shared between the two authors, Kelsey and Veronica, in 2018 and 2019. Veronica is an Afro-Costa Rican woman who has lived and farmed on the Talamanca coast for the past forty years. Kelsey is a white woman scholar from the United States who conducted eleven months of ethnographic research in Talamanca. We chose to cowrite because we hoped that collaborating across our different positionalities—Veronica as a farmer and a member of the Afro-Costa Rican community and Kelsey as a scholar and visitor—would allow us to produce a more accountable and relational telling of Afro-Costa Rican women's food practices. Geographic distance, technology constraints, and different educational backgrounds were real challenges to cowriting, but we prioritized collaborative analysis and thinking through WhatsApp phone calls and during Kelsey's visits to Talamanca. The specific data we reflect on include Veronica's own experiences as well as multiple successive interviews conducted by Kelsey with five other Afro-Costa Rican women in Talamanca.

The chapter is divided into four main sections. First, we provide a brief history of Afro-Costa Ricans in Talamanca and show how the recent expansion of tourism has impacted the community. Second, we situate our discussion theoretically within the field of Black Geographies. Third, we explore three ways that Afro-Costa Rican women describe the goals of their contemporary agrarian food practices: (1) to rebuild a community practice of food sharing, (2) to protect their health (bodily and environmental), and (3) to preserve generational, gendered knowledge. Finally, we consider what opportunities exist for Afro-Costa Rican women in the recent emergence of agritourism (e.g., farm visits) in Talamanca. Throughout the chapter, we draw attention to Afro-Costa Rican women's largely unrecognized labor, knowledge, and political will and their struggle for gender and racial equity in their country.

Afro–Costa Ricans and Emerging Tourism in Talamanca

Afro–Costa Ricans living in the country's Caribbean region trace their lineage to the free migrations of Afro-descendants from Caribbean countries in the late nineteenth century. The largest number came from Jamaica on contract with US businessman Minor Keith to build a railroad between Costa Rica's inland capital and the Caribbean port of Limón. For decades they worked building the railroad and growing bananas for Keith's United Fruit Company.[8] Although they were free laborers, most never received the full terms of their contract agreement: at times they went for months without pay, were denied the promised paid voyage back to Jamaica, were compensated in company currency only accepted at company stores, and were encouraged to farm land near the railroad in place of pay, an arrangement mirroring sharecropping.[9] Thus, Afro-Caribbean migrants' early farming experiences in Costa Rica were infused with "plantation logics."[10]

It was Afro-Caribbean populations who founded present-day towns on the Talamanca coast, the southernmost part of Costa Rica's Caribbean coastline.[11] Particularly after the United Fruit Company temporarily pulled out of the region in the 1930s because of the impacts of banana diseases, Afro-Caribbean populations established subsistence farms in the region and began growing cacao for export on a small scale, securing a reliable source of cash for the community.[12] The eight small communities they founded along the Talamanca coastline lived on the food they grew and hunted, which they shared among themselves. Economically and politically, these communities were largely autonomous from the rest of Costa Rica for the first half of the 1900s. Afro-descendants in Talamanca maintained a strong Afro-Jamaican culture, speaking English creole in a Spanish-speaking country, attending Protestant churches rather than Catholic, and continuing a number of Jamaican cultural traditions.[13]

Although Afro–Costa Ricans in Talamanca are proud of their ethnocultural identity, they have had to struggle for equal treatment as citizens in a country that prides itself on being "exceptionally white" within Central America.[14] To uphold the national mythology of Costa Rica's population as ethnically homogenous and of European ancestry, Afro-descendants in the Caribbean were written out of the national identity for years. When the Caribbean region was included, it was described as a crime-ridden, dangerous place.[15] Afro-descendant women also held gendered positions within racist national discourses that placed a disproportionate responsibility on women for representing themselves as pure and virtuous to advance Black ascent in the racist country.[16]

Afro-Caribbean migrants were not offered Costa Rican citizenship until the 1950s, and government-funded infrastructure including electricity and roads did not reach coastal Talamanca until the 1980s and later.[17] Just as the government was beginning to extend more infrastructure to Talamanca in the 1980s, Afro–Costa Ricans' cacao farms were hit by a moniliasis fungus that wiped out their crops in two years.[18] Receiving little economic support from the government, most sold or abandoned their farmlands over the next decade to investors from Costa Rica's capital or abroad. Then, in the 1990s and 2000s, tourists and leisure-seeking migrants from North America and Europe began arriving, drawn by lower prices than other parts of Costa Rica and responding to advertisements showcasing Costa Rica's Caribbean region as a more "exotic" destination than the Pacific.[19] The arrival of these comparatively wealthy foreigners provided important new sources of employment for Talamanca populations following the collapse of the cacao, but new jobs were primarily in the service sector and notably low-wage. Further, the tourism service economy reinforced gendered and racialized imaginaries of Afro-descendants in Talamanca that limited Black women's options by positioning them primarily as domestic workers, industrious and safe to employ in the house.

Because of the arrival of investors from elsewhere, many Afro–Costa Ricans no longer own land upon which they can grow food. Further, the rapidly changing population of the area has caused a decline in neighborhood relationships and food sharing. Most Afro–Costa Ricans now buy imported food, deepening their reliance on cash income. Prostitution and the trafficking of illicit drugs as forms of tourism adjacent livelihoods have also increased. It is within this historical and contemporary context that Afro–Costa Rican women give meaning to their agrarian food practices as part of a vision to reconstruct a particular type of community—one that shares, is characterized by bodily and environmental health, and preserves generational knowledge.

Black Agrarian Geographies

Situated within work on Black Geographies and specifically Black agrarian geographies, our chapter asks what geographical knowledges about food and farming Afro–Costa Rican women impart and how these knowledges can inform the creation of more just food systems. The field of Black Geographies centers the "spatial imaginaries, space-making practices, and senses of place rooted in Black communities."[20] By making Black spatial experiences and imaginaries the starting point, this work confronts violent, racist sociospatial organizations and highlights the placemaking of Black people in resistance to these racist dynamics.[21] Applied to geographies of food and agriculture, a Black Geographies approach reveals racial inequities embedded in contemporary food systems as well as the ways Black people creatively navigate these inequities.[22]

Afro-descendants in the Americas hold complex relationships with farming. Africans, and particularly African women, brought expert agrarian knowledge with them across the brutal middle passage that they put into practice growing and preparing food within the oppressive conditions of enslavement in the Americas.[23] For centuries, the plantation political economy constrained Afro-descendants' relationship to land and food across the Americas and initiated an enduring sociopolitical system and set of ideologies that have extended Black dispossession and anti-Black violence into the present.[24] However, the plantation is also a site of rupture and struggle, and it is within the oppressive context of the plantation that many Black spatial practices of survival, resistance, subsistence, kinship, and social mobilization emerged.[25] Contemporary Black relations to food in the Americas, including Afro–Costa Rican women's food practices in Talamanca, should thus be contextualized in relation to a history of colonialism, enslavement, and struggle.

Yet, these Black agrarian practices have not taken the same form in all geographic contexts. Instead, there is a plurality of "ways in which Black people have . . . sought to enact spaces of Black liberation" around the world.[26] Afro–Costa Rican women's food practices in Talamanca respond to the particular gendered and racialized violence of "white exceptionalism" in Costa Rica and show that community food-sharing practices and Afro-Caribbean food knowledges can create thriving, autonomous communities in such contexts. Afro–Costa Ricans' experiences also demonstrate the potentials and limits of agritourism for extending communal food growing and sharing practices. Attending to Afro–Costa Rican women's agrarian practices in this context extends our understanding of the role of Black women in global food systems and responds to calls to expand Black Geographies scholarship outside of North America.[27]

Afro–Costa Rican Women's Agrarian Food Practices

Afro–Costa Rican women who participated in this research shared three core aspirations for their agrarian food practices: (1) to recreate a community that shares with one another, (2) to protect the bodily and environmental health of the community, and (3) to preserve the familial and gendered knowledge that has been passed down through generations. These aspirations explicitly link food practices to particular ideas of "community." Afro–Costa Rican women's definition of community, we argue here, developed in response to the particular plantation logic and racism that their grandparents and great-grandparents navigated after arriving in Costa Rica. We believe the visions for community food practices expressed by Afro–Costa Rican women offer ways of building more just and equitable food practices globally.

A COMMUNITY THAT SHARES

Afro–Costa Rican women situate their everyday food practices within a hope to return to past practices of sharing food with one another. They describe how until the 2000s, the community depended on sharing food freely between themselves. The idea of *return* here is important. Afro–Costa Rican women express their belief in the effectivity and equitability of a sharing economy that Afro-descendants developed in Talamanca in the twentieth century because of their isolation from state services. Effectively confined to the Limón province by a 1934 government decree forbidding the hiring of people of color in the Pacific regions, Afro-descendants in Talamanca developed a means of living independent from others, sharing food from their farms freely across the community.[28] As one interviewee, Lyla, expressed, they feel "it was more beautiful then. You used to just go borrow something from your neighbor, but now you do not know who your neighbor is."[29] Reflections such as Lyla's were shared across the women participating in this research, and although they reveal a romanticized idea of the past, they also show a commitment to practices of cultural resistance originating in histories of marginalization.

Veronica and her husband have recently returned to their family farm, which they had moved away from following the cacao collapse in the 1980s. As they replant and open their farm to agritourists, Veronica describes their efforts as a dream to re-create a sharing community by stating, "I'm not thinking about planting to sell to big markets or export, that is not in my future. My planting is *to farm community*, so we can do like in the past. You give [to] me, I give [to] you, we exchange seeds, exchange plants, exchange food instead of buying." Like Veronica, several of the women interviewed expressed a desire for the community to grow and share food in order to reduce dependence on imported foods. Further, they see re-creating a sharing economy as an opportunity to rebuild an old sense of community, which they feel has been fractured and splintered by the arrival of new residents and tourists. As Lyla described in the earlier quote, they no longer know who their neighbors are. Thus, many understand food practices as critical to strengthening family and community bonds. For example, another interviewee, Jamia, started a small restaurant five years ago at the same time that she adopted her son from another Afro–Costa Rican community member who was unable to care for him. She rented the property and built the restaurant as both a business and a home. She included a bed and play space for her young son.

Jamia described her decision to open the restaurant as deeply connected to the adoption of her son. "I wanted to create a restaurant that was also a home. I wanted to be with my adopted son. And to be like my grandmother, always cooking for all the family and neighbors, everyone around. I rented this property, and then I built this house, I built it to be with my kids. I have a bed for them in the back, all their toys, I want them to be close. I want to cook for all my family and friends."

While the restaurant is an important source of livelihood for Jamia, to her, its greater importance rests in its ability to facilitate community. By linking the founding of the restaurant with the decision to adopt her son, she is showing that both are conscious choices built on the desire for a community in which members care for one another without looking for help from outside. Her vision emerges out of the specific experiences of Afro–Costa Ricans in Talamanca who for generations had to live without the support of a central government and in resistance to oppressive conditions in plantation economies.

BODILY AND ENVIRONMENTAL HEALTH

The Afro–Costa Rican women participating in this project connect their food practices to aspirations for both human and environmental health. Specifically, they emphasize their desire to use natural food to protect the health of the body and to care for the environment through sustainable practices. Interviewee Brianna has a small yard in which she grows enough plants to make more than twenty teas, some for detoxing, others for the stomach, nerves, or coughs. She explained that the leaves of many of her favorite tropical fruit trees such as papaya, mango, and soursop can be boiled to make herbal tea remedies. Brianna's planting choices reflect her desire to meet all her physical needs in her garden. Although she does purchase food and medicines from local stores, her starting place is her yard.

For Veronica also, who chooses to cook and eat only vegan food, the farm can provide complete sustenance (fig. 8.1). Further, Veronica desires to care for the land just as the land provides for her, describing it as a reciprocal relationship. Veronica and her husband use permaculture practices on their farm. She contrasts their farming practices with those of industrial food companies

FIGURE 8.1. Veronica with produce from her farm. Photo by Veronica Gordon.

by noting that the industrial food companies are the ones "that start producing in mass amounts, and then their minds start changing because [they think] it is better the money than the food, and the earth is being violated. [The earth needs] to rest just like our bodies, but now it is planting, planting, planting, and pouring on chemicals. No permaculture." Veronica links her vision of a permaculture, nonindustrial farm to her Seventh-Day Adventist faith.[30] She describes how God originally put Adam and Eve in the Garden of Eden, where they were meant to both learn from and care for the garden. She models many of her practices after principles she finds in the Bible, such as letting the land rest periodically just as God rested on the seventh day in the creation story and eating a plant-based diet, which was the first diet prescribed by God in Genesis. For Veronica, the physical, emotional, and spiritual health of people are deeply interconnected, and they are linked to environmental health through food cultivation and dietary practices. Her vision is to use food-based practices she finds in the Bible to achieve interconnected human and environmental health.

In the 1990s, following the collapse of the cacao and beginning to see a growth in tourists, Veronica and her husband temporarily left their farm to start a Caribbean-style restaurant. Although the restaurant was an important means of livelihood during a financially stressful time, Veronica describes her desire to start the restaurant as being equally about sharing "the message of healthy eating." By cooking delicious and primarily vegetarian dishes, she hoped to "revolutionize the eating habits of as many people as [she] could," reducing meat consumption and using foods naturally grown in Talamanca to build health.[31] After running the restaurant for nearly twenty years, Veronica and her husband returned to their farm a few years ago. She has begun hosting agritourists, offering a cooking class, and growing food for subsistence again. At both the restaurant and the farm, Veronica's food practices have been a source of economic livelihood as well as a means to promote health and act out her faith.

Both Brianna and Veronica are also committed to eliminating food waste, a practice that has been core to generations of Afro–Costa Rican women. They expressed pride in how their grandmothers and mothers would take the same few ingredients and prepare them in so many ways that "you never felt you were eating the same thing twice," in Veronica's words. Afro–Costa Rican women's knowledge of food preparation techniques has been built from years of creative experimentation and time spent developing varied dishes. During the period when Talamanca was largely isolated from the rest of Costa Rica, these food preparation techniques were part of developing an independent, self-sustaining local food system.

PRESERVING GENDERED KNOWLEDGE

The five women participating in this research all described how they learned about plant uses and food preparation techniques from their mothers and grandmothers. Although men in the community are also involved, interviewees referenced the important roles of women in their families in preserving this knowledge. Brianna describes how her grandmother used to cook for forty people. She described her as a "food specialist, so perfect in cooking." Brianna's grandmother played a key role in educating family and community members on food preparation techniques using knowledge brought from the Caribbean islands on how to use all the plants that grow in a tropical biome without the need for imported foods. Although Brianna's daughter has moved

FIGURE 8.2. Veronica teaching her granddaughter about the plants on the farm. Photo by Veronica Gordon.

to Switzerland, she has prioritized learning her mother's food preparation knowledge, and they are compiling a recipe book together.

Similarly, Maya, Jamia, and Veronica all spoke of their mothers and grandmothers as their source of knowledge regarding local plant uses, growing practices, and cooking techniques. And they are carrying on the tradition, passing on knowledge to their own daughters and granddaughters (fig. 8.2). In some cases, they have had to be creative in finding ways to carry on these agrarian practices. For example, Maya's grandmother previously owned multiple hectares of land along the coast that she farmed, but she sold it after the collapse of the cacao. Although Maya no longer has access to that land, many of the plants they had grown there are still found along the dirt roads bordering her grandmother's historic property. Today Maya makes a living by selling "plant walks" to tourists, in which she walks tourists along those roads and describes the various uses for these plants. Her creative practice not only recognizes and preserves the knowledge her grandmother passed on to her, but it also allows her to make a living from her knowledge of the land, despite her lack of official land ownership.

Although Maya and many other Afro–Costa Rican women would like to grow their own food as their grandparents did for both health and livelihood purposes, limited land access is a key challenge that prevents many of them from pursuing these goals. Much of the land the Afro–Costa Rican community farmed was purchased or claimed by investors from elsewhere after the collapse of the cacao economy. Significant land speculation and an increasing use of land for tourism in Talamanca since the 1990s have caused dramatic increases in property prices and made it untenable for most Afro–Costa Rican women to buy or rent land from the new owners. In Jamia's case, the insecurity of renting led her to quit her restaurant business. When her five-year rental agreement was up, the owner refused to renew, even though Jamia had built the restaurant/home on the premises. Instead, the foreign owner tore down the building and replaced it with an organic food market, an ironic replacement for an Afro–Costa Rican woman's community food gathering place. As is evident in Jamia's story, accessing land on which to plant, cook, or sell food remains a key struggle for Afro–Costa Rican women and prevents many of them from acting upon their agrarian food visions.

As demonstrated in these brief examples, Afro–Costa Rican women, with their aspirations for extending the practices of their mothers and grandmothers, are key actors in maintaining food knowledges. Further, these examples reveal the labor and time Afro–Costa Rican women have committed to preserving these practices and knowledges, labor and time which too often goes unseen. One way that Afro–Costa Rican women are creating livelihood opportunities is by inviting tourists to their farms or kitchens to learn about local food and its preparation. While food-based tourism provides exciting opportunities for increased recognition of Afro–Costa Rican women's roles in food systems, the potential for these opportunities to create more just food systems is limited by the gendered and racialized dimensions of the neoliberal tourism industry, as we explore in the next section.

Agritourism and Afro–Costa Rican Women's Food Practices

Farm visits and related forms of agritourism have grown significantly worldwide in recent years.[32] A growing interest in agricultural experiences by tourists to Talamanca is creating new opportunities for Afro–Costa Rican women to make a living while sharing their food knowledge, practices, and aspirations. Three of the five women participating in this research engage in some form of agritourism: Maya offers "plant walks," Brianna collects local ingredients with tourists as part of her cooking class, and Veronica hosts tourists on her farm, where they engage to varying extents with daily farm practices.

Agritourism provides an important means for Maya, Brianna, and Veronica to earn money from their food knowledges and practices. Further, it provides opportunities for them to share their extensive knowledge and receive recognition for their agrarian labor. These opportunities are particularly important for women in the community, given that employment provided by tourism in Talamanca is highly gendered and racialized, embedded in the region's history that has located Black women in positions of "respectable" domestic service and men as providers of exotic cultural encounters. Thus, women's significant roles within the emerging agritourism industry are notable and exciting. We are enthusiastic about the positive potential of agritourism for Afro–Costa Rican women.

However, agritourism makes only limited strides toward facilitating Afro–Costa Rican women's aspirations for building communal food practices. The emergence of agritourism in Talamanca has been facilitated in part by Costa Rica's neoliberal economic reforms since the 1990s that aim to grow the country's international tourism industry. As Michelle Christian demonstrates, Costa Rica's purportedly color-blind neoliberal tourism policies obscure the ongoing workings of racial power in the country's tourism economy. For example, by booking with foreign-owned guides and hotels in Talamanca, national and international travel agencies market the "consumption of black Costa Rican tourism spaces" through "white guidance and expertise."[33] Further, the branding of the Caribbean as an ethnic space and the representation of Afro-Caribbean people as tied to that space ignores Afro–Costa Ricans' capacity to enact large-scale societal transformation or affect state policies.[34] Thus, while we are hopeful for the possibilities of agritourism to create opportunities for Afro–Costa Rican women to pursue their agrarian aspirations, our optimism is tempered by a recognition of the ongoing racism inflected in (agri)tourist representations of the region. We would like to see Afro–Costa Rican women recognized as architects of their own food systems with lessons for global food systems.

Conclusion

Afro–Costa Rican women's agrarian food practices and visions for their futures on farms provide insight into how they have navigated oppressive conditions and state neglect and built a thriving, healthy community despite these conditions. Their stories demonstrate their immense knowledge of local foods developed over years of hard labor and creative experimentation. Afro–Costa Rican women's hopes for food-sharing economies, local and natural food consumption, and agricultural knowledge preservation offer important insights into Black agrarian geographies. These food practices have been and are still used by Afro–Costa Ricans to resist the oppression of plantation economies, state neglect, and tourism industries that too often profit from the production of gender and racial inequalities. Black agrarian geographies around the globe such as those of Afro–Costa Rican women demonstrate both the need for and the potential of achieving more equitable food access.

NOTES

1. McCutcheon, "Fannie Lou Hamer's Freedom Farms."
2. Gudmundson and Wolfe, *Blacks and Blackness*.
3. Freire et al., *Afro-descendants in Latin America*, 16.
4. Chomsky, *West Indian Workers*.
5. Palmer, *What Happen*.
6. Hawthorne, "Black Matters."
7. McKittrick, "Plantation Futures"; Ramirez, "Elusive Inclusive."
8. Chomsky, *West Indian Workers*.
9. Chomsky, *West Indian Workers*; Mosby, *Place, Language, and Identity*.
10. McKittrick, "Plantation Futures."
11. Palmer, *What Happen*.
12. Palmer, *What Happen*.
13. Palmer, *What Happen*.
14. Sandoval-García, *Threatening Others*.
15. Christian, "'. . . Latin America.'"
16. Foote, "Rethinking Race."
17. Palmer, *What Happen*.
18. Phillips-Mora, Ortiz, and Aime, *Fifty Years*.
19. Christian, "'. . . Latin America.'"
20. Hawthorne, "Black Matters," 5.
21. McKittrick and Woods, *Black Geographies*.
22. McCutcheon, "Fannie Lou Hamer's Freedom Farms"; Ramirez, "Elusive Inclusive"; Reese, "We Will Not Perish"; Reese, *Black Food Geographies*.
23. Carney, *Black Rice*; McCutcheon, "Fannie Lou Hamer's Freedom Farms."
24. McKittrick, "Plantation Futures"; Ramirez, "Elusive Inclusive."
25. McKittrick, "Plantation Futures"; Woods, *Development Arrested*.
26. Bledsoe and Wright, "Pluralities of Black Geographies," 420.
27. Hawthorne, "Black Matters," 8.

28. On the decree, see Koch, *Ethnicity and Livelihoods*.

29. All interviewee names, except Veronica's, are pseudonyms to protect anonymity.

30. Seventh-Day Adventism is a Protestant Christian denomination that observes the Sabbath on Saturday, the seventh day of the week. The denomination arrived in Jamaica and Costa Rica from the United States in the late 1800s and early 1900s, respectively. Members of the church have been noted for their focus on healthy foods. See Land, *Historical Dictionary*.

31. Gordon and Chapman, *Veronica's Table*, 69.

32. Barbieri et al., "Agritourism, Farm Visit, or . . . ?"

33. Christian, "Racial Neoliberalism," 174.

34. See Rivera Cusicanqui, "*Ch'ixinakax utxiwa*," for a discussion of how the labeling of Bolivian Indigenous peoples as "original peoples" relegates them to specific ethnic spaces.

WORKS CITED

Barbieri, Carla, Shuangyu Xu, Claudia Gil Arroyo, and Samantha Rozier Rich. "Agritourism, Farm Visit, or . . . ? A Branding Assessment for Recreation on Farms." *Journal of Travel Research* 55, no. 8 (November 2016): 1094–108.

Bledsoe, Adam, and Willie Jamal Wright. "The Pluralities of Black Geographies." *Antipode* 51, no. 2 (March 2019): 419–37.

Carney, Judith A. *Black Rice: The African Origins of Rice Cultivation in the Americas*. Cambridge, MA: Harvard University Press, 2001.

Chomsky, Aviva. *West Indian Workers and the United Fruit Company in Costa Rica, 1870–1940*. Baton Rouge: Louisiana State University Press, 1996.

Christian, Michelle. "'. . . Latin America without the Downside': Racial Exceptionalism and Global Tourism in Costa Rica." In "Rethinking Race, Racism, Identity, and Ideology in Latin America," special issue. *Ethnic and Racial Studies* 36, no. 10 (October 2013): 1599–618.

———. "Racial Neoliberalism in Costa Rican Tourism: *Blanqueamiento* in the Twenty-First Century." In *States and Citizens: Accommodation, Facilitation and Resistance to Globalization*, 157–89. Vol. 34 of *Current Perspectives in Social Theory*, edited by Jon Shefner. Bingly, UK: Emerald Group, 2015.

Foote, Nicola. "Rethinking Race, Gender and Citizenship: Black West Indian Women in Costa Rica, c. 1920–1940." *Bulletin of Latin American Research* 23, no. 2 (April 2004): 198–212.

Freire, German, Carolina Diaz-Bonilla, Steven Schwartz Orellana, Jorge Soler Lopez, and Flavia Carbonari. *Afro-descendants in Latin America: Toward a Framework of Inclusion*. Washington, DC: World Bank, 2018. https://openknowledge.worldbank.org/handle/10986/30201.

Gordon, Veronica, and Ruth C. Chapman. *Veronica's Table*. Middletown, DE: Independently published, 2016.

Gudmundson, Lowell, and Justin Wolfe, eds. *Blacks and Blackness in Central America: Between Race and Place*. Durham, NC: Duke University Press, 2010.

Hawthorne, Camilla. "Black Matters Are Spatial Matters: Black Geographies for the Twenty-First Century." *Geography Compass* 13, no. 11 (November 2019): 1–13.

Koch, Charles W. *Ethnicity and Livelihoods: A Social Geography of Costa Rica's Atlantic Zone*. Ann Arbor, MI: University Microfilms International, 1981.

Land, Gary. *Historical Dictionary of the Seventh-Day Adventists*. Metuchen, NJ: Scarecrow, 2005.

McCutcheon, Priscilla. "Fannie Lou Hamer's Freedom Farms and Black Agrarian Geographies." *Antipode* 51, no. 1 (January 2019): 207–24.

McKittrick, Katherine. "Plantation Futures." *Small Axe* 17, no. 3 (November 2013): 1–15.

McKittrick, Katherine, and Clyde Woods, eds. *Black Geographies and the Politics of Place*. Toronto, ON: South End, 2007.

Mosby, Dorothy E. *Place, Language, and Identity in Afro–Costa Rican Literature*. Columbia: University of Missouri Press, 2003.

Palmer, Paula. *What Happen: A Folk-History of Costa Rica's Talamanca Coast*. Miami, FL: Distribuidores Zona Tropical, 2005.

Phillips-Mora, Wilbert, Carlos F. Ortiz, and M. Catherine Aime. *Fifty Years of Frosty Pod Rot in Central America: Chronology of Its Spread and Impact from Panama to Mexico*. San José, Costa Rica: 15th International Cocoa Research Conference, 2006.

Ramirez, Margaret M. "The Elusive Inclusive: Black Food Geographies and Racialized Food Spaces." *Antipode* 47, no. 3 (June 2015): 748–69.

Reese, Ashanté M. *Black Food Geographies: Race, Self-reliance, and Food Access in Washington, D.C.* Chapel Hill: University of North Carolina Press, 2019.

———. "'We Will Not Perish; We're Going to Keep Flourishing': Race, Food Access, and Geographies of Self-Reliance." *Antipode* 50, no. 2 (March 2018): 407–24.

Rivera Cusicanqui, Sylvia. "*Ch'ixinakax utxiwa*: A Reflection on the Practices of Decolonization." *South Atlantic Quarterly* 111, no. 1 (Winter 2012): 95–109.

Sandoval-García, Carlos. *Threatening Others: Nicaraguans and the Formation of National Identities in Costa Rica*. Athens: Ohio University Press, 2002.

Woods, Clyde. *Development Arrested: The Blues and Plantation Power in the Mississippi Delta*. London: Verso, 1998.

PART 3

Food Security, Health, and Well-Being

LATRICA E. BEST

THE FINAL SECTION of this book, "Food Security, Health, and Well-Being," explores the importance of family and community in Black women's quest to procure foodstuff for themselves and others. Either directly or indirectly, each chapter chronicles the significance of Black women's social and economic contributions to their families and communities and the impact their relationship with food has on their health and well-being. These thoughtful essays illustrate a holistic understanding of health and well-being and the ways in which food can impact wellness in various ways. Health is not merely the absence of disease; it encompasses "a state of complete physical, mental and social well-being" that takes into consideration sociocultural and individual perceptions of entities such as economic concerns and people's abilities to preserve their health and well-being, even when faced with difficult circumstances.[1] Each chapter in this section extends the discussion of Black women's health and well-being by addressing the financial, cultural, and social factors that shape women's relationship with food. This relationship with food is uniquely expressed in the lived experiences of the voices represented in this chapter, from Latrica E. Best's discussion of how population health researchers frame research on Black women and "modifiable" food-related health concerns (chapter 9) to Hanna Garth's analysis of the impact of Black women's attempts to balance work, family, and food procurement and preparation in spite of psychological and, at times, health constraints (chapter 10) and Shelene Gomes's ethnography of Caribbean Rastafari migrant women's attempts to establish economic independence via culinary entrepreneurship in Ethiopia (chapter 11). These chapters highlight three important themes: the role of food in Black women's reimagining of their health and well-being, food as economic security, and the intergenerational nature of food and community building and sustainment.

The Role of Food in Reimagining Black Women's Health and Well-Being

Research regarding Black women's relationship with food and its connection to health and well-being often neglects the heterogeneity and lived experiences of Black women not only within their communities but within countries and across the Diaspora. The chapters reflect on these experiences and provide the background in which researchers can better contextualize and reimagine their work on Black women's wellness, particularly as it relates to food. The first chapter in this section, "Black Women, Food, and Health: Exploring the Importance of Intersectionality in Population-Based Health Studies," surveys the intersectional approaches to Black women's wellness in both population-based and food studies. In this piece, Best argues for the greater inclusion of intersectionality theory and food studies in population health research on Black women's health, particularly as it relates to health conditions in which food consumption has often been deemed a culprit of disease and Black-white health disparities. Understanding Black women's health and well-being goes beyond operationalizing and controlling for variables such as socioeconomic status or physical activity, for example. Recentering Black women's voices and experiences in every step of the research process is a must if researchers are to fully realize how social, cultural, and demographic characteristics shape health outcomes.

Rich qualitative and mixed methodologies that skillfully unpack Black women's relationships with food can be beneficial to understanding the well-being of Black women, their families, and their communities. In "I Put Food on Everyone's Table: Food Provisioning, Domestic Work, and Business across Three Generations of Black Women in Santiago de Cuba," Garth examines three generations of Black women in a low-income family in Santiago to capture the role of the grandmother in providing the necessary support for others to successfully engage in the labor force. Garth expertly illustrates how one grandmother's connection to food—as a cook for wealthy white Cubans, as a raiser of livestock, and as the primary cook for her family—sustains multiple generations. This grandmother provides sustenance despite the financial, social, and cultural constraints she faces as an older Black Cuban woman. Research on caregiving is mixed, but studies have shown that women carry much of the burden of caregiving and that their health may suffer from the strain of multiple roles.[2] Black women caregivers are particularly vulnerable to experiencing stress related to care.[3] Though the grandmother in Garth's analysis began to lose her eyesight due to glaucoma, she continued to raise and sell livestock to make ends meet for her family.

The experiences related to Black women's relationship with food can provide great insight into individual- and community-level wellness and a sense of belonging. In "Tasting Freedom: The Rastafari Family Food Beit in Ethiopia," Gomes chronicles the experiences of Black Rastafari woman-run *meghib beitoch*, or family restaurants, in Shashamane, Ethiopia. Through ethnographic fieldwork, Gomes explores Rastafari immigrants' attempts to craft an *ital*, or healthy, lifestyle in their new home. The attempts to merge traditional ways of cooking and food consumption within the context of Ethiopian culinary and taste preferences are, in a sense, their way of maintaining and, in some cases, reimagining what a healthful lifestyle encompasses. Achieving a healthy lifestyle, according to Gomes, is influenced by the accessibility of goods, which often falls outside of Western notions of healthy and clean living. Rastafari women who run a family food *beit* play an integral role in preserving their multicultural identity, cultivating an ital lifestyle, and melding Caribbean culinary tastes with local cuisine.

Food as Economic Security

Black women's roles in securing and preparing food, as discussed in the previous section, represent their importance in both formal and, often, informal economies. Their labor is crucial and is shaped by the expectations and constraints societies place on Black women's work. Black women's engagement in food-related activities for economic security for themselves and their families must be analyzed from an intersectional perspective, as, according to Best, this allows Black women's voices to be centered in understanding how their multiple roles can impact other realms of their lives as well as the lives of others. An intersectional approach to Black women's relationships with food also provides a clearer view of how the subjugation of their labor produces financial inequities. As Gomes contends, Rastafari women's domestic labor, like that of many other Black women, is considered "less valuable than men's 'productive' labor in public." This is the case even though Rastafari women are more likely to participate in waged labor than men in this Ethiopian locale. In this context, though Rastafari women own and operate beitoch, landownership and leasing in Ethiopia are not feasible without a considerable amount of foreign funds. Thus, Rastafari women's presence as entrepreneurs, culinary providers, and cultural tastemakers does not neatly translate into economic security for these women.

Similar to Gomes's analysis of the economic and culinary contributions of Rastafari women in Ethiopia, Garth chronicles how Black women in one family engage in both formal and informal food-related labor in order to maintain a living. Aside from the matriarch of the family, the grandmother Carla, whose "formal" occupation is a domestic worker who cooks and cleans for wealthy white Cuban families, each of the three women utilizes food as a means of securing income outside of their formal occupations. For this generation of women, preparing and selling food as a side job underscores not only Black women's contributions to Cuba's economy but also their ability to contribute to local food systems, even during times in which the Cuban state was less tolerant of such economic endeavors.

The Intergenerational Nature of Food, Community Building, and Sustainment

This book and particularly the chapters in this section have displayed the ways in which food, from its preparation to its sale and consumption, is an important fixture in the lives of Black women. For many of the subjects in this section, food helps shape their identities, provides nourishment and economic security, and acts as an anchor with which women sustain and nourish personal and familial relationships as well as strengthen community ties. To fully comprehend the intergenerational and interconnected nature of food in Black women's lives, Best contends that not only must we consider an intersectional approach to research, activism, and policy, but we should also contextualize the connections between Black women, food, and wellness from a life course perspective. This perspective or theory "links human development and behavior to socio-historical contexts that are embedded within social and personal relationships and processes."[4] The life course theory seeks to situate and explain individuals' experiences through the key principles and concepts of human development throughout the life span, human agency, historical time and place, the timing of lives, and linked lives.[5] Although life course research is well established within the social sciences, with a few exceptions research framing Black women's lives with this approach, especially as it relates to food, is less extensive. The chapters in this section capture holistically the sentiment of some of the key principles of life course theory and are outlined briefly below.

Each chapter explores the importance of human agency, as women attempt to sustain themselves, their families, and their communities via food. They exert their "agency within structure" as they navigate the social, cultural, and familial norms and constraints of their environment.[6] This point is particularly true for the Rastafari women beit owners in Ethiopia who use food to acclimate to the community's social, cultural, and economic ways of operating. These women attempt to preserve Rastafari ital living while simultaneously catering to the traditional and evolving tastes of Ethiopia. Likewise, the Black Cuban women introduced in Garth's analysis use food as a means to secure their livelihood in heavily gendered and racial spaces.

The importance of historical time and place, the timing of lives, and linked lives are particularly salient in this section's chapters. Significant events, such as wars, pandemics, and social movements, can impact individuals and groups in different ways. Garth contextualizes these key aspects of life course theory in her characterization of the grandmother, Carla, who was born before Cuba's socialist revolution in 1959. Carla ruminates on life pre- and post-revolution and its economic impact on her family. Carla was able to witness firsthand the economic issues Cuba experienced during the dissolution of the Soviet Union, its primary trade partner at the time. As Garth notes, this "Special Period" impacted both the quantity and quality of food available. According to life course theory, these events can impact Carla's responses to the scarcity of quality food in a way that is different from her daughter's and granddaughter's perceptions of food quality and security. At any rate, the lives of the three women are inextricably linked via food. Not only do they use food as a "side hustle" in their quest to become economically secure, but these women also use food as a means of nourishing and caring for each other. Carla continues to cook for her offspring so that her daughter and granddaughter can be free to pursue professional and social endeavors.

As Best highlights in the opening piece, scholars must intentionally identify and examine Black women's intersecting identities and experiences to fully understand the issues and concerns regarding their health and well-being. The intentional centering of Black women's experiences provides the space to highlight their agency. The essays in this section and the entire volume underscore that, regardless of their existing circumstances, Black women manage to exert their agency as it relates to food. This remains true, even as scholars have not always been diligent in highlighting and including meaningful analyses of Black women's agency and power. Gomes's analysis of Black Rastafari women who migrated to Ethiopia from Trinidad and Tobago and Jamaica provides an excellent example of women exerting their agency within the structure of their existing locale. Though these women are managing businesses as migrants, or "repatriates," they are intentional in their preservation of Rastafari ital living and social, food-related practices that, according to Gomes, reproduces Caribbean notions of "real" womanhood and wifehood. Gomes sees the reproduction of these ideologies and practices within her discussions of second-generation Rastafari girls, thus illustrating the ways in which Black women's agency can impact subsequent generations.

Concluding Thoughts

The ensuing essays all reflect on three key themes: the role of food in Black women's reimagining of their health and well-being, food as economic security, and the intergenerational nature of food and community building and sustainment. These pieces underscore the need to think broadly about what health and well-being mean to Black women and how those perceptions are influenced by their relationship with food. For the women highlighted in this section, food represents not only nourishment but also economic security. The food-related endeavors these women engage in illustrate the intergenerational nature upon which patterns of food practices and consumption originate and continue across women's lives and their communities. The ways in which these women utilize food to provide for themselves and their communities as well as to maintain familial and cultural relationships are indicative of the key tenets of life course theory. As previously mentioned, life course theory has been employed to study various aspects of individuals' lives, particularly as it relates to health and well-being. However, there is a lack of critical research in this arena that uses life course theory to fully explore Black women's experiences with food, from food access and security to production and consumption, and how it impacts their physical, mental, emotional, and financial well-being. These essays provide insight into the ways in which we can utilize Black women's experiences to reimagine what health and well-being mean within communities.

NOTES

1. "Constitution," World Health Organization, accessed December 1, 2021, www.who.int/about/governance/constitution; Zautra, Hall, and Murray, "Resilience."
2. Lee, "Health, Stress and Coping."
3. Wallace Williams, Dilworth-Anderson, and Goodwin, "Caregiver Role Strain."
4. Chatters, Taylor, and Taylor, "Racism," 113.
5. Elder, Johnson, and Crosnoe, "Emergence and Development"; Elder and George, "Age, Cohorts."
6. Settersten, *Lives in Time.*

WORKS CITED

Chatters, Linda M., Harry O. Taylor, and Robert Joseph Taylor. "Racism and the Life Course: Social and Health Equity for Black American Older Adults." *Public Policy and Aging Report* 31, no. 4 (2021): 113–18.

Elder, Glen H., and Linda K. George. "Age, Cohorts, and the Life Course," In *Handbook of the Life Course*, edited by Jeylan T. Mortimer and Michel J. Shanahan, 59–85. Boston: Springer, 2003.

Elder, Glen H., Monica J. Johnson, and Robert Crosnoe. "The Emergence and Development of Life Course Theory." In *Handbook of the Life Course*, edited by Jeylan T. Mortimer and Michael J. Shanahan, 3–19. Boston: Springer, 2003.

Lee, Christine. "Health, Stress and Coping among Women Caregivers: A Review." *Journal of Health Psychology* 4, no. 1 (1999): 27–40.

Settersten, R. A. *Lives in Time and Place: The Problems and Promises of Developmental Science.* New York: Routledge, 2018.

Wallace Williams, S., Peggye Dilworth-Anderson, and P. Y. Goodwin. "Caregiver Role Strain: The Contribution of Multiple Roles and Available Resources in African-American Women." *Aging and Mental Health* 7, no. 2 (2003): 103–12.

Zautra, Alex J., John Stuart Hall, and Kate E. Murray. "Resilience: A New Definition of Health for People and Communities." In *Handbook of Adult Resilience*, edited by John W. Reich, Alex J. Zautra, and John Stuart Hall, 3–29. New York: Guilford, 2009.

CHAPTER 9

Black Women, Food, and Health

Exploring the Importance of Intersectionality in Population-Based Health Studies

LATRICA E. BEST

Introduction

The popularity of intersectionality as a theoretical framework and methodological tool for understanding how social identities and characteristics intersect to produce and sustain inequalities throughout individuals' lives has increased exponentially in recent years. This recognition is evident in the widespread discussion of intersectionality in various academic and nonacademic settings. Nowhere is the increasing prevalence of intersectionality more apparent than in health research. In a recent article outlining the future steps needed to adequately integrate intersectionality into quantitative population health research, Madina Agénor notes that a search for articles discussing intersectionality in the PubMed database produced over 700 hits, a far cry from the forty-nine hits generated by a similar search in 2011.[1] Though intersectionality has played a more prominent role in public and population health research, much of the work incorporating this theory has used qualitative methodological approaches to understand health disparities and inequities. To many researchers, using qualitative methodology to examine intersectionality-driven research is intuitive, as qualitative strategies provide the freedom to interrogate "complex and dynamic understandings of socially constructed dimensions of difference and context."[2] Though the richness of qualitative inquiry into population health research remains vital to understanding the complexities of the health experience, recent research has explored intersectionality's usefulness in more quantitatively focused work.

At its core, population health is an interdisciplinary field of study that seeks to address the physical, social, psychological, and policy-related factors that contribute to health for both individuals and groups of people. Specifically, Robert A. Hummer and Erin R. Hamilton define population health as "the documentation of patterns and trends in health within specifically defined geographic places; the explanation of such health patterns and trends in those specific places using a multilevel set of determinants; and the translation of population health research findings into action to improve the health of those specific populations."[3] Quantitative methodology is often the default method of scientific inquiry for many population health researchers. Though there is quantitative population health research that engages intersectional and feminist theoretical frameworks, incorporating these frameworks into a study's design and question formation, data collection, data management and analysis, conclusions, and policy considerations is not the norm. However, the growth of articles advocating for the inclusion of intersectional approaches to population health suggests a shift in how researchers are reckoning with the health experiences and inequities facing multiple, marginalized identities and the social structures they inhabit. This possible paradigm shift in intersectional approaches and health disparities and inequities has also been championed by the National Institutes of Health, which recently advocated for more sound research and clearer grant applications regarding intersectionality in public and population health research.[4]

Why Food?

Within the context of health research, it is important to think not only about how intersectionality can be more broadly incorporated into population health but also about how intersecting, multiple identities and experiences are understood within non-health-related experiences. One important area worth exploring as it relates to health is food studies. Similar to population health, food studies is interdisciplinary in nature and takes a multilevel approach to understanding how individuals and communities engage with food, from the production, distribution, and consumption of food to the ways in which food, or the lack thereof, shapes other facets of their physical, psychological, and social lives. The growth of food studies has led to more meaningful efforts to address how multiple identities experience and shape food systems. Scholars and activists within the Black Geographies field have led the charge in reimagining food within Black spaces by connecting Black bodies to the land, both past and present, while providing the foundation for imagining a just Black future.[5]

From a health perspective, understanding Black women's relationship with food is necessary, as Black women often serve an integral role in the well-being of families and communities. The health of Black women undoubtedly impacts the health of others within their familial and social networks. Previous research has shown that Black women in the United States are overburdened with chronic health conditions, such as type 2 diabetes and hypertension, when compared to their white counterparts.[6] In many cases, quantitative-based population health studies often relegate such differences to lifestyle or other social risk factors. This is particularly true for what researchers consider "modifiable" health issues, such as obesity, diabetes, and hypertension, conditions that are often linked to diet. Though there are studies that examine these health concerns within an intersectional framework, the number of studies that incorporate a meaningful intersectional analysis into population-based studies is still lacking.[7] Furthermore, existing population-based studies examining Black women's health do not contend with the nuances of their relationship to food and their contributions to global food systems, areas in which food studies could greatly contribute. Specifically, researchers must think about how food, food systems, and health are intertwined in gendered and racialized environments that ultimately complicate notions of seemingly straightforward solutions and "modifiable" health concerns.

This chapter provides a brief overview of research in both population health and food to explore how researchers theorize, analyze, and make meaning of the relationship between food and health among Black women in the United States. Specifically, I offer an assessment of the inclusion of intersectionality theory in these two scholarly arenas. Finally, I argue that more quantitative population health studies would benefit from incorporating intersectionality and more nuanced perspectives of food into their studies and provide suggestions for doing so.

Intersectionality and Health

As previously discussed, health scholars have made concerted efforts to incorporate intersectionality in public and population health research.[8] This increase in the inclusion of intersectionality into population health has been most pronounced in quantitative population health research and is the focus of this chapter. Although qualitatively driven research is not discussed here, it is important to recognize that qualitatively minded health researchers should also be sensitive to the theoretical, methodological, and ethical considerations of creating and carrying out an intersectionally sound research study. Despite their different approaches, qualitative and quantitative researchers share similar concerns, from addressing implicit, intersectional responses in sometimes less desirable data to interpreting and making meaning of the complexities of the multiple social identities and inequalities present in the data.

Does intersectionality have a place within population health research, which is rooted in "positivistic assumptions implicit in quantification"?[9] The nature by which quantitatively driven scholars view and interpret health data can create potentially ideological and methodological discord. In addressing this issue, Lisa Bowleg contends "that the positivist paradigm that undergirds much (but not all) quantitative research appears to be orthogonal to the complexities of intersectionality."[10] For instance, previous quantitative research has shown that social identities that are often examined within intersectionality, such as race, can change, and have changed, over time and within different historical and social contexts.[11] Quantitative population health researchers need to think critically about their measurements and subsequent results and situate them appropriately in their time and place. Though not all quantitative population health research will call for the use of intersectionality, the use of its approach is possible. Data limitations should not hinder researchers' discussion of such limitations and should provide context as to what an intersectional approach to a given study should address.

In considering the inclusion of intersectionality in quantitative population health research, scholars must grapple with important population health concepts and, in particular, how inequality and difference are handled in their research. To revisit the core components of population health presented earlier in the chapter, much of the work in population health centers on finding and documenting patterns of health across various geographic locations and times as well as explaining the patterns and trends within any given data. Because of its focus on groups of people, population health research seeks to establish these patterns and trends by further delineating people into groups based on some sociodemographic characteristic(s), such as examining diabetes incidence rates in a population by race, gender, or age. As such, many population health researchers aim to identify populations at risk for certain health concerns and how inequalities arise and persist both within and between different groups of people. Thus, for population health research that is concerned with examining differences or disparities, the goals are often to define or detect existing disparities or differences, understand or contextualize such differences, and ultimately reduce or eliminate them. However, according to Amy M. Kilbourne and colleagues, much of our health disparities research disproportionately addresses defining and detecting inequalities without meaningfully taking the additional steps needed to fully understand, reduce, or eliminate them.[12]

Though adequately theorizing this line of research is equally important, much of the discussions regarding the incorporation of intersectionality into quantitative population health research are focused on methodological concerns. While there is a growing amount of literature focused on specific issues related to data quality, construct measurement, discriminatory accuracy, and the appropriateness of methodological techniques such as regression analyses with interaction terms, multilevel modeling, and cluster analyses, the focus of this chapter is to provide insight into the ways in which intersectionality can contribute to research on food and population health.[13] Lexi Harari and Chioun Lee's recent systematic review of the use of intersectionality in quantitative health disparities research provides a comprehensive look into how others have conceptualized and incorporated intersectionality into their work. This research, however, collectively illustrates the limitations, according to Harari and Lee, that quantitative population health researchers must consider.

One limitation of existing studies is the way in which intersectionality is defined and operationalized. The inherent intercategorical nature by which researchers assess differences between groups obscures the potentially rich heterogeneity that exists within groups.[14] This issue cannot be rectified by merely studying the differences in health among those with intersecting social identities. Additionally, in thinking about groups for analysis, quantitative population health researchers must think about the specific aims of their research and what groups best fit the study as well as the comparison of identified groups. Harari and Lee find in their review that most research focuses heavily on the "big three," or race or ethnicity, sex or gender, and some measure(s) of socioeconomic status. This particular reading of intersectionality is very confined and is reflective of intersectionality's growth in race, class, and gender studies. In fact, according to Patricia Hill Collins, "because intersectionality does not specify the configuration of categories or even the number of relevant categories for a particular analysis, it seemingly offers more flexibility than race/class/gender studies."[15] Still, many researchers have limited their work to these three categories without exploring categories such as age, geographic location, and religion that could be more meaningful and suitable for their analyses. Given that power is a core construct of intersectionality, researchers have argued for the inclusion and more nuanced discussion of power and those who possess privilege in intersectional analyses.[16] In order for researchers to truly understand the ways in which power and privilege operate to exacerbate health inequalities and inequities, having a more informed perspective on both group- and institutional-level processes is important.

Also, a careful reconsideration of other significant measures, such as explanatory and outcome variables, is just as vital to health research as intersectional measures. Identifying and accurately operationalizing key variables is crucial for contextualizing the mechanisms between groups of interest and health outcomes. Harari and Lee note that approximately a third of the journal articles that incorporated intersectionality into quantitatively driven health disparities research did not provide an explanation of the mechanisms that link respondents to the health outcomes of interest. This lack of explanation not only thwarts the validity of a research study but also undermines the ability to work toward equitable health. As Harari and Lee contend, "When no explanatory mechanisms are specified, the intersectional groups under investigation are often treated as proxies for explanatory mechanisms that might contribute to observed health disparities. This invariably leads to an implicit assumption that intersectional group membership can independently explain variation in health, and therefore membership in such groups becomes 'risky' to health in and of itself. If explanatory mechanisms are not explored, it is impossible to identify modifiable factors that contribute to health (in)equity, making it difficult to assist in the formulation of health-promoting interventions."[17] To be sure, researchers cannot and should not account for every explanatory variable or mechanism by which health disparities may arise within a given intersectional group. However, researchers can be more realistic and forthcoming with the scope and limits of their research studies.

Relatedly, intersectional quantitative population health research could greatly benefit from the increased use of both theoretical and methodological considerations of life course perspectives. From a theoretical standpoint, a life course approach can provide much-needed context to the complexity and fluidity of the lived experiences of those with intersecting identities. Within health disparities research, life course frameworks have been useful in scholars' attempts to contextualize inequalities in health, from identifying the critical periods throughout the life course where social circumstances may more profoundly impact life chances and subsequent health outcomes to understanding how social factors can accumulate and increase the risk of disease over time. Data availability and appropriate longitudinal data sets are issues that can understandably dictate the scope/premise of studies. However, using other forms of methodology and data from Black women in the Diaspora, similar to the research found within this book, would help scholars to understand more clearly the intersections that are pertinent to examining the links between food and various aspects of health.

Intersectionality, Food, and Health

Women's identities and relationships are closely intertwined with food. As Patricia Allen and Carolyn Sachs aptly note in "Women and Food Chains: The Gendered Politics of Food,"

> Throughout history, the social relations of food have been organized along lines of gender. Today, in most societies women continue to carry the responsibility for the mental and manual labor of food provision—the most basic labor of care. Women's involvement with food constructs who they are in the world—as individuals, family members, and workers—in deep, complex, and often contradictory ways. Women perform most food-related work, but they control few resources and hold little decision-making power in the food industry and food policy. And, although women bear responsibility for nourishing others, they often do not adequately nourish themselves.[18]

This sentiment rings true, especially for Black women, whose contributions are often devalued because of their social identities and status. Efforts to bring Black women's voices to the forefront of food scholarship and activism have become more prominent in recent years, as awareness of the importance of intersectional perspectives in academia continues to grow. However, scholars have long discussed women's relationship to food and the connection to their other social identities, though many of these works did not specifically name or fully employ key tenets of intersectionality. Relatedly, various scholars have produced important work that examines the complexities of Black women's experiences regarding food, yet within more mainstream spaces in food studies this work has often been overlooked.

For years, Black women have provided meaningful social narratives of their lives through food. The first Black woman–authored cookbook, *What Mrs. Fisher Knows about Old Southern Cooking* (1881) by Abby Fisher, goes beyond providing instructions for recipes to include personal accounts of the author's life as a Black woman.[19] Others have continued the tradition of marrying recipes with historical and sociocultural information about Black life and, namely, Black women. Perhaps the most compelling commentaries on food and Black women's agency are from Vertamae Smart-Grosvenor's writings that situate recipes and food-related discussions amid the backdrop of the racial reckoning of the 1960s and '70s. Originally published in 1970, Smart-Grosvenor's *Vibration Cooking: Or, The Travel Notes of a Geechee Girl* takes readers on a journey that prominently situates Black women and their roles in the center of African American culinary history.[20] Similarly, food scholars have sought to further add to feminist understandings regarding gender and food to examine Black women's roles in African American foodways. In an ethnographic study of Gullah women in the Sea Islands and adjacent mainland locales in South Carolina, Josephine Beoku-Betts utilizes Black feminist perspectives to combat the notion of food preparation as "women's work" and illustrates how Gullah women's engagement in food preparation for not only their families but also their communities is an act of community building, group survival and well-being, and cultural preservation.[21]

The intentional examination and naming of the relationship between gender, sexuality, class, and other intersecting identities within food research has been aided by work from scholars such as Psyche Williams-Forson, whose book *Building Houses Out of Chicken Legs: Black Women, Food and Power* explores the political nature of gender, food, and race, using the example of Black women's relationship with chicken. Williams-Forson uses a historical lens to examine Black women's use of chicken to highlight how it serves as "a means of gaining a modicum of economic self-sufficiency," all while these women are constantly subjected to racist and sexist stereotypes related to their relationship with this foodstuff.[22] Williams-Forson further expounds upon how the kitchen itself can symbolize Black women's agency and identity in her autoethnographic account of intercultural food experiences and exchanges with her spouse in "Other Women Cooked for My Husband: Negotiating Gender, Food, and Identities in an African American/Ghanaian Household." Though the presence of Black women in kitchen spaces historically has been synonymous with their social and cultural identities, Williams-Forson illustrates that the freedom she finds from disengaging from certain aspects of cooking and allowing others to do this task "opened up loci of commonality" while helping her family create new cultural traditions.[23]

While the rich history of Black women's contributions to food studies research is evident, researchers must be mindful of the nuances of these experiences and adequately capture them in health research. Both intersectionality and food studies are crucial to our understanding of the health of communities. Food is an integral part of our lives, and its impact on health outcomes and overall well-being must be fully understood within the full scope of intersecting identities and experiences of communities across the Diaspora. In thinking of how to best capture the complexities of intersectional approaches in studying food and health at the population level, I echo Williams-Forson's questions regarding the responsibilities and issues of studying Black women and food: "Who *else* is in the kitchen? Who should be there, but isn't?"[24] Similarly, health researchers, particularly at the population level, must contend with questions related to who their subjects are and how their relationship with food impacts their well-being.

Access to food is an important and well documented factor of health disparities. Health researchers most often conceptualize and measure access by assessing whether the proximity of affordable, healthy food options from one's residence is over one mile (food deserts) or by evaluating whether people or households can afford healthy foods (food security). Food accessibility has been linked to a host of health outcomes throughout the life course, from anemia, cognition, and aggression and anxiety issues in children to depression, sleep issues, and chronic health conditions such as hypertension in adulthood and later life.[25] Additionally, racial segregation has fostered a geographical and economic environment that leads to a greater number of fast-food restaurants and a scarcity of stores selling fresh fruits and vegetables in Black communities. This scenario, according to previous research, can lead to a greater likelihood of consuming fast food, which subsequently leads to an increased risk of health problems.[26]

To examine food access and health inequities, many population health researchers utilize geospatial analyses to capture the existence, or lack thereof, of physical food sources, such as supermarkets, restaurants, and corner stores, in marginalized communities. Though the ability to geographically define and situate food-related spaces within communities undoubtedly provides a wealth of information for understanding the links between food and health, additional context is needed. In a recent opinion piece in the *American Journal of Public Health*, a team of geographers argues for research on food access to move beyond mapping physical spaces, as maps may oversimplify the physical environment. Specifically, though useful in many ways, maps may obscure the nature by which people move within and outside of their communities to travel and shop.[27] Moreover, geospatial analyses may not capture the temporality of both the structural determinants of health and health outcomes. Community-level factors and policies can change over time, and the assumption that both homes and food spaces are appropriate proxies for how people live and engage with food could misrepresent key connections to health. To account for these considerations, Jerry Shannon and colleagues call for a more participatory approach to geospatial analysis that includes more longitudinal analyses, incorporates qualitative methodology, and integrates critical and feminist perspectives in geographical information systems.[28]

Including the voices of Black women and their perceptions of food access could nicely complement quantitatively driven population health studies focused on health in Black communities. In an examination of perceptions of food and water access among Black women in Flint, Michigan, Kellie Mayfield and colleagues center Black women's voices by employing a womanist theoretical framework to illuminate their food-related barriers, feelings of discrimination, and health concerns. This study also highlights Black women's experiential knowledge and the strategies they used within the constraints of a city experiencing consequential lead contamination in its water system and the closure of five large grocery stores within an eighteen-month period.[29]

Concluding Thoughts: Incorporating Intersectionality into Research on Food and Health

In summation, this chapter seeks to provide theoretical and methodological insight into the ways in which intersectionality can benefit population health research focused on food-related health concerns among Black women. The work presented here is merely a snapshot of the extensive amount of emerging research on intersectional approaches to population health. My goal in this chapter is to extend those conversations to include the intersectional work of food studies scholars. Their voices have and will continue to be important for our understanding of health conditions that are closely linked to food, from production to consumption.

In order to fully incorporate intersectionality within quantitative population-based studies, we have to recenter Black women's voices in every aspect of the research design process, from the creation of questions and theory implementation to data collection and analysis. There are a growing number of scholars who are committed to examining how various methodological and statistical analyses can more accurately depict intersectional approaches.[30] From a theoretical perspective, quantitative research studies need to move beyond their primary focus of the three core intersectional constructs of social inequality, relationality, and complexity.[31] As Agénor notes, many studies highlight multiple identities as their way of examining intersectionality within their work, with little focus on the inequalities that exist.

The role of sexuality in discussions on intersectionality, food, and health is essential to our understanding of research on health inequities. Black trans women's and queer people's relationships with food and its impact on identity and health are crucial areas of exploration. Research in queer ecology and eco-queer movements highlights the difficulties in queer individuals' abilities to secure and maintain sustainable food spaces.[32] Being both Black and queer interrupts heteronormative roles of mothering and nurturing and needs to be contextualized in research that often defaults to long-held beliefs regarding Black women and risk behaviors for health conditions. Voices of Black trans women such as Ceyenne Doroshow, who serves in a mothering role to Black transgender people and chronicles her life via recipes, are vital to a host of conversations on topics from food access to health and well-being.[33]

As previously mentioned, the increasing popularity of intersectionality in population health research is promising. The focus of this growing research has been on what Patricia Homan and colleagues call structural intersectionality, which is defined as "the conceptualization and measurement of intersecting systems of oppression (e.g., structural racism, structural sexism, and classism) and their joint effects on population health."[34] This approach would allow for researchers to think about and measure how racism and sexism, for instance, change over time, thus providing greater social context for examining one's lived experience. New approaches to intersectionality within population health can lay the groundwork for more theoretically engaging statistical approaches that move us beyond more descriptive levels of understanding how Black women's relationships with food impact their health and the health of their communities.

NOTES

1. Bowleg, "*Women and Minorities*"; Agénor, "Future Directions."
2. Misra, Curington, and Green, "Methods of Intersectional Research," 14.
3. Hummer and Hamilton, *Population Health in America*, 7.

4. Alvidrez et al., "Intersectionality in Public Health."
5. Jones, "Dying to Eat?"; Reese, *Black Food Geographies*.
6. Assari et al., "Socioeconomic Status"; Hines, Zare, and Thorpe, "Racial Disparities in Hypertension."
7. Himmelstein, Puhl, and Quinn, "Intersectionality."
8. For an overview of intersectionality, please see the introduction of this book.
9. Bowleg, "When Black + Lesbian + Woman," 317.
10. Bowleg, "When Black + Lesbian + Woman," 317.
11. Best and Byrd, "All Marked-Up."
12. Kilbourne et al., "Advancing Health Disparities Research."
13. Green, Evans, and Subramanian, "Can Intersectionality Theory Enrich."
14. McCall, "Complexity of Intersectionality."
15. Collins, *Intersectionality*, 40.
16. Cole, "Intersectionality and Research"; Harari and Lee, "Intersectionality in Quantitative Health."
17. Harari and Lee, "Intersectionality in Quantitative Health," 8.
18. Allen and Sachs, "Women and Food Chains," 23.
19. Fisher, *What Mrs. Fisher Knows*; Zafar, "Signifying Dish."
20. Smart-Grosvenor, *Vibration Cooking*.
21. Beoku-Betts, "We Got Our Way."
22. Williams-Forson, *Building Houses*, 7.
23. Williams-Forson, "Other Women Cooked," 458.
24. Williams-Forson and Wilkerson, "Intersectionality and Food Studies," 7.
25. Eicher-Miller et al., "Food Insecurity"; Cohen et al., "Effect"; Melchior et al., "Food Insecurity"; Wu and Schimmele, "Food Insufficiency and Depression"; Ding et al., "Food Insecurity"; Beltrán et al., "Food Insecurity and Hypertension."
26. Kwate, "Fried Chicken."
27. Shannon et al., "More Than Mapping."
28. Shannon et al., "More Than Mapping."
29. Mayfield et al., "African American Women's Perceptions."
30. Bauer, "Incorporating Intersectionality Theory"; Bauer et al., *Harnessing the Power*.
31. Agénor, "Future Directions."
32. Leslie, "Queer Farmers"; Sbicca, "Eco-queer Movement(s)."
33. Doroshow, *Cooking in Heels*.
34. Homan, Brown, and King, "Structural Intersectionality."

WORKS CITED

Agénor, Madina. "Future Directions for Incorporating Intersectionality into Quantitative Population Health Research." *American Journal of Public Health* 110, no. 6 (2020): 803–6.

Allen, Patricia, and Carolyn Sachs. "Women and Food Chains: The Gendered Politics of Food." In *Taking Food Public: Redefining Foodways in a Changing World*, edited by Psyche Williams-Forson and Carole Counihan, 23–40. New York: Routledge, 2012.

Alvidrez, Jennifer, Gregory L. Greenwood, Tamara Lewis Johnson, and Karen L. Parker. "Intersectionality in Public Health Research: A View from the National Institutes of Health." *American Journal of Public Health* 111, no. 1 (2021): 95–97.

Assari, Shervin, Maryam Moghani Lankarani, John D. Piette, and James E. Aikens. "Socioeconomic Status and Glycemic Control in Type 2 Diabetes: Race by Gender Differences." *Healthcare* 5, no. 4 (2017): 83–93.

Bauer, Greta R. "Incorporating Intersectionality Theory into Population Health Research Methodology: Challenges and the Potential to Advance Health Equity." *Social Science and Medicine* 110 (June 2014): 10–17.

Bauer, Greta R., Lisa Bowleg, Setareh Rouhani, Ayden Scheim, and Soraya Blot. *Harnessing the Power of Intersectionality: Guidelines for Quantitative Intersectional Health Inequities Research*. Technical report. London, ON: University of Western Ontario, 2014.

Beltrán, Sourik, Marissa Pharel, Canada T. Montgomery, Itzel J. López-Hinojosa, Daniel J. Arenas, and Horace M. DeLisser. "Food Insecurity and Hypertension: A Systematic Review and Meta-Analysis." *PLOS ONE* 15, no. 11 (2020): e0241628.

Beoku-Betts, Josephine A. "We Got Our Way of Cooking Things: Women, Food, and Preservation of Cultural Identity among the Gullah." *Gender and Society* 9, no. 5 (1995): 535–55.

Best, Latrica E., and W. Carson Byrd. "All Marked-Up in the Genetic Era: Race and Ethnicity as 'Floating Signifiers' in Genetic and Genomic Research." In *Genetics, Health and Society*, edited by Brea Perry, 45–69. Vol. 16 of *Advances in Medical Sociology*. Bingley, UK: Emerald Group, 2015.

Bowleg, Lisa. "The Problem with the Phrase *Women and Minorities*: Intersectionality—an Important Theoretical Framework for Public Health." *American Journal of Public Health* 102, no. 7 (2012): 1267–73.

———. "When Black + Lesbian + Woman ≠ Black Lesbian Woman: The Methodological Challenges of Qualitative and Quantitative Intersectionality Research." *Sex Roles* 59, no. 5 (2008): 312–25.

Cohen, J. F. W., M. T. Gorski, S. A. Gruber, L. B. F. Kurdziel, and E. B. Rimm. "The Effect of Healthy Dietary Consumption on Executive Cognitive Functioning in Children and Adolescents: A Systematic Review." *British Journal of Nutrition* 116, no. 6 (2016): 989–1000.

Cole, Elizabeth R. "Intersectionality and Research in Psychology." *American Psychologist* 64, no. 3 (2009): 170–80.

Collins, Patricia Hill. *Intersectionality as Critical Social Theory*. Durham, NC: Duke University Press, 2019.

Ding, Meng, Margaret K. Keiley, Kimberly B. Garza, Patricia A. Duffy, and Claire A. Zizza. "Food Insecurity Is Associated with Poor Sleep Outcomes among US Adults." *Journal of Nutrition* 145, no. 3 (2015): 615–21.

Doroshow, Ceyenne. *Cooking in Heels: A Memoir Cookbook*. Brooklyn, NY: Red Umbrella Project, 2012.

Eicher-Miller, Heather A., April C. Mason, Connie M. Weaver, George P. McCabe, and Carol J. Boushey. "Food Insecurity Is Associated with Iron Deficiency Anemia in US Adolescents." *American Journal of Clinical Nutrition* 90, no. 5 (2009): 1358–71.

Fisher, Abby. *What Mrs. Fisher Knows about Old Southern Cooking*. 1881. Reprinted with notes by Karen Hess, Bedford, MA: Applewood Books, 1995.

Green, Mark A., Clare R. Evans, and S. V. Subramanian. "Can Intersectionality Theory Enrich Population Health Research?" *Social Science and Medicine* 178 (April 2017): 214–16.

Harari, Lexi, and Chioun Lee. "Intersectionality in Quantitative Health Disparities Research: A Systematic Review of Challenges and Limitations in Empirical Studies." *Social Science and Medicine* 277 (May 2021): 113876.

Himmelstein, Mary S., Rebecca M. Puhl, and Diane M. Quinn. "Intersectionality: An Understudied Framework for Addressing Weight Stigma." *American Journal of Preventive Medicine* 53, no. 4 (2017): 421–31.

Hines, Anika L., Hossein Zare, and Roland J. Thorpe. "Racial Disparities in Hypertension among Young, Black and White Women." *Journal of General Internal Medicine* 37, no. 8 (2022): 2123–25.

Homan, Patricia, Tyson H. Brown, and Brittany King. "Structural Intersectionality as a New Direction for Health Disparities Research." *Journal of Health and Social Behavior* 62, no. 3 (2021): 350–70.

Hummer, Robert A., and Erin R. Hamilton. *Population Health in America*. Oakland: University of California Press, 2019.

Jones, Naya. "Dying to Eat? Black Food Geographies of Slow Violence and Resilience." *ACME: An International Journal for Critical Geographies* 18, no. 5 (2019): 1076–99.

Kilbourne, Amy M., Galen Switzer, Kelly Hyman, Megan Crowley-Matoka, and Michael J. Fine. "Advancing Health Disparities Research within the Health Care System: A Conceptual Framework." *American Journal of Public Health* 96, no. 12 (2006): 2113–21.

Kwate, Naa Oyo A. "Fried Chicken and Fresh Apples: Racial Segregation as a Fundamental Cause of Fast Food Density in Black Neighborhoods." *Health and Place* 14, no. 1 (2008): 32–44.

Leslie, Isaac Sohn. "Queer Farmers: Sexuality and the Transition to Sustainable Agriculture." *Rural Sociology* 82, no. 4 (2017): 747–71.

Mayfield, Kellie E., Marsha Carolan, Lorraine Weatherspoon, Kimberly R. Chung, and Sharon M. Hoerr. "African American Women's Perceptions on Access to Food and Water in Flint, Michigan." *Journal of Nutrition Education and Behavior* 49, no. 6 (2017): 519–24.

McCall, Leslie. "The Complexity of Intersectionality." *Signs* 30, no. 3 (2005): 1771–800.

Melchior, Maria, Jean-François Chastang, Bruno Falissard, Cédric Galéra, Richard E. Tremblay, Sylvana M. Côté, and Michel Boivin. "Food Insecurity and Children's Mental Health: A Prospective Birth Cohort Study." *PLOS ONE* 7, no. 12 (2012): e52615.

Misra, Joya, Celeste Vaughan Curington, and Venus Mary Green. "Methods of Intersectional Research." *Sociological Spectrum* 41, no. 1 (2021): 9–28.

Reese, Ashanté M. *Black Food Geographies: Race, Self-Reliance, and Food Access in Washington, D.C.* Chapel Hill: University of North Carolina Press, 2019.

Sbicca, Joshua. "Eco-queer Movement(s): Challenging Heteronormative Space through (Re)Imagining Nature and Food." *European Journal of Ecopsychology* 3 (2012): 33–52.

Shannon, Jerry, Ashanté M. Reese, Debarchana Ghosh, Michael J. Widener, and Daniel R. Block. "More Than Mapping: Improving Methods for Studying the Geographies of Food Access." *American Journal of Public Health* 111, no. 8 (2021): 1418–22.

Smart-Grosvenor, Vertamae. *Vibration Cooking: Or, The Travel Notes of a Geechee Girl*. New York: Doubleday, 1970. Reprinted with a foreword by Psyche Williams-Forson and a new preface. Athens: University of Georgia Press, 2011.

Williams-Forson, Psyche A. *Building Houses Out of Chicken Legs: Black Women, Food, and Power*. Chapel Hill: University of North Carolina Press, 2006.

———. "Other Women Cooked for My Husband: Negotiating Gender, Food, and Identities in an African American/Ghanaian Household." *Feminist Studies* 36, no. 2 (2010): 435–61.

Williams-Forson, Psyche, and Abby Wilkerson. "Intersectionality and Food Studies." *Food, Culture and Society* 14, no. 1 (2011): 7–28.

Wu, Zheng, and Christoph M. Schimmele. "Food Insufficiency and Depression." *Sociological Perspectives* 48, no. 4 (2005): 481–504.

Zafar, Rafia. "The Signifying Dish: Autobiography and History in Two Black Women's Cookbooks." *Feminist Studies* 25, no. 2 (1999): 449–69.

CHAPTER 10

I Put Food on Everyone's Table

Food Provisioning, Domestic Work, and
Entrepreneurship across Three Generations of
Black Women in Santiago de Cuba

HANNA GARTH

Introduction

On a hot summer afternoon in Santiago de Cuba, I sat with Carla in her home.[1] While the pressure cooker hissed as the afternoon meal's yuca softened, we began to talk about her life and the ways being a woman in Cuba had changed over the years. Carla, who identified as a Black, low-income woman from Santiago de Cuba, was born before Cuba's 1959 socialist revolution. I asked her if she felt that her day-to-day life had improved over the course of her lifetime. To my surprise, she said that she did not feel that any policies, pre- or post-revolution, had made a difference:

> I have worked my whole life. Since I finished the fourth grade—that was the last year of school I did before working as a domestic in

people's houses. I worked in houses before the revolution and after; nothing changed. I always had to come home after cooking and cleaning on the other side of town to do the same thing in my house. I raised my four kids; their father was in the street. It was really hard, but I worked, I worked for everything. I went to the market. I made the food. I raised pigs and chickens to sell for us. Now I am almost seventy years old and I don't work outside the home anymore, but I still do everything around here. I am raising my grandkids and great-grandkids—they are here all the time, and do you see their mothers? I work and work and work.

Carla spoke with a tone of anger and annoyance. She had stopped her schooling to work, cleaning and cooking for wealthy families on the other side of the city. By underscoring that her children's father was "in the street," she stressed that without much help from him, she also did all of the work to raise her children, cook, clean, and maintain the household.[2] While she may have been annoyed at the naivete of my questions, which implied that things *should* have changed over her life course and after significant political events, she nevertheless strongly affirmed that nothing had changed in her life. She described her life as revolving around paid and unpaid labor, outside and inside of the home, drawing little distinction between the two.

Carla's narrative runs counter to the notion that the status of women may be "falling back," losing the gains in social equity and labor involvement over the past few decades, and instead shows that for many Cuban women, particularly those with darker skin and of lower socioeconomic status, constant work within and outside of the home has been their reality for generations. Despite nearly fifty years of policy efforts toward women's equality, in Cuba women still undertake the vast majority of unpaid household labor and, often, work outside the home for pay either in full-time, state-based employment or in part-time non-state-based work. While state pensions, the state provisioning system, and other entitlements allow many Cubans the opportunity to retire from jobs outside the home at age sixty, many of these seniors continue to bear a burden of household tasks, such as childcare, cleaning, and meal preparation. However, as in Carla's case, for many of these seniors, their time is not spent purely on leisure but on other household tasks such as childcare. Carla's reflections are typical of the matrifocal ways of framing Black womanhood and mothering in Cuba and the Caribbean; the standards of womanhood placed upon Carla and women like her are distinct from the white-racialized forms of virtuous womanhood.[3]

Based on long-term ethnographic research, this chapter draws on three generations of Black women from a low-income family in Santiago de Cuba, of which Carla is the matriarch. I detail their household labor done to feed the family; their paid domestic labor cooking and cleaning in the homes of wealthier white Cubans; and their entrepreneurial endeavors, such as raising pigs and selling prepared food to generate income. With the collapse of the Soviet Union in the 1990s and the loss of its most significant trade partner, Cuba entered a period of economic hardship known as the Special Period. Although the quantity and quality of rationed food have significantly improved since then, supplies have not returned to Soviet-era levels. Ten years after the worst scarcities of the Special Period, many of my research participants reported that they continued to live with food shortages and economic hardship.

This chapter focuses on one of the twenty-two families included in the broader study. Carla, the oldest woman in the family, born in 1943, remembers life before the socialist revolution. Her daughter Gema has been living with her mother since her husband left her over thirty years ago. Gema's daughter, Yaicel, works at a local state-run factory, has a second job as a dancer in a local folkloric troupe, and also works with her mother selling food. Analyzing the lives and work of these three women, I demonstrate the various forms of labor that Black women engage in to ensure that food gets on the table and households are well maintained. Race, gender, and class must be understood intersectionally as mutually constitutive and foundational to Black women's subjectivities in contemporary Cuba.[4] Specifically, I analyze the role of grandmothers in maintaining the household, teaching the skills of household labor and entrepreneurship, and providing childcare for younger generations to be able to work outside the home. I argue that through their matriarchal roles, Black grandmothers teach the skills necessary for *luchando la vida* ("struggling for life"), and therefore their work is central to the alleviation and prevention of poverty, hunger, and malnutrition.

Theoretical Context: (White) Women and Work in Cuba

This chapter builds upon feminist scholars of Latin America who have demonstrated the ways in which the reproductive and productive labor of women in the household continues to be undervalued.[5] Before the 1959 socialist revolution, women's participation in the Cuban workforce was relatively high compared to that in other Latin American countries.[6] After 1959, Cuba's approach to gender equity was incorporated with the Marxist ideologies driving the socialist revolution. For Fidel Castro, the women's movement was to be a "revolution within the revolution" and not apart from it; thus, an autonomous feminist movement that empowered women to work toward equality was never established in Cuba. Several policies were put in place to "liberate," including encouraging women to work outside the home through the provision of equal work and educational opportunities, creating programs to help with domestic work and childcare, and mobilizing women into positions within the Communist Party.

However, there were fractures between Marxist ideology and Cuban cultural norms. Traditionally, the home was thought to be a social area over which women have control and are kept safe from the dangers of life in public spaces, or "the street." The *casa/calle* divide is used to mark the distinction between women's space and men's space, with "men dominant in the public sphere and women in the private sphere of the household."[7] The notion of the casa/calle division of gendered spaces has persisted since Cuba's independence from Spain.[8] This approach to women's place in the world is often linked to white bourgeois Spanish thinking; however, it can be seen across racial lines throughout various economic classes in Cuban society.[9]

Many previous analyses of women's lives in Cuba have not adequately analyzed the specific subject positions of Black Cuban women. Gendered subjectivities are often racialized in a way that excludes nonwhite people from both the constraints of these understandings of proper gendered behavior.[10] The ideals of gendered spaces in the contemporary landscape can be traced to a history of racialized, white European hegemony during the colonial period. While postcolonial Cuba attempted to shed Spanish colonialisms, some, such as those related to the virtues and vices of gendered subjectivity, have been very difficult to eradicate even through the socialist period. These deeply ingrained "notions of respectability" were part of the "intimate in colonial rule" that remain central to Cuban understandings of womanhood.[11] We must understand "the mutually constitutive role of race and gender in constructing subject positions, technologies of violence and understandings of social order."[12]

Black feminist theory, drawn from research in the United States and the Caribbean, has documented the ways in which Black women are continually affected by the trifecta of racial, gender, and economic oppression.[13] As Saidiya Hartman notes, "The systematic violence needed to conscript black women's domestic labor after slavery required locking them out of all other sectors of the labor market, a condition William Patterson described as economic genocide."[14] Moreover, Theresa Rajack-Talley has found a great need to understand the intersection of race, gender, and economic issues not only at the level of policy and demographics but also through the personal experience of struggle. The Cuban women in this chapter struggle through poverty collectively and intergenerationally.[15] Offering collective agency as a theoretical framework, Monica White argues that history and commitment to communally produced solutions are a manifestation of self-reliance and self-determination. Ashanté Reese argues that the "self" in these articulations is less about the individual and more about the ways the community itself can produce alternatives, though they may be limited in scope and sustainability.[16] Although Cuban women, and in particular Black Cuban women, face many obstacles, they continue *luchando la vida*.

In the sections that follow I detail the lives of Carla, Gema, and Yaicel, analyzing how their care work and labor inside and outside the home—preparing food for their own families, for the families they work for, and for public sale—is shaped by social expectations for Black women's labor and the ways in which they work within these expectations to build meaningful lives for themselves. After detailing the forms of food-related and care-related work that these three women engage in, I offer my analysis of the ways in which their working lives document the fundamental role of Black women's labor in sustaining their families, communities, and Cuban society.

The Women

CARLA

Seventy-year-old Carla remembers life before Cuba's socialist revolution. While she acknowledges the benefits of the revolution, such as free education, free health care, low-cost housing, utilities, and a food ration, she also is sure to underscore that she worked her whole life, for others and in her own home, and the revolution did not change that. In addition to those forms of labor, Carla always maintained "side hustles" to bring money into the household, from running an illegal lottery and using her landline as a pay phone to raising pigs and goats to sell for meat.

She began working for pay outside the home when she was around twelve years old. Although she cannot remember the details about what exactly she started doing, she remembers working in the homes of wealthy white families on the other side of the city from the age of twelve into her late thirties. She cooked, cleaned, did laundry, ran errands, and lovingly cared for the children of dozens of white families. She usually worked from 7 a.m. to 8 p.m., sometimes having to stay late as well. She never made a lot of money but always enough to keep her own household going. After she had her own children, she was the sole income earner for many years; she was very proud to have made enough money to purchase the home that she and her family still live in today. Although she complained that her husband was always "in the street" and never helped around the house, she stayed married to him until he died, and she never remarried. As a Black woman, although her husband was "in the street," Carla was not kept away safely to run her home but rather expected to cook, clean, and care for other households as a domestic laborer. As she moved in and through the streets to conduct this labor, the casa/calle divide did not apply to her as a Black woman. Her husband found work off and on but never had a reliable income.

Carla had always done additional work to make ends meet in the evenings and on her days off. For many years she worked as a seamstress in her living room, repairing garments, hemming, and taking clothes in and out for friends, neighbors, and the occasional wealthy client from the other side of town. She did this until her eyesight began to fail as her glaucoma worsened. In addition, she has always maintained livestock in and around her home, for the family to either consume or sell. She has raised chickens, pigs, and goats to eat as well as pigeons to sell for sport.

While laboring outside the home and maintaining several other side jobs, Carla also raised four girls. When they were very young, her mother helped take care of them, but once Carla bought her own place and the girls were in school, she did everything on her own. She would wake up before dawn to prepare breakfasts and lunches for her family before catching the bus to her job. The girls would come home after school, and their father was supposed to keep an eye on them, but they were mostly on their own. Carla would prepare a late dinner after her shift, usually a light soup or a simple sandwich for everyone. After cleaning the kitchen, she would dedicate the rest of her waking hours to her side jobs before collapsing into bed each night.

In Carla's opening quote in this chapter, she testifies to the endless labor that she has done over the course of her life. She has truly worked hard to earn what little she has to her name, and as she asserts, despite the changes to women's labor under the socialist revolution, Carla and many Black Cuban women continued to serve in the same roles of domestic laborer for white families, as the improvements in working conditions for women were really focused on white women. Even as Carla has stopped doing most formal paid labor, she continues to raise animals to sell, uses her phone as a community pay phone for extra money, and as she attests in the opening quote, is the primary caregiver for her grandchildren and great-grandchildren that live in her house. Although she speaks with a tone of annoyance about this, I also observed that she is very well respected by her family and community as a local fixture and matriarch. Nevertheless, Carla's labor, like that of many Black Cuban women of her generation, has been central to the building and maintenance of Cuban society. These women have provided the domestic support for white women to work outside the home and for their own kin to earn money, as Carla and her generation continue to provide childcare and household labor.

GEMA

Gema moved in with her mother, Carla, over three decades ago, when she divorced her first husband. Gema works as a nurse and, like her mother, had a side job of preparing food and selling it at a small stand in the evenings as well as during major local festivals such as Carnaval. Gema's hospital nursing job is difficult and exhausting; it involves long hours on her feet and a lot of walking. Although she is completely exhausted most evenings after her shift, she still prepares food and sets up her food stand almost every night on a busy corner near her home. She has been selling food this way for many years, sometimes having to sell food clandestinely when the Cuban state was less permissive to small businesses. Once the state became more open to small businesses, she took out a license. Gema then struggled to make enough money to ensure that she could pay the taxes and still make a profit. She explains to me, "I know that some months I don't make any money, but other times of the year I make a lot. And I don't just do it for money anymore; I do it because it gets me out of the house. I am very social, but I can't afford to go out to fancy places, and I'm not just going to sit on a bench in the park. Selling food gives me a reason to be out of the house; it allows me to see everyone even if no one is buying."

Between her two jobs, Gema spends very little time at home. She has always relied on Carla for childcare, and Carla has always cooked the household meals that Gema eats for breakfast, lunch, and dinner. Gema never assists with any cooking or cleaning, and only very rarely assists with food acquisition for the household. She does, however, dedicate some time to acquiring food for her business, which has yielded relationships that Carla can draw upon to access food on the black market or for bargains.

Although her family makes fun of her seemingly leisurely life, Gema dedicates most of her working hours to caring for others. Her work as a nurse is difficult, and she pours herself into caring for hospitalized people. Her evenings are dedicated to selling prepared foods, which is another form of care-based labor for the neighborhood and her community. Because of Carla's role as a caregiver in the home, Gema is able to dedicate herself to these other forms of labor and engage in very little household-based work or childcare.

YAICEL

Gema's daughter, Yaicel, born in 1983, has lived in her grandmother's house nearly her whole life, except for the first year or so, when she lived with her parents while they were still married. After her parents divorced when she was two years old, Yaicel never really saw her father. He lived in the area and she knew what he looked like, and she would bump into him and exchange awkward hellos from time to time.

Yaicel was raised primarily by her grandmother. During one visit, we sat on her grandmother's bed and chatted. She ran her hands along the bedspread and fondly recalled the many nights that she and her little brother had spent in the bed, snuggled up with Carla. In 2008, when I first met her, Yaicel had two children of her own that she was raising in the house—a toddler, Obalo, and eight-year-old Livia. Yaicel had quickly split up with Livia's father. After moving in with him for just under one year, she moved back into Carla's house. Except for that one year, Yaicel has lived there her whole life. In 2008, Obalo's father lived there with them as well.

As we sat on the bed that day, Yaicel called to Carla in the other room, "Mama, let's make some coffee." Without speaking, Carla moved toward the kitchen nook and started making the coffee. We moved to the living room and rocked on rocking chairs, and Obalo climbed into Yaicel's lap, pulling down her shirt to nurse. Yaicel had her first child, Livia, when she was in her late teens. She had just begun her career working as a dancer with a local folkloric dance troupe when she became pregnant. Between the pregnancy, birth, and parenting Livia during her early years, Yaicel took three years off from work. She was able to return to work with the dance troupe in large part because Carla was able to watch Livia while Yaicel trained in the afternoons and evenings. In the years since we first met in 2008, Yaicel has consistently worked as a dancer, again taking some time off for her second child, Obalo. In 2017, after Obalo's father left her for another woman, in order to support herself and her two children, Yaicel started to work in a local state-run factory, maintained her second job as a dancer in a local folkloric troupe, and earned additional money for the household selling prepared food with her mother, Gema.

Yaicel's labor caring for her children and working as a wage earner is actually a quadruple shift (*quadruple jornada*), even further extending the more common *triple jornada* of Latin American women.¹⁷ Unlike the generations before her, Yaicel's paid labor is not care based. As a dancer she benefits from the Cuban socialist revolution's investment and dedication to the arts. While this is a shift from previous generations of Black women's labor, the role of the folkloric dancer is often occupied by Black Cubans and seen by many Cubans as labor that is well suited to Black people, in contrast to ballet, which is predominantly white. Yaicel's factory job is also distinct from the types of work previous generations took up, and it clearly fits with the Cuban revolution's and Federation of Cuban Women's goals to move Cuban women into the socialist labor force. While most of Yaicel's work is distinct, her evenings selling food with Gema still tether her to the labor of food preparation and caregiving.

Conclusions: Care and Black Womanhood in Cuba

The role of Black women's labor in providing food and childcare, that is, filling the role of the quintessential Black matriarch, has been foundational to Cuban society since colonization and continues to be essential in the socialist and post-Soviet periods. Devyn Spence Benson has recently argued that "since the post-1989 economic crisis, uneven economic development has often seen black women's bodies re-sexualized or (re)mammy-fied, as shown in the sales of tourist T-shirts with black minstrel faces."¹⁸ While Carla's narrative and life story attest to the ways Black Cuban women have and continue to serve the roles of caregiver and domestic laborer for white Cuban families, her story also counters the idea that this is a new or reemerging phenomenon but rather an ongoing condition for women of Carla's generation.

While the lives of women from Carla's generation and socioeconomic status have not changed significantly, her own detailing of how much time she spends on her role as a grandmother reveals the ways in which the lives of her children may be different from her own. The labor of grandmothers plays a significant role in the functioning of Cuban society, particularly as younger women take on multiple jobs outside the home. Because of her labor, Carla's daughter and granddaughter spend less time on childcare than she does today and less than her generation did when they were younger. Carla's reflections illuminate the larger point that women have historically taken on the dual burden of housework and work outside the home. In her case, she continues to take on this labor, caring for the children so that their mothers have less of a work burden, a common situation in my study population.

The labor of Black Cuban women such as Carla allows for the younger generations of Cuban women, Black and non-Black, to work multiple jobs outside the home; many maintain a state job as well as an under-the-table or black-market way of earning money. In some cases, the childcare done by grandparents also allows younger generations to have relatively full social lives, spending their time dating if they are single or spending quality time with their partners, while someone else watches their children. In Yaicel's case, her own paid labor has moved away from the trend of Black women as care workers, but she is still ensconced in a typically Black role as a folkloric dancer and cultural producer.

The lives and labor of these three generations of Black Cuban women show the importance of understanding the role of Black women as laborers and caregivers in Cuba, both historically and today. These Black matriarchs pass down the skills of *luchando la vida* to future generations of Black women, who continue to work multiple jobs cooking, cleaning, and caring for households across Cuba. Much of the research on women's lives in Cuba has been focused on the lives and work of white Cuban women and has neglected to understand the ways in which the labor of Black women is essential to the functioning of Cuban households and part of what allows so many women to work outside the home. Although some scholars have argued that political and economic changes in Cuba have led Black women to revert to the roles of mammy or sexual object, the data presented here, on the one hand, show that the roles of Black women as caregivers and domestic laborers in the Cuban labor force may have remained steadily in place for older generations of Cuban women. On the other hand, younger generations, raised in the socialist period and post-Soviet period, have engaged in different forms of state-based wage labor than previous generations. However, they tend to remain in positions that are thought to be suited to Black women. Although the youngest generations have the skills it takes to put food on the table in Cuba, it is unclear whether they will continue in the role of caring for their own grandchildren and great-grandchildren in the future.

NOTES

1. All participant names are pseudonyms.

2. In Cuba, the saying that someone is "in the street" means that they are doing various things outside of the home, including acquiring goods and making social connections to get goods and services, but it can also refer to hanging out, drinking, and having sexual affairs. Garth, *Food in Cuba*.

3. Garth, *Food in Cuba*; Safa, "Matrifocal Family"; Pertierra, *"En Casa."*

4. Cooper, "Intersectionality"; Crenshaw, "Demarginalizing the Intersection."

5. Allen and Sachs, "Women and Food Chains"; DeVault, *Feeding the Family*; Page-Reeves, *Women Redefining the Experience*; Texler Segal and Demos, *Gender and Food*.

6. In 1953, women were nearly 13 percent of the labor force; one-quarter of these women were domestic servants (Smith and Padula, *Sex and Revolution*). In 1957, 48 percent of the Cuban service-sector employees were women.

7. Safa, *Myth of the Male*, 47–48.

8. Garth, "'Toward Being'"; Pertierra, *"En Casa"*; Smith and Padula, *Sex and Revolution*.

9. Stoler, *Carnal Knowledge*.

10. Stoler, *Carnal Knowledge*. See also Allen, *¡Venceremos?*; Roland, *Cuban Color in Tourism*; Roland, "T/racing Belonging"; and Saunders, "La Lucha Mujerista."

11. Thomas, *Exceptional Violence*. In contrast, the socialist revolution went to great lengths to inculcate the socialist "New Man" with a particularly socialist ideology of self-sacrifice. For Fidel Castro the New Man involved "an attitude of struggle, dignity, principles, and revolutionary morale" (Castro, *Informe central*, 59); for Che Guevara it was part of a "commitment to action" (Guevara, *El socialismo*). All Cubans were re-educated into this new morality via explicit programs (Blum, *Cuban Youth*). Notions of "honor" and "respect" from the colonial era still remain central to Cuban ideals of masculinity (Knight, *Slave Society in Cuba*).

12. Haley, *No Mercy Here*, 4. See also Cole, "Race toward Equality"; Fernandes, "Fear of a Black"; Fernandez, *Revolutionizing Romance*; and Finch, "Scandalous Scarcities."

13. Collins, *Black Feminist Thought*; Davis, *Women, Race and Class*; Marable, "Grounding with My Sisters."

14. Hartman, "Belly of the World," 170.

15. Rajack-Talley, *Poverty Is a Person*.

16. White, *Freedom Farmers*; Reese, "We Will Not Perish."

17. Garth, *Food in Cuba*.

18. Spence Benson, *Anti-racism in Cuba*, 1.

WORKS CITED

Allen, Jafari. *¡Venceremos? The Erotics of Black Self-Making in Cuba*. Durham, NC: Duke University Press, 2011.

Allen, Patricia, and Carolyn Sachs. "Women and Food Chains: The Gendered Politics of Food." *International Journal of Sociology of Food and Agriculture* 15, no. 1 (2007): 1–23.

Benson, Devyn Spence. "Representations of Black Women in Cuba." *Black Perspectives* (blog). African American Intellectual History Society, May 4, 2017. www.aaihs.org/representations-of-black-women-in-cuba.

Blum, Denise F. *Cuban Youth and Revolutionary Values: Educating the New Socialist Citizen*. Austin: University of Texas Press, 2011.

Castro, Fidel. "Informe central al segundo congreso [del Partido Comunista de Cuba]." *Bohemia magazine* (Havana), December 1980.

Cole, Johnnetta B. "Race toward Equality: The Impact of the Cuban Revolution on Racism." *Black Scholar* 1, no. 8 (1980): 1–22.

Collins, Patricia Hill. *Black Feminist Thought: Knowledge, Consciousness, and the Politics of Empowerment*. 10th anniversary ed. New York: Routledge, 2000.

Cooper, Brittany. "Intersectionality." In *The Oxford Handbook of Feminist Theory*, edited by Lisa Disch and Mary Hawkesworth, 385–406. Oxford: Oxford University Press, 2015.

Crenshaw, Kimberlé. "Demarginalizing the Intersection of Race and Sex: A Black Feminist Critique of Antidiscrimination Doctrine, Feminist Theory and Antiracist Politics." *University of Chicago Legal Forum* 1989, no. 8 (1989): 139–67.

Davis, Angela Y. *Women, Race and Class*. New York: Random House, 1981.

DeVault, Marjorie L. *Feeding the Family: The Social Organization of Caring as Gendered Work*. Chicago: University of Chicago Press, 1994.

Fernandes, Sujatha. "Fear of a Black Nation: Local Rappers, Transnational Crossings, and State Power in Contemporary Cuba." *Anthropological Quarterly* 76, no. 4 (2003): 575–608.

Fernandez, Nadine. *Revolutionizing Romance: Interracial Couples in Contemporary Cuba*. New Brunswick, NJ: Rutgers University Press, 2010.

Finch, Aisha K. "Scandalous Scarcities: Black Slave Women, Plantation Domesticity, and Travel Writing in Nineteenth-Century Cuba." *Journal of Historical Sociology* 23, no. 1 (2010): 101–43.

Garth, Hanna. *Food in Cuba: The Pursuit of a Decent Meal*. Stanford, CA: Stanford University Press, 2020.

———. "'Toward Being a Complete Woman': Reflections on Mothering in Santiago de Cuba," *UCLA Center for Study of Women Newsletter*, December 2010.

Guevara, Ernesto. *El socialismo y el hombre en Cuba*. Montevideo, Uruguay: Semanario Marcha, 1965.

Haley, Sarah. *No Mercy Here: Gender, Punishment, and the Making of Jim Crow Modernity*. Chapel Hill: University of North Carolina Press, 2016.

Hartman, Saidiya. "The Belly of the World: A Note on Black Women's Labors," *Souls* 18, no. 1 (2016): 166–73.

Knight, Franklin W. *Slave Society in Cuba during the Nineteenth Century*. Madison: University of Wisconsin Press, 1970.

Marable, Manning. "Grounding with My Sisters: Patriarchy and the Exploitation of Black Women." In *How Capitalism Underdeveloped Black America: Problems in Race, Political Economy, and Society*, 69–104. Boston: South End, 1983.

Page-Reeves, Janet. *Women Redefining the Experience of Food Insecurity: Life off the Edge of the Table*. Lanham, MD: Lexington Books, 2014.

Pertierra, Anna Cristina. "*En Casa*: Women and Households in Post-Soviet Cuba." *Journal of Latin American Studies* 40, no. 4 (2008): 743–67.

Rajack-Talley, Theresa Ann. *Poverty Is a Person: Human Agency, Women and Caribbean Households*. Kingston, Jamaica: Ian Randle, 2016.

Reese, Ashanté M. "'We Will Not Perish; We're Going to Keep Flourishing': Race, Food Access, and Geographies of Self-Reliance." *Antipode* 50, no. 2 (March 2018): 407–24.

Roland, L. Kaifa. *Cuban Color in Tourism and La Lucha: An Ethnography of Racial Meanings*. New York: Oxford University Press, 2011.

———. "T/racing Belonging through Cuban Tourism." *Cultural Anthropology* 28, no. 3 (2013): 396–419.

Safa, Helen. "The Matrifocal Family and Patriarchal Ideology in Cuba and the Caribbean." *Journal of Latin American Anthropology* 10, no. 2 (2005): 314–38.

———. *The Myth of the Male Breadwinner: Women and Industrialization in the Caribbean*. Boulder, CO: Westview, 1995.

Saunders, Tanya L. "La Lucha Mujerista: Krudas Cubensi and Black Feminist Sexual Politics in Cuba." *Caribbean Review of Gender Studies* 3 (November 2009): 1–20.

Smith, Lois M., and Alfred Padula. *Sex and Revolution: Women in Socialist Cuba*. New York: Oxford University Press, 1996.

Spence Benson, Devyn. *Anti-racism in Cuba: The Unfinished Revolution*. Chapel Hill: University of North Carolina Press, 2016.

Stoler, Ann Laura. *Carnal Knowledge and Imperial Power: Race and the Intimate in Colonial Rule*. Berkeley: University of California Press, 2002.

Texler Segal, Marcia, and Vasilikie Demos, eds. *Gender and Food: From Production to Consumption and After*. Bingley, UK: Emerald Group, 2016.

Thomas, Deborah A. *Exceptional Violence: Embodied Citizenship in Transnational Jamaica*. Durham, NC: Duke University Press, 2011.

White, Monica M. *Freedom Farmers: Agricultural Resistance and the Black Freedom Movement*. Chapel Hill: University of North Carolina Press, 2018.

CHAPTER 11

Tasting Freedom

The Rastafari Family Food Beit in Ethiopia

SHELENE GOMES

Introduction

On a typical weekday around noon in the town of Shashamane in Ethiopia, Sister Pauletta's yard will be packed with customers.[1] In this well-built house, Pauletta expanded her food *beit*, or restaurant, over decades. Despite being in yard spaces, some *beitoch* (the plural of beit) are licensed restaurants. For sale was "food," in the Jamaican meaning of cooked, filling meals anchored by a starch—rice, potatoes, eddoes (taro), yams, or plantains (bananas). Added would be peas with cabbage, carrots, stewed beef, oxtail, or fish seasoned with *berbere*, an Ethiopian peppery spice. Curried goat and white rice accompanied by *ital* (healthy) or vegetarian options such as stewed peas were sold as well. Interspersed were ritual Ethiopian foods such as *doro wat* (chicken in red sauce with boiled eggs and injera, the staple bread made of teff). These meals were prepared by Pauletta, her grown male and female children, and a local Ethiopian *serratena* (female domestic worker). Around payday, the food beit would be especially crowded. Another example of a licensed food beit was Sister Faith's. Her menu was similar to Pauletta's but catered more to tastes from Trinidad and Tobago.[2] Pauletta and Faith are Black Rastafari women who migrated, or "repatriated," to Ethiopia from Jamaica and Trinidad and Tobago, respectively.

These initial observations of woman-run *meghib beitoch* (family restaurants) capture the empirical and conceptual concerns of this chapter.[3] I examine the interrelation of women's work, cooking, eating, socializing, and cultural identity among Rastafari repatriates in the Jamaica Safar, a multiethnic neighborhood in Shashamane, Ethiopia. A gendered analytical approach helps understand the interconnections between work and sociocultural values that are evident in women's roles and food-related activities. These roles are situated in a hierarchical distinction, positioning women's reproductive and domestic labor in the household as less valuable than men's "productive" labor in public. While this gendered and class distinction between productive and reproductive work persists in both Rastafari and Rastafari–local Ethiopian households, women also engage in more regular waged labor outside the yard than men. Pauletta's and Faith's beitoch are examples of this pattern, with nuances that are specific to Rastafari and Caribbean value systems, which I will discuss.

The chapter draws on ethnographic fieldwork undertaken between 2008 and 2009 and again between 2012 and 2015. Ethnography is characterized by in-depth investigation through fieldwork aimed at understanding, interpreting, and analyzing informants' experiences from their perspectives. I undertook the technique of participant observation to collect information, observing participants' daily activities, including household activities such as cooking, cleaning, and going to the weekly market to shop for food, while I lived in one Rastafari Twelve Tribes yard in 2008–09. I also attended ritual and community events such as Rastafari celebrations and a subdistrict meeting, among others.

I visited different yards in the Jamaica Safar to meet and interview household members, thereby undertaking rudimentary household surveys. Through participant observation, unstructured and semistructured interviews with repatriates and Ethiopian-born youth, basic household surveys, and life narratives, I became familiar with at least one member each of seventy-three first- and second-generation households. The primary language of communication was Jamaican Patois, which I learned quickly, with English as my mother tongue. Amharic and Amharic-patois speech combinations are also used between Ethiopian-born children and grandchildren, as noted by Giulia Bonacci, and I developed a very basic Amharic vocabulary.[4] Among Rastafari generally in this area, communication was in Caribbean Patois (not necessarily derived from Jamaica) and English.

From 2012 to 2015, I worked at a regional public university in the neighboring urban locale of Hawassa, the capital of the Southern Nations, Nationalities, and Peoples Region. During these years, I visited Shashamane about once a month, or more often if there was an event such as a birthday or funeral, and I continued to attend community events. While I primarily draw on my observations from Faith's and Pauletta's food houses, I also make peripheral references to thirteen additional family restaurants, shops, and cooking experiences where the primary income comes from the sale of homemade food, except at the soya factory and hotel businesses. These examples indicate patterns of work in food industries among the Rastafari migrant population. The small number of microlevel cases in this essay provides an avenue to discuss insights into the historical conditions of global food systems as these intersect with changing culturally specific practices in a migration setting. Interrelated considerations are conceptions of health and well-being, livelihood practices, gendered ideals of morality, womanhood, and division of labor in migrant-local relationships. In this case, the migration is to the sacred place of Ethiopia, motivated by Rastafari spiritually centered demands for freedom and autonomy.

Within the precarious livelihoods of many Rastafari in Shashamane, selling food earns a reasonable, consistent income. Precarity also means that menus do not always reflect consistent tastes, and with an unpredictable supply of ingredients and flavors, there is experimentation among cooks. Rastafari cooking is a site that reflects a stew of changing goods and tastes while catering to an ital imperative. This insight is not a particularly novel one. The function of food in social reproduction more generally and in cultural transmission specifically within migrant communities in multicultural states has been well researched.[5] However, it is at the microlevel that attention to these studies can be used to analyze culture and sociality around the food beit.

Following a brief discussion of the theory of food, in the next sections I present Rastafari notions of ital living to situate particular concerns around cooking, eating, and selling food. I also highlight changing food tastes among residents of the multicultural Jamaica Safar with Rastafari migration, demonstrating how food is an avenue for maintaining cultural identity and integrating into this sacred place in contemporary Ethiopia. I consider who does the cooking in the food beit attached to the home, in light of the gendered division of labor that has historically characterized Caribbean societies. These roles are rooted in a hierarchical distinction, positioning women's reproductive and domestic labor in the home as less valuable than men's "productive" labor in public. Women's multiple roles in the diasporic Caribbean are observable in this locale. With gender roles situated in the value systems of the modern Caribbean and its plantation economies, this case in particular highlights the disjuncture between the division of "productive" and "reproductive" labor that feminists and other scholars have interrogated. Global food production in early capitalism and the function of the West Indies in shaping these material conditions for tastes are evident in the case presented here.

The Material Conditioning of Taste

Ethnographers have long paid attention to the materialism and symbolism in the anthropology of food and eating. One of the most influential ideas is Sidney Mintz's argument about "tasting food and tasting freedom." I draw on this analogy to analyze the role of food in Rastafari repatriation as it relates to generating income that supports the desire for an ital lifestyle characterized by freedom and autonomy. As Mintz has articulated, early capitalism depended on forced labor on the plantations of the Americas.[6] Sugar production, for instance, entailed specialized knowledge at each stage from Caribbean fields to European tables: when to cut the sugar cane, how best to transport it to the factory, how long to boil and refine it in producing gradients of sugar, and so on. According to Mintz, taste in its literal sense had to be highly refined both in commercial production and in the domestic preparation of food for the master class and the enslaved class.

Food presented a medium through which human abilities, capacities, rights, and privileges associated with full-human status (denied to enslaved populations) were drawn on and experienced. The individuality—of tastes and talents—with the oppressive conditions under which people struggled to survive is evident in foodways or the societal context in which food is sourced, cooked, distributed, and eaten. As Mintz summarizes, "The ability to render judgments of food, to develop comparisons, to calibrate differences in taste— and to be prevented from doing so—help to suggest that something of the taste of freedom was around before freedom itself was."[7] Creating a cuisine, or what became "typical" foods in the Caribbean and in particular islands and territories, was shaped by material conditions, as I noted at Pauletta's and Faith's restaurants. Such complex sets of knowledge necessary in cooking were developed by subordinated groups who were literally denied freedom. Effectively, "tasting food" was dependent on hierarchies of class and race engrained in modern, global food production. And as Rachel Slocum and Arun Saldanha point out, the racialization of food persists in contemporary globalization.[8] Disparities in production of and access to nutritious food are a glaring way for bodies to be viscerally categorized as "healthy" or "unhealthy" and for sensory expressions of food as "smelly" or "ethnic" to be coded in the Global North.

In the case of Rastafari repatriates in Ethiopia, subaltern acts of collective and personal reinvention are evidenced in the actual move to Ethiopia and — the focus of this chapter — in the continuity and change of Caribbean foodways in Shashamane. With a population of approximately 100 million, Ethiopia has a high degree of food insecurity, including undernutrition exacerbated by climate change. With an agriculture-based economy expanding into manufacturing and services, food sources are also tenuous for Rastafari. Like many poor Ethiopian women, when money was severely low, second-generation Ethiopian Rastafari women cooked injera to sell. Although this item generated very little income, there were low cost and labor inputs. All these factors were present in the interactions I had with residents as they sought to become involved in microentrepreneurial activities that straddled the informal and formal economies in Ethiopia. In addition to Faith's and Pauletta's restaurants, I encountered two family-owned bakeries, one family ital food operation producing dried fruits and juices, a juice beit, two small combination dry goods shops and meghib beitoch, three exclusively dry goods shops, three Rastafari women who independently sold baked goods, one Rastafari male migrant who made wine for sale, two sizable Rastafari-owned hotels (one was later sold), and a soya factory.[9]

Rastafari, Repatriation, and Ital Living

Rastafari emerged in Jamaica with the 1930 coronation of Ras Tefari Mekonnen as His Imperial Majesty Emperor Haile Selassie I, King of Kings and Lion of Judah. As an anticolonial movement for Black empowerment in British colonial Jamaica, Rastafari saw themselves in the image of this Ethiopian emperor, rejecting racist Eurocentric ideology and instead centering Africa as the locus of civilization.

For Rastafari adherents, Ethiopia and Africa are the origin of humankind as well as a divine and sacred place known as the promised land. Personified in His Majesty, "Rastafarians," or "Rastafari," in Jamaica took this name, actively reimagining themselves. Rastafari in Shashamane today identify as "Ethiopians."[10] Pauletta and Faith self-identified as Black women, Faith's ethnically mixed African and Indian family in Trinidad and Tobago notwithstanding.

In Ethiopia, although the name "Jamaica Safar" reflects the greater number of Rastafari who moved from Jamaica, Rastafari from the English-speaking and French-speaking Caribbean, North America, and Europe "returned" to the symbolic homeland of Ethiopia over the past six decades with the hope of achieving freedom and spiritual and material well-being. Although the latter has not been achieved by the community generally, in their efforts to realize freedom, food has enabled Rastafari to maintain a distinct cultural identity by reproducing mores and habits, evident in foodways, and to integrate into the Jamaica Safar.

This neighborhood is composed of Rastafari residents from the four organizations of the Ethiopian World Federation, the Twelve Tribes, the Theocratic Order of Nyahbinghi, and the Ethiopia Africa Black International Congress, or Bobo Ashanti. There are also local Ethiopian residents of Oromo, Gurage, Amhara, Tigray, and Wollaita ethnicities, among others, and multicultural Ethiopian-born children.[11] This repatriation was motivated by the granting of five *gashas* (200 hectares) to "black people of the world" in the 1950s by His Imperial Majesty Emperor Haile Selassie I. The land was given in appreciation for their opposition to the Italian occupation of Ethiopia from 1935 to 1941.[12] Since the 1970s especially, there have been Rastafari-Ethiopian intermarriages and childbearing relationships showing continued Rastafari residence in Ethiopia despite political coups d'état in 1974 and 1991 as well as the leadership change in 2018 to Abiy Ahmed as prime minister.[13] Anecdotal estimates of the Rastafari population in Shashamane range from 200 to 1,000.

Moving or repatriating to Ethiopia entailed a spiritual, physical, and financial resolve to building lives on this land. A healthy, natural, vital, or ital (in Rastafari speech) lifestyle realizes this adherence to uplifting the spirit and body and stabilizing livelihoods through different degrees of ital living. As literature and cultural studies scholar Annika McPherson explains, "Livity has various descriptions, ranging from 'a code of relationships with God, nature, and society' to a consciousness or 'living according to the strict principles of Rastafari.'"[14] Religious studies scholar Ennis Edmonds observes that "ital living is . . . a commitment to using things in their natural or organic states. . . . The Rastafarian ideal proscribes the use of synthetic materials and chemically treated foods. I say 'ideal,' because the economic reality of life for most Rastas makes strict ital living difficult, if not impossible. . . . Rastas believe that the entire universe is organically related and that the key to health, both physical and social, is to live in accordance with organic principles."[15]

Rastafari embody ital living in different ways. Some adhere to the moral emphasis on living well with people and doing "good works" or behaving in a morally upright manner to ensure future salvation. They prioritize less eating foods grown organically or dietary prohibitions other than avoiding pork, which is followed by all Rastafari. Some repatriates do espouse a strict vegetarian or vegan diet and refrain from seafood, meat, salt, and dairy. Nyahbinghi and Boboshanti Rastafari, for example, often adhere to the biblical food taboos in Leviticus 11 and Deuteronomy 14, while Twelve Tribes Rastafari avoid pork and shellfish. In Mary Douglas's analysis of Judeo-Christian dietary prohibitions, she argued that taboos that distinguish between "pure" and "impure" animals and those "good to eat," to quote Marvin Harris, reflect the social order, inclusive of moral systems and the relationship between humanity and the divine. For Rastafari who adhere to such taboos, keeping the body "clean" reinforces a greater sense of goodness and proximity to divinity. These examples emphasize "food, dietary practices, and environmental as well as spiritual consciousness [that] thus form an entity."[16]

Bonacci notes that the differences in dietary proscriptions contribute to the division between Nyahbinghi and Twelve Tribes Rastafari in Shashamane, pointing to the diversity in Rastafari practice as well as microconflicts within the Rastafari community. Disagreements over homogenizing multiple nationalities into one, that of Jamaican, are subsumed when locals refer to Caribbean food, whether made by Rastafari from Trinidad and Tobago or from Jamaica, as "Jamaican." This usage introduces multiethnic local Ethiopians to new foods and fosters an overarching Caribbean identity in this destination.

One core item in all Rastafari diets is ganja (cannabis), or the "holy herb," as Rastafari say, which is consumed in teas or more commonly smoked for its medicinal and religious properties. As historian Monique Bedasse states, such consumption habits are "in keeping with their [Rastafari] pursuit of a natural lifestyle that depends on nature's bounty and translates into an 'ital' diet, which consists of organic, unprocessed foods and usually the omission of salt in cooking." Dietary practices and observances also differ among Rastafari.[17] Among the second generation, ganja is added to items such as baked goods for personal eating. This behavior is more in keeping with production and consumption habits in the Global North, as ganja becomes increasingly decriminalized and legalized outside of Ethiopia.

Changing Food Tastes

The sale of cooked food is one important source of cash earnings for repatriates with constrained income-generating opportunities. Rastafari run mostly small food houses, such as Pauletta's and Faith's, selling savory and sweet foodstuff that is easy to eat on the go and on the street, such as small flour-based pies (fried or baked) filled with vegetables, soya, or beef. Popular items also include bread, coconut drops, dried fruit, and luxuries such as cake or ice cream.[18] Whether a sizable businesses such as a hotel or factory or a small-scale food beit, such ventures are funded by repatriates' savings and informal loans from other Rastafari.

Understanding how food is commodified and integral for survival and cultural reproduction is critical in the Jamaica Safar, though not special to this locale. "Street food" is common across Ethiopia and the Global South, which equates to "cheap food." In urban Ethiopia, this encompasses items such as roasted corn, *dabo colo* (bite-sized bits of roasted flour), lentil *sambusas* (similar to Indian samosas), and now French fries. Compared to fashionable street food in cities of the Global North, food sold on the roads of Shashamane and other cities in Ethiopia is made for the poor, reinforcing how cooking and food consumption, even on a small scale, are racialized and classed.

The precarity of work across formal and informal sectors generally, and especially for Rastafari in Shashamane, is a reality for repatriated women and men, with many households generating income from multiple sources. Shopkeeping or selling dry goods of locally manufactured or packaged foods is a common form of self-employment for both Rastafari and local Ethiopians. At a basic level, it mitigates hunger, provided there are goods in the shop. As 18 percent of youth were unemployed in urban Ethiopia in 2011 and about 50 percent of youth were underemployed, working in the family food beit can be a source of financial security. Pauletta's and Faith's children, some of whom are university graduates but temporarily unemployed or underemployed, can work in the family food beit, for example.[19]

Pauletta's food beit originated as a one-room shop, or souk, with concrete walls at the front of her family's yard. Built into the zinc fence, the shop window allowed customers to buy cooked food, bringing their own takeaway bowls. By 2008, a small seating area with two or three colorful plastic tables and chairs had been added. Local beers and wines were added to the menu, and it became a popular *limin*, or socializing, spot for young people, including those who were Rastafari and non-Rastafari, born in Ethiopia or abroad.

Expanding from the shop was a successful livelihood strategy for Pauletta and her family. Not all Rastafari owners of dry goods shops aim to get into this work, but it provides a steady income, given the macroeconomic factors previously noted. When combined with the much-needed remittances of money and goods from Rastafari abroad, occasional gifts from visitors, and the sale of items such as clothing (often with iconographic images of the Lion of Judah, Bob Marley, or red, gold, and green colors) or toiletries (perfumes), the earnings from the shop stretch further. Though Pauletta's restaurant was located off the main road heading south into Shashamane's town center, within a short walking distance of public transportation, Faith's food beit was farther into the neighborhood along an unpaved road. By 2013, when I returned to Shashamane while working in the neighboring city of Hawassa, Faith had moved residence closer to the main road, and her food beit had become more popular. Location was likely one reason for this increased clientele, because her menu had remained the same. Faith had added a few chairs and tables to the courtyard, and it became another limin spot for Rastafari.[20]

The popularity of Pauletta's food beit with local customers indicates changing food tastes in Shashamane. Typical Jamaican meals cooked with local spices have gradually become familiar to local Ethiopians in Shashamane. With fried fish and beef common in Ethiopia and the increasing popularity of rice (locally grown and imported from India), Caribbean additions of *escovitch* fish or turmeric-based curry powder present new flavor combinations and hybrid dishes (fig. 11.1). For instance, a local Ethiopian master's student writing on Rastafari settlement in Shashamane reflected on his surprise when he realized that he was eating a very tasty meal consisting of oxtail that would be unusual in his family.[21] Although oxtail and cow foot used to be discarded by local Ethiopians, now these parts are sold by butchers, demonstrating the cultural and economic impact of Caribbean culinary habits in Shashamane. "Strange" Caribbean foods, from the perspective of local Ethiopians, are transformed into everyday foods. Most of the customers at Pauletta's restaurant were, in fact, local Ethiopians who lived and worked in the surrounding area. Local Ethiopians buy Rastafari-made foods, fruit juices (of mango, small plum, star apple, orange, clementine, sorrel or hibiscus, soursop, pineapple, and peanut), and homemade wines for personal consumption. These are all made with locally grown and available items familiar to Rastafari from tropical climates.

Analysis and Discussion

Taste, affordability, and performance all coalesce in eating habits in the family food beit. As Pierre Bourdieu's seminal work argues, class is a factor when considering the enactment and embodiment of taste.[22] In this ethnographic case, it is difficult to distinguish class in Shashamane among the Rastafari community.

FIGURE 11.1. *Escovitch* fish with rice and peas, lime, and avocado prepared and served at a food beit in Shashamane. Photo by Tamara Brathwaite.

Repatriates are excluded from privately owning or leasing property in Ethiopia unless they qualify for an investor license, which requires proof of large sums of foreign currency. Waged work is uncertain and sporadic for most repatriates. Although diet is a basic indicator of class, the performative aspect of class through food tastes that Bourdieu identified is not apparent in the same way.

An intergenerational analysis is useful. Food tastes among the mostly internationally immobile second generation in the Jamaica Safar have been cultivated not only for sustenance but also through programs on cable television, gifts from visitors, and remittances of goods. "As Bourdieu points out, these class tastes are bound together into systems, with internal logic and structure, by sentiments and dispositions rooted in childhood and a lifetime of learning."[23] In the 1970s–'90s when Richard Wilk did fieldwork in urban and rural Belize, he found that there was "no consensus" on "highbrow" versus "lowbrow" food.[24] While this finding is similar for diasporic Caribbean Rastafari in Shashamane, there are luxury food items that the average resident of Shashamane would not be able to afford. Ice cream is one, and there are ritual-associated expensive dishes, such as doro wat, which can be prepared only by families who can afford the ingredients and the cooking equipment (whether charcoal, electric, gas, or wood). For example, even in Rastafari households of modest means, on certain occasions such as birthdays, families who receive remitted funds or are financially better off in the long term or short term will serve cake or ice cream. The food eaten in the household and the food beit, as well as the purchasing power of Rastafari families, serves to distinguish status within the Rastafari community. As noted, the food eaten indicates intergenerational changes in taste and current youth expectations. In the simple example of serving ice cream to guests at a birthday party, the host needs to have access to a freezer and a regular supply of electricity or ice for it to remain frozen, which also points to status.

Extending this discussion of taste in terms of social structure and the individual and intra-Caribbean cooking practices and foods, the differences between Faith's beef pies and another Rastafari sister's beef patties in taste, texture, and appearance can indicate both national and personal differences within Caribbean culinary traditions.[25] Among Black women childminders in well-off households in Brooklyn, New York, sociologist Tamara Mose Brown suggests that cooking West Indian food and cultivating certain eating habits bonds workers from different Caribbean countries together. Women from Grenada, Trinidad and Tobago, and Guyana with slightly different tastes and food preparation techniques cultivate a Caribbean identity, as evidenced when a childminder remarks, "We are West Indian and eat with our hands."[26]

The adjustments that cooks make to the spices and ingredients they use in times of scarcity evidence their local and trans-local networks, abilities to source items, and finances. For instance, the curry-powder-and-pimento spice made in the English-speaking Caribbean and in Diaspora businesses in the Global North is brought to Ethiopia by visitors and internationally mobile repatriates. When it is unavailable or unable to be brought, cooks in Shashamane use turmeric bought in Addis Ababa, the Ethiopian capital. Decades earlier, during the Derg government between 1974 and 1991, sugar was a scarce commodity and repatriates used their local networks, money, personal items, and bargaining skills to acquire it, according to Rastafari. This combination of material conditions, social circumstances, and individual attributes continues to be important to Rastafari survival and ital living in Ethiopia. Examining who cooks in the food beit and in the home and how this work relates to a sexual division of labor is another significant aspect of this discussion.

Who Cooks?

Small-scale agriculture and the sale of food have historically been a source of income generation in the colonial West Indies for poor and working-class families. The usually Black Caribbean woman seller of cooked street food and produce from the garden—known as a higgler or marketeer—has traditionally been a mobile income generator in households and grows and sells produce to support her family. This dual role of women in productive and reproductive labor, as well as women's multiple roles, can be analyzed in terms of the historical conditions of the modern, protocapitalist Caribbean plantation. Starting in the sixteenth century, women were brought to and arrived in the colonial Caribbean specifically for their labor in plantation production and were encouraged to reproduce this labor source.[27]

Anthropologist Christine Ho aptly delineates the convergence of capitalism and patriarchy, whereby "the dual roles performed by Caribbean women for centuries as workers and as mothers render fuzzy the Western feminist distinction between the public world of work and the private domain of the home."[28] These gender relations are situated in an unequal distinction, positioning women's reproductive and domestic labor in the home as less valuable than men's "productive" labor in public—even while women do both. One such case of "fuzziness" is the cooking such laborers do both for household eating and for sale. Cooks were and still are women in Caribbean insular and diasporic households. Postcolonial Caribbean gender roles and normative expectations reproduced in the diasporic Caribbean are observable in Shashamane among first- and second-generation Rastafari. In Twelve Tribes Rastafari households in Shashamane, this pattern differs: both men and women in Rastafari and Rastafari–local Ethiopian homes cook for daily family consumption to maintain an ital diet. In contrast, a gendered division of labor is adhered to in Boboshanti and Nyahbinghi homes.

"What constitutes work is problematic partly because the income-earning activities of working-class women do not lend themselves easily to measurement and partly because they perform a wide range of economic activities."[29] This nexus is captured in Pauletta's and Faith's food beitoch. The commodification of cooking food for sale parallels the blurred roles and categorical distinctions of "productive" and "unproductive" labor that were institutionalized in industrial capitalism and the plantation economy. The division of productive and reproductive labor that conceptualizes gendered work in capitalist economies is inadequate to theorize the experiences of everyday Caribbean women. I use the distinction, however, to draw attention to persistent material connotations of lower wages and social status for women as a group.

While this gendered distinction between productive and reproductive work persists in Rastafari yards and Rastafari–local Ethiopian households, women also engage in more regular waged labor outside the yard than men, taking on the breadwinner role that is associated with a patriarchal-derived ideal of masculinity. A class analysis is critical, because productive and reproductive work overlap in poor households. As well as doing domestic work, more women are involved in small-scale food selling than men. Among the thirteen independent, small-scale businesses that I have listed, men, singly and jointly with their women partners, ran or owned the modest juice beitoch, a bakery, the dry goods shops, the soya factory, and the hotel, and they also make wine.[30] Cooking food to sell was done by women only, except in the two bakeries, where both men and women contributed their labor to baking and selling the items. These examples indicate patterns of work in the food sector among Rastafari migrants in which women cook food and sell small items and men cook for the family in the home, particularly among those of the Twelve Tribes.

Planting and harvesting for family consumption goes hand in hand with cooking and eating habits. The ability to grow small crops such as potatoes, cabbages, and mangoes facilitates an ital lifestyle, but space is needed. Since there is no communal or neighborhood small garden, for Rastafari who live in one room or a communal yard with shared lavatory facilities and do not have the space for kitchen gardens, the lack of space to grow subsistence crops inhibits mitigating against hunger in the way persons with bigger yards are able to. Combined with an increased dependence on the marketplace for staple goods that require cash to purchase, these social and spatial factors increase the vulnerability of Rastafari with modest and irregular incomes to macroeconomic and social changes.[31]

In patriarchal societies, cooking is a form of women's oppression that cannot be reductively analyzed either in Caribbean Rastafari households in Ethiopia or in the English-speaking Caribbean with a history of women's and men's labor exploitation. In Ethiopia, "women and less educated individuals are disproportionally more likely to be employed in the informal sector," and in 2011 "41 percent of employed women were employed in the informal sector," thereby increasing their economic and social vulnerability.[32]

In the case of women childcare workers from the English-speaking Caribbean in New York, Mose Brown argues that having knowledge of typical West Indian foods and the ability to feed children adequately and nutritiously are measures of parenting that West Indian women use to challenge their subordination in mainly well-off, white employers' households. Preparing Caribbean foods that young white American children in their care prefer to eat also subverts the inequality of the employer-employee relationship. As Mose Brown argues, "Providers made food preparation a measure of mothering ability against which their employers were found wanting, as well as a means of asserting control within the employers' household."[33]

This criterion of "real" Caribbean womanhood and wifehood is reproduced in the Jamaica Safar, as a conversation among second-generation girls indicates, taken from my field notes. The inability of local Ethiopian women to adequately care for and feed their repatriated Rastafari husbands emerged in the remarks that local Ethiopian women "can't cook the food that the men like, they don't know how to keep the house clean or how to keep their man looking good."[34] I was skeptical that this adversity affected every man in this type of relationship, and I brought up two Ethiopian wives who cook popular Jamaican foods well. The young women responded that these two women were exceptions to the rule. For the multicultural second generation, food is an avenue of cultural reproduction and culture change in urban Ethiopia.

Relatedly, domestic ability is one basis for cultural comparison between local Ethiopian and Rastafari women, in which Rastafari women are presented as exhibiting superior qualities to local Ethiopian women. While the contrasting aspects of self-identity emerged forcefully in this conversation, there were other everyday examples in which Rastafari behaviors and beliefs were presented as superior to those of local Ethiopians. Rastafari women's judgments of local Ethiopian women's morality and personal hygiene were likewise tied to cooking skills, unpaid domestic work (as above, where it was framed as a duty for a woman to keep her house clean and organized), and all-around mothering and wifely abilities. These are attitudes that reinforce the gendered expectations that women be mothers and wives who prioritize reproductive work, while the reality is that women do income-generating work that is indispensable to family sustenance.

Reinforcing the interconnection of moral systems with symbolic and material dimensions, food has the potential to distinguish and unify individuals and groups. This connection is apparent in the cooking and eating of foods among Rastafari and between Rastafari and local Ethiopians in the Jamaica Safar. For instance, in local Ethiopian–Twelve Tribes Rastafari intercultural households, diet is usually a mixture of popular Ethiopian and Caribbean meals and those particular to an ethnic group. For example, *kitfo*, or mostly raw meat, is typical of the Gurage ethnic group, as are beans for the Wollaita. While the first is unfamiliar to Rastafari, who view it as unclean and do not prepare it, the second is a popular ingredient. Food not only reflects identity but is integral to the active making of such categories through everyday behaviors. Food preparation and eating reinforce a cultural identity for Rastafari, reflect national Jamaican orientation, and indicate local Ethiopian wives' integration into the Rastafari community.

Based on interviews with West Indian women married to Ghanaian men, Obiagele Lake suggests that one factor in the social integration of West Indian wives in Ghana was the women's ability to cook local foods.[35] Similarly in Shashamane, Rastafari husbands and partners teach local wives to cook typical Jamaican meals with a meat or ital option of stewed beef or peas to accompany rice. Food is a means through which Rastafari assert cultural differences from local Ethiopians (a multiethnic group) and create new foods by mixing cuisines and ingredients. As Mintz and Christine DuBois succinctly emphasize, "Like all culturally defined material substances used in the creation and maintenance of social relationships, food serves both to solidify group membership and to set groups apart."[36] Food creates community by reinforcing cultural contrast and exchange through the creation of new foodways.

Concluding Remarks

This ethnographically based discussion centered the food cultures of Caribbean Rastafari migrants and the multicultural second generation to extend the anthropology of food and eating. In migrating or repatriating to the symbolic home of Ethiopia, Rastafari from the Caribbean have embodied freedom in its spiritual sense. Situated within Caribbean modernity, this example demonstrates how cooking and eating facilitate cultural reproduction as well as individuality within the particular context of Rastafari dietary habits. The individualism and collectivism cultivated in modern plantation production in the Caribbean are reflected in the Rastafari worldview and the culinary practices of first- and second-generation Rastafari in Ethiopia. Food is a critical component of fulfilling an ital, or healthy, lifestyle, which is circumscribed by moral and dietary guidelines. While food is fundamental to bodily survival, selling cooked and preserved food is also a crucial source of income, and is done mostly by women, as seen in the examples of Pauletta's and Faith's food beitoch.

Rastafari women's roles in cooking and eating, food production, and consumption as rooted in colonial gender systems in the Caribbean demonstrate the inadequacy of a distinction between productive and reproductive labor, even while women structurally are disadvantaged by this elitist distinction. This line of argument is recognized in Caribbean gender ideologies.[37] Women have historically done both types of work and continue to, as evidenced by the examples from a diasporic multicultural Caribbean community in Ethiopia. From this analytical grounding, the small number of microlevel cases in this essay provides insights into the contemporary implications of global food systems as these intersect with changing culturally specific practices in a migration setting.

In facilitating ital living by cooking food for household members and to sell to local Ethiopian and Rastafari customers, Rastafari repatriates express varied tastes. In using their skills and choosing ingredients such as spices to create new tastes for multicultural residents, cooks in the Jamaica Safar express human inclinations and draw on techniques of preparation, consumption habits, and socialized tastes, all of which elucidate the interconnections of historical conditions and contemporary change. These changing tastes underscore how tasting food and tasting freedom are intertwined, to quote Mintz. The individuality—of tastes and talents—situated in the precarious livelihoods of Rastafari repatriates in Ethiopia today is evident in foodways or the societal contexts in which food is sourced, cooked, distributed, and eaten. The vulnerability of the poor to food insecurity, especially in the Global South, presents common conditions confronted by all peoples in Ethiopia and specific habits developed in one migrant-local setting.

For Rastafari women, cooking food presents an opportunity for autonomy as well as maintenance of domestic labor based on Caribbean ideals of womanhood and motherhood in this diasporic setting. Cooks maintain a cultural identity as Rastafari as well as a pan-Caribbean identity, thereby distinguishing themselves from local Ethiopians. Food is also important in building intercultural community ties between Rastafari of various nationalities and multiethnic local Ethiopians. The unique circumstances through which this multicultural neighborhood has developed, as well as the features it shares with other migration locales, help us consider how foodways are constantly being shaped by multiple mobile and sedentary actors.

NOTES

1. Rastafari refer to each other as "Brother" and "Sister" to indicate relationships of fictive kinship. Out of respect, I have maintained this use when I introduce residents. The names used in this chapter are pseudonyms.

2. Such dishes included sweet and savory pastries such as beef patties and jam tarts. Meals of white rice, vegetables, beef, and lentils were also staples. Faith and her two grown children, a son and daughter, prepared an expanded menu of curried beef and ital potato and chickpeas with roti (South Asian–style flour-based bread) as well.

3. A literal translation of "meghib beitoch" from Amharic to English would be "food houses."

4. Bonacci, *Exodus!*, 378.

5. Cook, "Geographies of Food"; Goody and Goody, "Food and Identities"; Johnston and Longhurst, "Mixed Feelings"; Marte, "Dominican Migrant Cooking"; Mose Brown, *Raising Brooklyn*; Parasecoli, "Food, Identity."

6. Mintz, *Tasting Food, Tasting Freedom*, 37.

7. Mintz, *Tasting Food, Tasting Freedom*, 37.

8. Slocum and Saldanha, *Geographies of Race*.

9. Many of these income-generating activities were not licensed with the local district or regional authority, although the better-established food beitoch run by Faith and Pauletta were registered, as were the hotels and factory.

10. To adhere to this emic Rastafari meaning, I use "local Ethiopian" to refer to persons who were born in Ethiopia, whose parents and immediate ancestors were all born in a territory of Ethiopia, and who have multiple generations in the home speaking a language native to Ethiopia. This could include, e.g., Afan Oromo and not only Amharic, which is widely spoken. Although the Ethiopian-born children of repatriates speak Amharic fluently, their parents learned Amharic in Ethiopia, and parent-child communication is primarily in English and in Caribbean patois. Children with one local Ethiopian parent usually speak both patois and at least one local language, such as Amharic, Afan Oromo, Wollaita, or Tigrinya, to name a few.

11. Chevannes, *Rastafari*, 142.

12. Bonacci, *Exodus!*, 270–71.

13. This change was particularly noteworthy as Ahmed is ethnically Oromo, a group that has historically been materially dispossessed and discursively juxtaposed as the antithesis of the civilized northern Abyssinian ethnic groups of Amhara and, more recently, Tigray.

14. McPherson, "'De fuud dem produus,'" 287; Chevannes, *Rastafari*, 169; Edmonds, *Rastafari*, 60.

15. Edmonds, *Rastafari*, 60.

16. McPherson, "'De fuud dem produus,'" 290.

17. Bedasse, *Jah Kingdom*, 30.

18. The pies can be filled with vegetables, such as cabbage and carrots, which are inexpensive, or minced beef, which is more costly. Coconut drops are baked with flour and flavored with coconut in a small, dense circular shape.

19. Broussard and Tekleselassie, "Youth Employment."

20. Since then, Faith has left Shashamane for family and financial reasons.

21. Soroto, "Settlement and Integration."

22. Bourdieu, *Distinction*.

23. Bourdieu; Wilk, "'Real Belizean Food,'" 251.

24. Wilk, "'Real Belizean Food,'" 252.

25. A beef pie in Trinidad and Tobago tends to be smaller and with less yellow coloring than a beef patty in Jamaica, which is bigger, indicating differences between similar Caribbean foods.

26. Mose Brown, *Raising Brooklyn*, 99.

27. Reddock (*Women, Labour and Politics*), Peake and Trotz (*Gender, Ethnicity and Place*), and Safa (*Myth of the Male*) develop this line of argument with reference to the English- and Spanish-speaking Caribbean. The labor of Indigenous women was similarly hyperexploited as that of enslaved and indentured women workers who arrived in the West Indian colonies.

28. Ho, "Caribbean Transnationalism," 39.

29. Ho, 39.

30. Shopkeeping was done by women, men, and children of both genders, including at Sister Pauletta's shop attached to the family food beit. In line with microentrepreneurial activities, family members who were able and skilled all worked in these modest family businesses. Specifically, women, men, and older children worked at the front of the shop selling. Men or women—whoever spoke Amharic more fluently—ordered and bought stock for the shop or ingredients for cooking and liaised with local officials regarding taxes and permits.

31. John Mazzeo ("La Viché," 115–29) notes that this is a similar constraining factor in maintaining a subsistence supply of food in households, although in rural Haiti.

32. Broussard and Tekleselassie, "Youth Employment."

33. Mose Brown, *Raising Brooklyn*, 81.

34. Field notes, July 15, 2008.

35. Lake, "Toward a Pan African," 29.

36. Mintz and DuBois, "Anthropology," 109.

37. For an elaboration of this point, see Barrow, *Family in the Caribbean*; Massiah, *Women as Heads*; Momsen, *Women and Change*; Rajack-Talley, *Poverty Is a Person*; and Safa, *Myth of the Male*.

WORKS CITED

Barrow, Christine. *Family in the Caribbean: Themes and Perspectives*. Kingston, Jamaica: Ian Randle, 1996.

Bedasse, Monique A. *Jah Kingdom: Rastafarians, Tanzania and Pan-Africanism in the Age of Decolonization*. Chapel Hill: University of North Carolina Press, 2017.

Bonacci, Giulia. *Exodus! Heirs and Pioneers, Rastafari Return to Ethiopia*. Translated by Antoinette Tidjani Alou. Kingston, Jamaica: University of the West Indies Press, 2015.

Bourdieu, Pierre. *Distinction: A Social Critique of the Judgement of Taste*. Cambridge, MA: Harvard University Press, 1984.

Broussard, Nzinga H., and Tsegay Gebrekidan Tekleselassie. "Youth Employment: Ethiopia Country Study." Working Paper. International Growth Centre, April 2012.

Chevannes, Barry. *Rastafari: Roots and Ideology*. Syracuse, NY: Syracuse University Press, 1994.

Cook, Ian. "Geographies of Food—Mixing." *Progress in Human Geography* 32, no. 6 (2008): 821–33.

Douglas, Mary. *Purity and Danger: An Analysis of Concepts of Pollution and Taboo*. New York: Praeger, 1966.

Edmonds, Ennis. *Rastafari: From Outcasts to Culture Bearers*. Oxford: Oxford University Press, 2003.

Goody, Jack, and Esther Goody. "Food and Identities: Changing Patterns of Consumption in Ghana." *Cambridge Journal of Anthropology* 18, no. 3 (1995): 1–14.

Ho, Christine G. T. "Caribbean Transnationalism as a Gendered Process." *Latin American Perspectives* 26, no. 5 (September 1999): 34–54.

Johnston, Luke, and Robyn Longhurst. "Mixed Feelings: Women's Experiences of Food, Eating and Home in Hamilton, Aotearoa New Zealand." *Hagar: Studies in Culture, Polity and Identity* 11, no. 1 (2013): 121–13.

Katzin, Margaret Fisher. "The Jamaican Country Higgler." In *Work and Family Life: West Indian Perspectives*, edited by Lambros Comitas and David Lowenthal, 3–26. New York: Anchor Press/Doubleday, 1973.

Koç, Mustafa, Jennifer Sumner, and Anthony Winson, eds. *Critical Perspectives in Food Studies*. North York, ON: Oxford University Press, 2017.

Lake, Obiagele. "Toward a Pan African Identity: Diaspora African Repatriates in Ghana." *Anthropological Quarterly* 68, no. 1 (January 1995): 21–36.

MacLeod, Erin. *Visions of Zion: Ethiopians and Rastafari in the Search for the Promised Land*. New York: New York University Press, 2014.

Marte, Lidia. "Dominican Migrant Cooking: Food Struggles, Gendered Labor, and Memory-Work in NYC." *Food and Foodways* 20, no. 3–4 (2012): 279–306.

Massiah, Joceylin. *Women as Heads of Households in the Caribbean: Family Structure and Feminine Status*. Paris: UNESCO, 1983.

Mazzeo, John. "La Viché: Haiti's Vulnerability to the Global Food Crisis." In "The Global Food Crisis: New Insights into an Age-Old Problem," edited by David Allen Himmelgreen and Satish Kedia, special issue. *Annals of Anthropological Practice* 32, no. 1 (2009): 115–29.

McPherson, Annika. "'De fuud dem produus me naa go iit it!': Rastafarian Culinary Identity." In *Caribbean Food Cultures: Representations and Performances of Eating, Drinking and Consumption*, edited by Wiebke Beushausen, Anne Brüske, Ana-Sofia Commichau, Patrick Helber, and Sinah Kloß, 279–98. Bielefeld, Germany: Transcript Verlag, 2014.

Mintz, Sidney W. *Tasting Food, Tasting Freedom: Excursions into Eating, Culture and the Past*. Boston: Beacon, 1996.

Mintz, Sidney W., and Christine DuBois. "The Anthropology of Food and Eating." *Annual Review of Anthropology* 31 (2002): 99–119.

Momsen, Janet. *Women and Change in the Caribbean: A Pan-Caribbean Perspective*. Kingston, Jamaica: Ian Randle, 1993.

Mose Brown, Tamara. *Raising Brooklyn: Nannies, Childcare and Caribbeans Creating Community*. New York: New York University Press, 2011.

Parasecoli, Fabio. "Food, Identity, and Cultural Reproduction in Immigrant Communities." *Social Research* 81, no. 2 (2014): 415–39.

Peake, Linda, and Alissa D. Trotz. *Gender, Ethnicity and Place: Women and Identity in Guyana*. London: Routledge, 1999.

Rajack-Talley, Theresa Ann. *Poverty Is a Person: Human Agency, Women and Caribbean Households*. Kingston, Jamaica: Ian Randle, 2016.

Reddock, Rhoda. *Women, Labour and Politics in Trinidad and Tobago: A History*. London: Zed Books, 1994.

Safa, Helen. *The Myth of the Male Breadwinner: Women and Industrialization in the Caribbean*. Boulder, CO: Westview, 1995.

Slocum, Rachel, and Arun Saldanha, eds. *Geographies of Race and Food: Fields, Bodies, Markets*. London: Routledge, 2013.

Soroto, Solomon. "Settlement and Integration of 'Rastafarians' in Shashemene, Oromia Region Ethiopia." Master's thesis, Addis Ababa University, 2008.

Wilk, Richard. "'Real Belizean Food': Building Local Identity in the Transnational Caribbean." *American Anthropologist* 101, no. 2 (June 1999): 244–55.

World Food Programme. "Climate Risk and Food Security in Ethiopia: Analysis of Climate Impacts on Food Security and Livelihoods." Accessed August 10, 2019. https://documents.wfp.org/stellent/groups/public/documents/newsroom/wfp269379.pdf.

CONCLUSION

Exercising Agency, Navigating Marginalization, and Maintaining Silent Control in Global Food Systems

THERESA RAJACK-TALLEY, LATRICA E. BEST, AND PRISCILLA McCUTCHEON

WRITTEN MOSTLY BY BLACK WOMEN of the African Diaspora, the chapters in this book offer a comprehensive picture of how women navigate under the persistent gazes of colonial, patriarchal, and racial histories and conditions. The authors in this edited work collectively agree that women's desire to control their own destiny within patriarchal and racialized food production and distribution systems is linked to the social responsibility of feeding families and communities. Within these chapters, the authors uncover the many colorful and challenging roles women play within global food systems, at the kitchen table and beyond. The themes in the three sections of the book collectively exhibit that while women have been assigned "kitchen table" roles throughout history, this social positioning creates a double-edged sword of disempowerment and empowerment. As Shelene

Gomes demonstrates in chapter 11, the function of cooking can be a form of women's oppression, with the kitchen table as a symbol of domestication. Women's reproductive occupation is isolating from power, decision-making, and resources in their private and public spheres. However, this book illustrates how women use the kitchen, food preparation, and food production as sites to negotiate the subjugation, marginalization, and poverty of themselves and their families. Further, these chapters reveal how women silently maintain elements of power, freedom, and self-sufficiency. Innately, women strive for food justice and sustainable food production in ways that impact households, communities, and society at large.

Resilient, Resistant, Transformative, and Hopeful

Women's kitchen table responsibilities spill over into decisions regarding what to grow and the need for women to engage in food production and educate others on agricultural practices that are environmentally sustainable and safe. The collective roles that women play require the deployment of their agency in ways that integrate, according to Gloria Sanders McCutcheon (chapter 3), the economic viability of their households and environmental sustainability of their farms, with the social values and responsibilities of families and communities. According to Eveline M. F. W. Sawadogo/Compaoré and Sakiko Shiratori (chapter 2), determining what meal to prepare, how to prepare it, whom to feed, and when creates opportunities for women to make major decisions about family diets, consumption patterns, hunger, health, nutrition, and well-being. Oftentimes kitchen table responsibilities can either dictate women's needs to earn additional household incomes or reduce the need for monetary purchases.

The research and voices of the women in this book help us with the micro- and macrogendered understandings of many under-studied themes and levels of analyses of global food systems. Latrica E. Best (chapter 9) refers to the micro-macro intersectionality in the way women are connected to food and health by interrogating how researchers situate the lives of Black women in their health research. Though many chapters employ an intersectional lens in analyzing various aspects of global food systems, the richness of intersectional perspectives is in its use of narrative methods that amplify the stories and voices of researchers. The telling of stories was strongly encouraged, including those of the authors. According to Claudia J. Ford (chapter 7), stories are forms of investigation, inquiry, and analysis, a way to counteract historical mechanisms that have attempted to silence women's voices. The women's stories in this book unearth complex gendered activities and power struggles around growing, cooking, feeding, and celebrating women who take care of families and communities while navigating their exclusion from resources, decision-making, and macrolevel policies—spaces where women are treated as if they "do not belong." The experiences of the women across the Diaspora show that in all aspects of the global food system, women remain resilient, engaged in resistance, and transformative, grasping hope because they must ensure that food gets on the table and households are well maintained.

Debunking the Myth of Women as Secondary to Household Economies

The work cited throughout this book debunks many myths about women's roles on and off the farm and inside of and outside of the kitchen. Gomes explains that "these roles are rooted in a hierarchical distinction, positioning women's reproductive and domestic labor in the home as less valuable than men's 'productive' labor in public." Not only is labor in the house undervalued, but it is a common belief that women around the world are relegated to the kitchen and portrayed in a role of feeding families, even as we recognize this as a vitally important role. Even where women, in particular rural women, engage in farming, Lydia Kwoyiga and Agnes Atia Apusigah (chapter 1) explain that this is often seen as women playing a "secondary" or "supplementary" role in the household economy. This myth continues to be perpetuated, although women's studies and feminist perspectives for decades have pointed out the repercussions that pitting reproductive roles against productive roles have had on devaluing or undervaluing women's roles in the household economy and in families and society at large. Moreover, women often engage in both forms of labor by performing multiple tasks, moving "seamlessly" between the informal and formal sectors. This engagement is reflected in several chapters in this book. Gomes refers to this as a disjuncture between the division of productive and reproductive labor of women. Hanna Garth, on the other hand, points out that women's multitasking of paid and unpaid work, while important to the household economy, is "tiring" (chapter 10).

Contrary to long-standing myths, women are active, vital, and inventive contributors to global food systems. Gomes stresses that in an unstable economy in Shashamane, Ethiopia, Rastafari women who sell food are often the only stable providers of income. Ford begins her piece with a powerful vignette about Leah Chase, a Black female restaurateur who opened Dooky Chase's, a famous restaurant in New Orleans. Chase opened the restaurant during the civil rights movement, when Black people had few dining options, and it became an economic engine in the community. Similarly, both Kelsey Emard and Veronica Gordon (chapter 8) and Garth underscore just how important women's contributions are to a nation's economy, as significant social and political shifts occur in local economies. Agriculturally, Campaore and Shiratori argue that in rural areas, women dominate in domestic food production that is no less economically worthy than the cash crop or livestock production men engage in for markets. Moreover, Sawadogo/Compaoré and Shiratori and Sanders McCutcheon both point out that women's roles in food production are at the "cutting edge" of agricultural production and innovation and are transformative globally. Yet, women farmers are left out of macroeconomic policy planning, and their economic contributions are not acknowledged as significant additions to countries' gross domestic product figures. Because their roles, as well as their skills and expertise, are not recognized, they are excluded from important productive resources such as land, loans, technology, and agricultural extension services. Both Kwoyiga and Apusigah and Kenia-Rosa Campo and colleagues (chapter 4) describe how, despite these limitations, women are still found at all levels of the food chain, mitigating changes in food systems in ways that enhance household consumption and economies.

Navigating Inequities and Exercising Agency

A consistent and strong thread that runs through the chapters in the book is the ways in which women across the Diaspora have consistently resisted marginalization and negotiated their experiences in specifically gendered ways. Because of gender and racial hierarchies, women operate at microlevels in agricultural production and food systems—in the kitchen, in the fields, and among local women's networks. There are several notable ways in which women outmaneuver their limited opportunities throughout global food systems. The examples referenced in the case studies on the African continent explain that while it is culturally expected that women work on their husband's or father's farmland, women often request their own farm plots. Though plots assigned to women are small and the least arable, they nonetheless allow women the freedom to decide what should be grown and what should be done with the produce, including spending the income earned from sales. In the case of cowpea production in Burkina Faso, Sawadogo/Compaoré and Shiratori raise the concept of "women's crops," and Kwoyiga and Apusigah discuss the importance of women in Ghana successfully advocating for their own plots of land to experiment with groundwater production systems. Sanders McCutcheon notes that in Zimbabwe, it was women who understood pest management, though men were often initially presented as the holders of knowledge to community visitors. Campo and colleagues draw a similar reference to a fish farming project in a rural part of the Caribbean island of Trinidad. These are all illustrations of women exerting their agency to branch out with their own food production projects and at the same time prevent family hunger; women's crops are also sometimes "hungry season crops."

The authors were also in agreement about why women feel the need to navigate their inequities and exercise their agency. Ironically, their reasons are similar to what governments have been forced to confront, that is, that rising costs and the need for imported and often processed foods in many developing countries present complex issues of threatened self-reliance and self-sufficiency. Linked to these concerns are persistent poverty and a decline in the health and well-being of populations across the African Diaspora and elsewhere. Cast in the prescribed roles of "nurturer" or "caretaker," women are the ones who primarily carry the load and love associated with these responsibilities. In a rich discussion of mothering in Black agrarian pedagogies, shakara tyler (chapter 6) addresses the ethical aspects of care discussed in Black feminist literature.

Carriers of Knowledge and Cultural Identities

In many ways, it is women who provide nutrition for families and feed communities by growing and selling basic produce or selling cooked food. But the "women's crops" and recipes they use also assist in maintaining the cultural identities and histories of families and ethnic groups. Ford considers the passing down of history as justice work and essential to food and agrarian history. Gomes makes this her core thesis in her discussions on the Rastafari family food *beit* in Shashamane. The sale of food at local Rastafari restaurants provides additional income for households and gives women an opportunity for autonomy, while the recipes they use reflect specific ethnic tastes and the racialization of food. We also observe that women are cultural custodians and ambassadors who pass on recipes as well as other forms of knowledge. Emard and Gordon illustrate how women preserve and share gendered knowledge that goes beyond food preparation and recipes to include safe food production practices. Sanders McCutcheon interprets this custom through her discussion of the Feminist Agri-food Systems Theory and gives numerous examples of women passing knowledge about sustainable agricultural practices down to their children and youth as a form of intergenerational learning. A common thread regarding the knowledge women keep and pass on is the focus not only on establishing sustainable and safe food practices but on creating just food systems while navigating a lack of land and other resources. Taking these points into consideration, Best argues for more research that contextualizes these identities and knowledge to better understand the health and well-being of women across the Diaspora.

Mothers, Grandmothers, and Othermothers

The thesis that women's roles are key to cultural continuance, as well as the survival and the education of youth and other family members, is linked by tyler to the concept of "mothering." She traces these nurturing functions to the historiography of mothering and Black agrarian pedagogies. The link to Black women's history in agriculture, and more so to just food systems, is made clear by Ashanté M. Reese and Dara Cooper (chapter 5), who argue that women hold leadership roles and make spaces within organizations to think and drive praxis-safe food practices. Similar to the emergent trend in the other chapters, women's dreams, agency, and desire for independence and freedom are linked to food justice possibilities.

While Reese and Cooper call the names of Black women ancestors and tyler compiles a historiography, Ford talks about the formidable and dedicated Black aunties who saw no one as a stranger and did not allow anyone to leave the kitchen table without a satisfied stomach and spirit. Garth takes on an intergenerational perspective by examining the work of three women in one family in Cuba. Garth's work highlights the crucial role of grandmothers not only in caregiving but also in passing down key labor skills and knowledge. Sanders McCutcheon also references the influence of her aunt and her mother in more direct and personal life experiences, women who encouraged and created a way for her to be a scientist during a time when few in academic spaces would. Collectively, the authors see their involvement with food and agriculture as a tool for consciousness-raising, transformation, mobilization, freedom, and independence or an opportunity for autonomy. The women across the Diaspora silently agree that Black women are not just feeding food but feeding knowledge.

Concluding Statement

To borrow Reese and Cooper's concept, the editors of this book "made spaces" for the freedom of the women who wrote the chapters telling their stories. The book is an attempt to bring together women's voices and analyze the various aspects of women's roles in the global food system. We were transformed and empowered while editing this book, and we hope that the authors in the collection feel this way too. We also hope that the natural conversations created between the chapters in this book continue a much-needed dialogue about our global food system. As we noted in the introduction to this book, there is an increasingly loud cry to listen to Black women. However, this cry cannot come only during times of crisis but must be consistent. As seen in our book, Black women are changing and transforming the food system globally in an array of circumstances. We intend for our book to be used by activists, scientists, and policymakers to see the importance of what is happening from the micro- and metalevels to the macrolevel regarding planning and involvement of the knowledge and experiences of women at the kitchen table and beyond.

Finally, we are completing this book during the COVID-19 pandemic and amid public outcries against state violence against Black people. These are not events that are operating separately from the contents of this book. The global food system is being affected by the pandemic through a slowing down of imports and exports in some countries, which is particularly impacting food workers who were already marginalized in our food systems. Many of these workers are women, women of color, and Black women. Inside of the home, women are caregivers whose livelihoods are being disproportionately impacted by COVID-19; we know that many women are being pushed to the breaking point as caregivers and have had to leave the formal workforce during this time. Black women are taking on these roles, all while fearing for the safety of themselves and their families, as they are keenly aware that they are not even safe in their own homes. Though we are all affected by these events, preliminary research has shown that, as public health and intersectionality scholar Lisa Bowleg contends, "we are not all in this together," despite the media- and government-backed COVID-19 campaigns that have been omnipresent in the United States since the start of the pandemic.[1] Not only have Black, Indigenous, and other people of color had their livelihoods adversely affected by the pandemic, but these same groups are especially vulnerable to contracting the virus and suffering health issues related to COVID-19. As Best argues, a more thorough understanding and inclusion of the lived experiences of Black women and their roles in the global food system is needed in order to fully improve the lives of these women, their families, and their communities. Moreover, this understanding should propel women's voices and involvement at all levels of the food chain—the micro, meta, and macro—as the health, safety, and security of food systems are linked to gendered ways of knowing and doing.

NOTE

1. Bowleg, "We're Not All."

WORK CITED

Bowleg, Lisa. "We're Not All in This Together: On COVID-19, Intersectionality, and Structural Inequality." *American Journal of Public Health* 110, no. 7 (May 2020): 917.

Contributors

Agnes Atia Apusigah is associate professor of cultural analysis and gender studies at the Faculty of Education of the University for Development Studies, Tamale, Ghana. She has worked at the University for Development Studies since completing her doctoral studies on cultural studies and curriculum studies from Queen's University, Kingston, Ontario, in 2002. As an academic, her research has been in the areas of political economy of African development, educational reform and development, Indigenous knowledge, and gender and women's studies. Her most recent work includes "Teacher Professionalism and Educational Quality" (2015), "Endogenizing Higher Education in Africa" (2015), "Community-Based Ecotourism in Ghana" (2017), and "Critical Notes on Northern Ghana's Development" (2018).

She is actively involved in community, national, and international development work and serves on several governing boards and steering committees, such as Sustainable Peace Initiative, G-RAP Gender, BESSFA Rural Bank, Ghana Water Company, Afrikids Ghana, and Star Ghana, as member, vice-president, or chair. She also worked as a consultant on gender, program development, and organizational assessment for International Labour Organization, UNICEF, Comic Relief, Christian Aid, Advertising Association of Ghana, SEND Ghana, and many more. As part of her community development work, she has collaborated with several local government authorities on various programs.

Neela Badrie is from Trinidad and Tobago and gives undergraduate and postgraduate lectures in the areas of microbiology, biotechnology, food safety and risk analysis, food product development, epidemiology and foodborne diseases, and international trade and food legislation at the Faculty of Food and Agriculture of the University of the West Indies – St. Augustine Campus. She is also an attorney-at-law admitted to practice law at the Supreme Court of Trinidad and Tobago. She is a fellow of the Caribbean Academy of Sciences and the World Academy of Sciences, Italy. She is the recipient of several awards such as the US Fulbright Study/Research Award, the Association of Commonwealth Universities scholarship, the Caribbean-Pacific Islands Mobility Scheme scholarship, European Union Lomé IV-CULP-UWI fellowship, United Nations University fellowship, and the Rudrunath Capildeo gold medal for applied science and technology of the National Institute of Higher Education, Research, Science and Technology. She has served as a guest editor for a special issue on food safety of the *International Journal of Consumer Studies* and is on the editorial board of several scientific journals.

Latrica E. Best is associate professor of sociology and African and African Diaspora studies at Boston College. With formal training in sociology, demography, and gerontology, she is a social demographer whose work focuses on how the intersection of social, biological, and demographic factors impact our understanding of health outcomes across the life course for Black people, particularly in the United States and Africa. She seeks to examine how to best capture the intersectional Black experiences in health research. As an investigator on a National Institutes of Health multiyear grant exploring culture, community, and fruit and vegetable consumption among Black Kentuckians, she coauthored peer-reviewed articles on African American eating practices, optimal social-marketing strategies of fruit and vegetable consumption, and methodological issues in researching African American communities.

Kenia-Rosa Campo holds a bachelor of science and master of science from the University of the West Indies. Kenia-Rosa has a strong passion for teaching and learning and provides agricultural consulting services to many farmers and farmer organizations. She is also interested in soil microbiology, molecular biology, and field diagnosis.

Dara Cooper is an activist, organizer, writer, and movement-vibe curator. She is the cofounder and former executive director of the National Black Food and Justice Alliance where she currently serves as strategic advisor. A founding member of the HEAL Food Alliance, Cooper also served on the Movement for Black Lives policy table and leadership team, helping to write and launch the Vision for Black Lives. She currently serves as a member of the Kataly Foundation's Environmental Justice Resource Collective and is involved in the distribution of about $50 million to BIPOC environmental justice organizations around the country. Previously, Cooper led the launch of

Fresh Moves (Chicago), an award-winning mobile produce market with community health programming, which quickly became a nationally recognized model for healthy food distribution and community self-determination.

Kelsey Emard is assistant professor (senior research) and instructor of geography at Oregon State University. Her scholarship examines how rural communities navigate and respond to global economic restructuring, environmental change, and conservation governance. She uses participatory approaches to center local knowledge and expertise in her work. She has published in *Progress in Human Geography*, *Geographical Review*, *Sustainability*, and *Gender, Place, and Culture*.

Claudia J. Ford has had a career in international development and women's health spanning four decades and all continents. Dr. Ford is professor and chair of the Department of Environmental Studies at State University of New York, Potsdam. She has a BA in Biology from Columbia University, MFA in creative nonfiction writing from Vermont College of Fine Arts, MBA in health administration from Antioch University, and PhD in environmental studies from Antioch University. Dr. Ford is a midwife and ethnobotanist who teaches, conducts research, and writes about traditional ecological knowledge, spiritual ecology, entheogenic plant medicine, women's reproductive health, and sustainable agriculture. She has served on the boards of the Soul Fire Farm Institute and the Black Farmer Fund Pilot Community; both organizations are committed to supporting Black farmers and ending racism and injustice in the food system. Dr. Ford is currently writing a book, *Black Ecological Wisdom*, which reveals the environmental traditions of the Black Diaspora for the purpose of planetary healing at this time of environmental crisis. She is a writer, poet, and visual artist, and a single mother who has shared the delights and adventures of her global travel with her four children and two grandchildren.

Hanna Garth is a sociocultural and medical anthropologist who studies food access and the global food system. Her recent work is focused on the connections between food systems, structural inequalities, health, and well-being. Specifically, she studies the ways in which changes in the global food system, international trade, and shifts in local food distribution systems impact communities, families, and individuals. She studies these questions in Latin America and the Caribbean and among Black and Latinx communities in the United States. She is assistant professor of anthropology at Princeton University. She published the book *Food in*

Cuba: The Pursuit of a Decent Meal, and coedited the volume *Black Food Matters: Food Justice in the Wake of Racial Justice* with Ashanté Reese.

Shelene Gomes, PhD, teaches social anthropology and the sociology of culture at the University of the West Indies – St. Augustine Campus in Trinidad and Tobago. Her monograph, *Cosmopolitanism from the Global South* (2021) traces Caribbean cosmopolitan sensibilities through Rastafari imaginaries and migration to Ethiopia. She is a member of the transcontinental Globalization, Accessibility, Innovation and Care Research Network. Her current interdisciplinary research centers the cultural logics of care in examining socially reproductive labor. Shelene's work is unified by a focus on contemporary solidarities, acts of agency, and place-making within the context of unequal historical conditions of modernity.

Veronica Gordon and her husband, Delroy Lewis Fisher, have been instrumental in implementing a dynamic health reform movement in Puerto Viejo, Costa Rica. Together with their five children they have established a successful ministry of healthy holistic living. Veronica is also the owner of *Veronica's Place*, a bed-and-breakfast style accommodation in Puerto Viejo.

Wendy-Ann Isaac is a Trinidadian and is senior lecturer in the Department of Food Production, Faculty of Food and Agriculture where she teaches in the areas of sustainable agronomy, weed science and ecology, seed technology, innovative farming technologies, including protected agriculture, and controlled environment agriculture to undergraduate and postgraduate students. She has authored and coauthored several papers and chapters on these topics, which have been published in both regional and international peer-reviewed journals. She has also coedited several books exploring these issues: *Sustainable Food Production Practices in the Caribbean* (2012), *Agricultural Development and Food Security in Developing Nations* (2016), and *Impacts of Climate Change on Food Production in Small Island Developing States* (2014). She serves on the editorial board of *Agronomy, Tropical Agriculture*, the *Journal of Agricultural Extension and Education, Frontiers in Sustainable Food Systems*, and others.

Lydia Kwoyiga is senior lecturer and head of the Department of Environment, Water and Waste Engineering of the University for Development. Kwoyiga holds a PhD in environmental science from Technische Universität Dresden, Germany. She has about ten years of professional working experience.

She works at the University for Development Studies, Tamale, Ghana, since 2013. Working in Ghana's only pro-poor university, she is concerned about promoting sustainable livelihoods in a well-balanced environment. She has a special interest in the sociocultural aspect of groundwater resources development and the global environmental impacts and hazards of climate change in Ghana and beyond. Her research areas straddle groundwater and rural livelihoods, local knowledge and groundwater development, institutions and climate change adaptation, women and food security, gender studies, solar-powered groundwater irrigation, and higher education. From 2020 to 2022, she served as a returned expert under the Programme/Expert Fund Migration and Diaspora (Germany) of the Deutsche Gesellschaft für Internationale Zusammenarbeit GmbH of the Centre for International Migration and Development. She has participated in the monitoring and evaluation of solar-powered irrigation projects in the Brong Ahafo, Volta, and Northern Regions of Ghana, and she has contributed to the development of a curriculum on solar-powered irrigation systems in Ghana, as part of the Green People's Energy Project sponsored by Gesellschaft für Internationale Zusammenarbeit. She has recently contributed to drafting the University for Development Studies gender policy.

Gloria Sanders McCutcheon has been working in environmental entomology for the past fifty years, with an interest in food systems and health disparities. Dr. McCutcheon is professor and chair of the Department of Biology at Claflin University, Orangeburg, South Carolina. She earned a BS in zoology and MS in entomology from Clemson University and a PhD in environmental entomology from the University of Georgia. She teaches, conducts research, and communicates with scientific and general audiences as she mentors students and faculty in the areas of biology, biotechnology, public health, and environmental science. Dr. McCutcheon has served on the boards of Columbia College and local schools, with an interest in enhanced educational opportunities. She serves on the Tri-County Health Network to address health disparities. She has served on journal editorial boards for sustainable agriculture and food systems. Dr. McCutcheon is well published in reducing toxic pesticide usage. Her research has been funded by the US Department of Agriculture, National Institutes of Health, and National Science Foundation. She is the recipient of the 2019 South Carolina Environmental Awareness Award. She is currently writing a book for children, revealing the flora and fauna of the small farm where she grew up in rural South Carolina, as well as a memoir. Gloria is married to a retired United Methodist Church pastor, which afforded her the opportunity to live and co-parent two daughters in several regions of South Carolina. She is happy to share her experiences with four grandchildren.

Priscilla McCutcheon, PhD, is assistant professor at the University of Kentucky in the Department of Geography and affiliated with African American and Africana Studies Program. She completed her master of arts and doctorate at the University of Georgia and her bachelor of arts at Spelman College. Much of her work has been with Black faith-based food programs in the US South, ranging from emergency food programs to Black nationalist sustainable farms. She has also completed archival work on food and agricultural programs of the civil rights and Black Power movements, including Fannie Lou Hamer's Freedom Farms and the National Council of Negro Women's Hunger Initiatives. This work has resulted in solo and co-authored publications in outlets that include the *Annals of the American Association of Geographers, Antipode, Black Perspectives, Environment and Planning D*, and *Southern Cultures*. She is increasingly interested in Black spiritual and religious geographies and how the "spirit" makes place in the US South's natural and built environment.

Theresa Rajack-Talley is professor of Pan-African studies and sociology and vice-provost for the Office of Equity and Inclusion at Dalhousie University. She is a senior administrator and scholar who works on issues of race and ethnicity, gender, social class, nationality, and their intersectionality with social inequality, equity, and inclusion. Her research, publications, and administrative work are centered on addressing all forms of oppression and discrimination.

Ashanté Reese is associate professor of African and African Diaspora studies at the University of Texas at Austin. She's the author of *Black Food Geographies: Race, Self-Reliance, and Food Access in Washington, D.C.* and coeditor of *Black Food Matters: Racial Justice in the Wake of Food Justice*.

Eveline M. F. W. Sawadogo/Compaoré holds a PhD in sociology and social policy (specialty in science, technology, and innovations studies) from the University of Nottingham in the United Kingdom. She is a senior researcher at the Institute of Environment and Agricultural Research in Burkina Faso since September 2015. Her research topics include agricultural innovation systems, approaches to the diffusion of innovations in agriculture and the environment, innovations and social inequalities, public policy, food systems policies, and gender and diversity. Dr. Sawadogo/Comparoé is a laureate of the African Women for Agricultural Research and Development award (2018).

Sakiko Shiratori is a senior researcher at the Information and Public Relations Office of the Japan International Research Center for Agricultural Sciences. She previously worked at the Japan International Cooperation Agency Research Institute. Her areas of interest are the linkages of agriculture, food consumption, human nutrition, and health, particularly in the context of developing regions. She holds a PhD in agricultural and applied economics from the University of Minnesota. She has an MS in agricultural development economics from the University of Reading, United Kingdom, and a BS of agriculture from the University of Tokyo.

shakara tyler is a returning-generation farmer, educator, and organizer who engages in Black agrarianism, agroecology, food sovereignty, and environmental justice as commitments of abolition and decolonization. She obtained her PhD in community sustainability at Michigan State University and works with Black farming communities in Michigan and mid-Atlantic states. She is currently a lecturer at the University of Michigan School for Environment and Sustainability. She explores participatory and decolonial research methodologies and community-centered pedagogies in the food justice, food sovereignty, and environmental justice movements. She also serves as board president at the Detroit Black Community Food Security Network, board member of the Detroit People's Food Co-op, cofounder of the Detroit Black Farmer Land Fund, and member of the Black Dirt Farm Collective.

Marquitta Webb is senior lecturer in human nutrition and dietetics at the University of the West Indies – St. Augustine Campus. She is also a registered dietitian and conducts research in nutrition prevention, management of chronic disease, and other related areas, including agriculture.

Index

Page numbers in italics refer to illustrations.

Africa. *See* Burkina Faso; Ghana; Zimbabwe
"African Diaspora Women" (Reagon), 107–8
Africa University, 67–68
Afro-Costa Rican food practices, 136–48
Afroecology, 101
agency: Black people, in local food systems, 99; collective, 177; decision-making and home demonstrations, 110, 112, 114, 117; decision-making power in Burkina Faso, 56; decision-making power in Trinidad, 80–82; efforts to increase, 37–39; kitchen as symbol for Black women's, 165–66; lack of, in Burkina Faso, 45, 48; measures of empowerment, 78; and opportunity structures, 35–37; and well ownership, 35; women's exercise of, 117–18, 209–10. *See also* empowerment, women's
Agénor, Madina, 158, 168
agritourism, 140, 146–47
agroecology, 62–63
Agyeman, Julian, 10
Allen, Erika, 102
Allen, Patricia, 164; "Women and Food Chains," 164
Alsop, Ruth, 31, 35
alternative food movements, 93, 130, 177. *See also* local food systems
Amharic speech patterns, 188–89
Anatomy of Female Power (Chinweizu), 30

Andrews, Donna, 102
animal exploitation, 102n9
Apperwhite, Estelle, 102
Apusigah, Agnes Atia, 9, 21, 22, 24–39, 208, 209, 210
aquaculture, 74–84, *77*
Asian Development Bank, 26

Badrie, Neela, 10, 21, 22, 74–84
Baker, Ella Josephine, 88, 127
Bandele, Owusu, 127
Baxter, Kirtrina, 102
Beal, Frances, 4
Beckford, Beatriz, 97–98
Bedasse, Monique, 192
Bennett, Evan P., 109–10
Benson, Devyn Space, 181
Beoku-Betts, Josephine, 165
Best, Latrica E., 1–15, 151–57, 158–68, 206–13
Beyond Settler Time (Rifkin), 88
Bilge, Sirma, 4, 5
Black agrarianism, 106–20
Black Dirt Farm Collective, 101
Black Farmers Urban Growers Conference, 101
Black feminism: definitions and overview, 89–91, 93–94; and diversity of Black mothering, 107–8; and food justice, 6, 92–102; framework of care, 94–97; theory, 176–77
Black Geographies, 6, 137, 160; Black agrarian geographies, 139–40

Black Oaks Center for Sustainable Renewable Living, 99
Black Panther Party (BPP), 110–11, 113, 115, 116, 118
Black Urban Growers, 130
Bonacci, Giulia, 188, 192
Bourdieu, Pierre, 194
Bowleg, Lisa, 161, 212
BRIDGE (Institute of Development Studies, United Kingdom), 25
Buhari, Muhammadu, 30
Building Houses Out of Chicken Legs (Williams-Forson), 89, 165
Bullard, Robert D., 10
Burkett, Darnella, 102
Burkina Faso: household food preparation, 52–56; methodology of study, 46–48; National Program for Economic and Social Development, 46; overview, 42–44; women's roles in food production, 44–46, 48–56

cabbage looper moths, 65–66
Campo, Kenia-Rosa, 10, 21, 22, 74–84, 209, 210
capabilities approach, 81–82
capitalism, critiques of, 89, 98–99, 119, 189, 197
caregiving: and gendered assumptions, 101; kinship care, 99; and mothering in Black agrarianism, 106–20; stress of, 153
Carter, Derrais, 96
casa/calle divide, 176, 178. *See also* public vs. private spaces
Castro, Fidel, 176
Chase, Leah Lange, 88, 124, 127, 209
chicken, as staple food, 165–66
childcare, cooperative, 112–13
Chinweizu, 30; *Anatomy of Female Power*, 30
Christian, Michelle, 147
churches as "homeplaces," 115–16
Cite Black Women Collective, 8
civil rights activism, and food activism, 126–27

class stratification: and discrimination, 5–6, 111, 163, 197; and food tastes, 189, 194–96
Clemson University Agricultural Experiment Station, 63–64
Clevenger, Lorrie, 130
Cobb, Pat, 64
Collier-Thomas, Bettye, 114
Collins, Patricia Hill, 4, 5, 112, 114, 117, 163
Combahee River Collective, 4–5
Cooper, Dara, 11, 89–90, 92–102, 211, 212
Costa Rica: background and overview, 136–39; Black agrarian geographies, 139–40; tourism in Talamanca, 139, 146–47; women's agrarian food practices, 140–46
COVID-19 pandemic, 20, 212–13
cowpea: cooking methods, 52–54, 53; processing in Burkina Faso, 49–52; as "women's crop," 21, 43, 45, 209–10
Crenshaw, Kimberlé, 4–5
crop diversity, 62–63, 67
Cuba: biological pest issues, 65–67; Black women and domestic work, 173–82
culinary histories, 165; and legacies of slavery, 189–90

Davis, Angela, 109
Davis, Kristin, 75
Detroit Black Community Food Security Network, 98, 99
domestic labor: and racialization in Cuba, 174–77, 178, 181; value of Rastafari women's, 154, 181, 188–89, 197
Doroshow, Ceyenne, 168
Douglas, Mary, 192
dry-season groundwater irrigation, 24–39
DuBois, W. E. B., 115

economic security and food, 89, 152, 153–54, 156
eco-queer movements, 168
Edmonda, Ennis, 191
Ekboir, Javier, 75

INDEX

Elmhirst, Rebecca, 76
Emard, Kelsey, 12, 89, 90, 136–48, 209
empowerment, women's, 10, 20, 107, 206; and aquaculture in Trinidad, 75, 78, 81–82, *81*; and feminist agri-food systems theory, 61; in Ghana, 26, 30–31. *See also* agency
entomology. *See* pesticide alternatives
environmental issues: agriculture and cropping systems, 62–63, 207; injustice and food system activism, 127–28; sustainable agriculture in Costa Rica, 142–44; in urban areas, 130, 132. *See also* pesticide alternatives
Ethiopia, Rastafari migrants, 186–201
ethnography, 187
Evans, Bob, 10

family farms, and cash income in Burkina Faso, 44–45
"farmer's friends" (natural enemies of pests), 66, 67–68. *See also* pesticide alternatives
farm plots in Africa, 44–45, 47, 48–49, 209–10
Feminist Agri-food Systems Theory (FAST), 60–63, 211
Fisher, Abby, 165; *What Mrs. Fisher Knows about Old Southern Cooking*, 165
fish production, 74–84
Florida Negro District home demonstrations, 110, 112, 114
Floyd, Edith, 131
Food and Agricultural Organization, United Nations (FAO), 8–9, 24, 25–26, 34, 38; fish production, 76–77, *77*
food deserts, 22, 166–67
food insecurity: in Africa, 28–29, 42, 44, 190; in United States, 129–30. *See also* hunger
food justice: and Black Feminist praxis, 92–102; Black women's leadership in United States, 124–33; overview, 10–12, 87–91
food security, 7–8, 12–15, 21–22, 44–46, 166–67

food studies, 10, 13, 152, 160, 165, 166
Ford, Claudia J., 11–12, 88, 124–33, 207–9, 210, 211
Frasier, Aleya, 102
Free Breakfast Program (Black Panther Party), 111, 113, 115, 116, 118, 121n48
Freedom Dreams (Kelley), 10
Freedom Farm Cooperative (FFC), 94–95, 111, 113, 114–15, 116–17, 118, 128–29
Freedom Quilting Bee (Alabama), 110, 112–13, 114, 117
Fulton, Alvenia, 101

Garden of Happiness, 130
Garth, Hanna, 14, 152–55, 173–82, 208, 211
Garvey, Amy Jacques, 5
gendered roles: in African Diaspora, 7–8, 109; in agritourism, 147; Black women in global food production, 1–2; care work, 96–97, 101; domesticity and home, 95; gender inequality, in Caribbean region, 74–75; gendered knowledge, 144–46, 210–11; mothering, 107–8. *See also* gendered roles in food production; mothering in Black agrarianism; public vs. private spaces
gendered roles in food production: Burkina Faso, 55; Ethiopia, 196–200; global statistics, 8–9; Trinidad, 82–83; "women's crops," 45; Zimbabwe, 68. *See also* cowpea
geospatial analysis, 166–67
Ghana: data gathered in 2019 study, 26–28; geography and climate, 25; groundwater irrigation, 28–29; overview, 24–26; women's agency and empowerment, 30–31, 35–39; women and household food provisioning, 29–30, 31–35
Gilmore, Georgia, 127
Gleason, Flavia, 117
Gomes, Shelene, 14, 152, 153–54, 186–201, 206–7, 208, 210

Gordon, Veronica, 12, 89, 90, 136–48, *143*, *145*, 209
Gray, Heather, 129
Graziano da Silva, Jose, 1
Great Migration, 6, 125, 131
groundwater irrigation, 24–39
Growing Joy Community Garden, 131
Gullah women, 165
Guthman, Julie, 3
Guy-Sheftall, Beverly, 5; *Words of Fire*, 5

Haile Selassie, 190, 191
Hamer, Fannie Lou, 88, 89, 94–95, 101, 111, 113, 118, 127–28
Hamilton, Erin R., 159
Harari, Lexi, 162–63
Harris, Marvin, 192
Hartman, Saidiya, 176
Hayes, Cynthia, 101
health: and Afro-Costa Rican practices, 142–44; health disparities, 2–3; ital lifestyles for Rastafari, 191–92, 200; "modifiable" health issues, 160; population-level health, 158–63, 166–68; role of food security, 12–15, 151–57
Heinsohn, Nina, 31, 35
Ho, Christine, 197
Hobart, Hiʻilei, 95–96
Homan, Patricia, 168
hooks, bell, 128
Horne, Savi, 101, 102
House, Callie, 127
household food provisioning in Ghana, 24–39
Hudson-Weems, Clenora, 5
Huggins, Erica, 118
Hummer, Robert A., 159
hunger, 20, 44. *See also* food deserts; food insecurity; malnutrition
hungry-season crops, 43
Hunter, Kanchan Dawn, 130
Hurston, Zora Neale, 88, 127

Indigenous Americans, 93
intergenerational sharing, 154–56

intersectionality: food and health, 4–6, 164–67; in health research, 158–64; and narrative methods, 207–8; of race, gender, and class in Cuba, 175, 176–77; theory, 4–5, 152, 154
irrigation, dry-season groundwater, 24–39
Isaac, Wendy-Ann, 10, 21, 22, 74–84

Jackson, Dean, 102
Jamaica Safar neighborhood (Shashamane, Ethiopia), 187–201
Jones, Claudia, 5
Journal of Negro Education, 114

Kabeer, Naila, 31
Katic, Pamela G., 34
Keith, Minor, 138
Kelley, Joan, 116
Kelley, Robin D. G., 10; *Freedom Dreams*, 10
Kilbourne, Amy M., 162
King, Deborah, 117
Kishore, Rosemarie, 80
kitchen table as symbol, 115, 165–66, 206–7
Kneese, Tamara, 95–96
knowledge-sharing, informal, 65–69, 106–20, 140; gendered, 144–46, 210–11
Kortatsi, B. K., 28
Kwoyiga, Lydia, 9, 21, 22, 24–39, 208, 209, 210

Land Loss Prevention Project, 99–100, 101
land ownership by women, 34. *See also* farm plots in Africa
Latin America, 136. *See also* Costa Rica
La Via Campesina, 132
Lawrence, Pauline, 64
Lee, Chioun, 162–63
Lewis, Desiree, 102
Lewis, Edna, 101, 127
life course theory, 155, 164
literacy, 113–14, 115

local food systems, 130; in United States, 99. *See also* alternative food movements
Lunsford, Lindsay, 102

Maathai, Wangari, 101
malnutrition, 3–4, 46, 76, 83, 175. *See also* hunger; nutrition
Marquez, Francia, 102
Marxism and Cuban culture, 175–76
Mayfield, Kellie, 167
McCutcheon, Priscilla, 1–15, 87–91, 102, 206–13
McKittrick, Katherine, 12
McPherson, Annika, 191
meat consumption, 52, 144, 199
Merkel, Angela, 30
migration: African men, 32–33, 36; to Costa Rica, 138; Rastafarian to Ethiopia, 187, 188, 200
Minas Rojas, Charo, 102
Mintz, Sidney, 189, 200, 201
Misra, Joya, 5–6
monocultures, 62
Mose Brown, Tamara, 196, 198
mothering in Black agrarianism, 11–12, 88, 106–20, 211; othermothering, 11, 107–8, 119, 211. *See also* gendered roles
Moyles, Trina, 65; *Women Who Dig*, 65
music and freedom songs, southern US, 116–17

Namara, Regassa E., 28–29
Nash, Jennifer, 93–94
National Black Food and Justice Alliance (NBFJA), 89, 97–100
National Council for Negro Women, 94
National Negro Health Week, 117
Negro Cooperative Extension Service, 127
Negro home demonstrations (Florida), 110, 112, 114, 116, 117
Nelson, Nadine, 102
neoliberalism, 146–47
Nettles-Barcelón, Kimberly, 102

New Communities farming collective, 129
Norman, Barbara, 131
nutrition: and aquaculture, 21–22, 76; determinants of nutritional status, *83*, 83–84; and global food systems, 2–3; and "women's crops" in Burkina Faso, 43, 46, 51–52. *See also* malnutrition

obesity, 61, 130
Obiagele, Lake, 199
Ochieng, P. A., 26
othermothering, 11, 107–8, 119, 211

Parks, Alsie, 102
Parrish, Alice, 102
patriarchal societies: Burkina Faso, 48, 52; and care work, 96–97; Ghana, 27, 30; Rastafari–local Ethiopian households, 197–98
Patterson, William, 176
Pennick, Edward, 129
Penniman, Leah, 20, 88, 101, 102, 127, 131
People's Defense League, 124
pesticide alternatives, 59–60; biological control in Cuba, 65–67; biological control in southeastern United States, 63–65; biological control in Zimbabwe, 67–69
pig bank (Freedom Farm Cooperative), 94, 111, 118, 128
plantation economies, 100, 103n23, 109, 138, 140–41, 148, 189, 197. *See also* slavery, legacy of
population health, 158–63, 166–68
poverty: and Freedom Farm Cooperative, 94–95, 119; gendered nature of, 2, 81–82; and "street food," 193; in United States, 129–30
Princess Pamela (Pamela Strobel), 127
prison system, 100
productive labor vs. reproductive labor, 189, 197, 199, 200, 208. *See also* gendered roles; gendered roles in food production

public vs. private spaces, 95, 176, 188–89, 197; domestic spaces, Cuba, 176, 181–82. *See also* casa/calle divide; gendered roles

quadruple jornada, 180–81
quantitative methodology, 159, 161–64
queer ecology, 168

racism: in Central America, 138–39; and food insecurity, 129–30; and health disparities, 2–3; racial segregation and access to food, 166–67
Rajack-Talley, Theresa, 1–15, 19–23, 176–77, 206–13
Ramsundar, Himawatee, 80
Rastafari: foodways, 192–93, *195*; gendered roles, 153, 154, 155; origins, 190–91
Reagon, Bernice Johnson, 107–8 109; "African Diaspora Women," 107–8
Redmond, LaDonna, 92–93, 102
Reese, Ashanté M., 11, 89–90, 92–102, 177, 211, 212
Reid, Debra A., 109–10
religious faith and food practices, 143–44
Resurreccion, Bernadette P., 76
Rifkin, Mark, 88; *Beyond Settler Time*, 88
Rise and Root Farm, 130

Sachs, Carolyn, 164; "Women and Food Chains," 164
Saldanha, Arun, 189–90
Samman, Emma, 31
Sanders, Hattie Mines, 59, 64, 69
Sanders McCutcheon, Gloria, 9, 22, 59–70, 207, 209, 210, 211
Santos, Maria Emma, 31
Sawadogo/Compaoré, Eveline M. F. W., 9, 21, 22, 42–56, 207, 209–10
Sbicca, Joshua, 10–11
Sen, Amartya, 31, 35
Sequeira, E. Jemila, 129
sexuality and intersexuality, 168
Shannon, Jerry, 167
sharecropping systems, 93, 110, 138

sharing economies, 141–42
Sharpe, Christina, 94, 96
Sherrod, Shirley, 101, 102, 127, 129
Shiratori, Sakiko, 9, 21, 22, 42–56, 207, 209–10
slavery, legacy of, 96, 100, 127, 128, 131, 136, 140, 176–77. *See also* plantation economies
Slocum, Rachel, 189–90
Smart-Grosvenor, Vertamae, 101, 127, 165; *Vibration Cooking*, 165
Smith, Melbah, 102
social context, and intersectionality, 5–6
social justice, 6. *See also* food justice
social responsibility, 61–62. *See also* food justice
Soul Fire Farm, 101, 131
Southeastern African American Farmers Organic Network, 99–100, 101
Southwest Georgia Project, 101
soybeans, 63–64
Spielman, David J., 75
Spillers, Hortense, 95
Spiral Gardens Community Food Security Project, 130
State of Food Security and Nutrition in the World (2021), 20
Strobel, Pamela (Princess Pamela), 127
Student Nonviolent Coordinating Committee, 111, 118
Sudarkasa, Niara, 29
sustainable agriculture, 62–63; women's roles in promotion of, 63–69

technology, access to, 38–39
Thiombiano, B. Gnoumou, 45
Thomas, Miessha N., 129
Thompson-Duchene, Brenda, 102
Trichogramma wasps, 66
Trinidad and Tobago, 187; fish production case study, 74–84; methodology of case study, 77–78; Nation Policy of Gender and Development, 75–76
triple jornada, 181
Truth, Sojourner, 4, 127
Tubman, Harriet, 127

Turnipseed, Sam, 65
tyler, shakara, 11, 88–89, 106–20, 210

United States: Black agrarianism, 106–20; food inequities, 93; food justice and Black feminism, 92–102; food justice and urban farms, 124–33; health research and intersectionality, 158–68
urban farms and gardens, 99, 130–31

Vibration Cooking (Smart-Grosvenor), 165
Villholth, Karen G., 25
Vitale-Wolff, Jonah, 131

Washington, Booker T., 117
Washington, Karen, 102, 130
Washington, Tiffany, 102
Webb, Marquitta, 10, 21, 22, 74–84
wellness. *See* health
What Mrs. Fisher Knows about Old Southern Cooking (Fisher), 165
White, Monica, 94, 102, 128, 131, 177
white supremacy, 96, 98, 128. *See also* racism

Wilk, Richard, 195
Williams-Forson, Psyche, 89, 102, 165–66; *Building Houses Out of Chicken Legs*, 89, 165
Wise, Dorothy, 101
"Women and Food Chains" (Allen and Sachs), 164
women's contributions to global food supply: challenges and barriers, 26; food security, 44–46; global statistics, 24; misrepresentation of, 25
women's roles. *See* gendered roles
Women Who Dig (Moyles), 65
Wood, Sylvia, 127
Words of Fire (Guy-Sheftall), 5
workforce, women's participation, 175–76, 181

Yakini, Malik, 98
Yeni, Sthandiwe, 102

Zafar, Rafia, 102
Z-HOPE (Zetas Helping Other People Excel), 62
Zimbabwe, 65–67

Printed in the USA
CPSIA information can be obtained
at www.ICGtesting.com
CBHW031541150624
10141CB00006B/609